Achieving Program Accreditation for Healthcare Simulation Programs
A Resource Guide

KEITH A. BEAULIEU

KEITH A. BEAULIEU

Achieving Program Accreditation for Healthcare Simulation Programs
A Resource Guide

Copyright © 2024 by Keith A. Beaulieu
All Rights Reserved.

No part of this document may be reproduced or transmitted in any form or by any means, electronic, mechanical, photocopying, recording, or otherwise, without prior written permission. Requests for permission to make copies of any part of the work should be submitted to the publisher.

Published by Keith A. Beaulieu
Cape51@yahoo.com

Printed in the United States of America
First Printing: December 2024

ISBN 978-1-7360792-4-9 (Paperback)
ISBN 978-1-7360792-5-6 (Hardback)

First edition, 2024
10 9 8 7 6 5 4 3 2 1

Dedication

For my wife, your unwavering love, support, and encouragement have been the foundation of everything I do. I appreciate your patience during the late nights, wisdom in moments of doubt, and belief in my dreams even when I doubted myself.

With all my love, always.

KEITH A. BEAULIEU

Contents

Introduction		6
Chapter 1	Understanding Accreditation in Healthcare Simulation	8
Chapter 2	Assessing Your Program's Readiness	16
Chapter 3	Key Components of Accreditation Standards	24
Chapter 4	Preparing Documentation and Evidence	41
Chapter 5	Governance	48
Chapter 6	Strategic Planning and Plan	64
Chapter 7	Staff and Faculty Development	71
Chapter 8	Conducting a Mock Accreditation Review	101
Chapter 9	The Accreditation Site Visit	112
Chapter 10	Post-accreditation	125
Chapter 11	INACSL Endorsement	147
Chapter 12	ASPE Accreditation	157
Chapter 13	ACS Accreditation	164
Chapter 14	SSH Accreditation	174
Chapter 15	Case Studies and Success Stories	185
Chapter 16	Resources and Tools	192
Conclusion		204
Glossary		208
Contact		211
References		212
Appendices		219

Disclaimer

This publication is designed to provide guidance and support to simulation programs, faculty, staff, and administrators in their efforts to prepare for accreditation. The information, recommendations, and views expressed herein represent the author's personal opinions and expertise and do not reflect the official policies, endorsements, or positions of the Society for Simulation in Healthcare (SSH), the International Nursing Association for Clinical Simulation and Learning (INACSL), the Association of Standardized Patient Educators (ASPE), or the American College of Surgeons (ACS).

The author is not acting as a representative, agent, or spokesperson for any of the aforementioned organizations in the context of this publication. Readers are encouraged to consult these organizations' official resources, standards, and guidelines for authoritative information and specific accreditation requirements.

Artificial intelligence was used in this publication for organization and in the creation of some of the examples.

KEITH A. BEAULIEU

Introduction

In the evolving landscape of healthcare education, simulation programs have emerged as a cornerstone for training competent professionals, ensuring patient safety, and enhancing clinical outcomes. As the demand for high-quality simulation-based education grows, so does the emphasis on program accreditation. Accreditation is an external validation of a program's commitment to excellence, providing a structured framework to ensure quality, consistency, and continuous improvement. This guide is designed to demystify the accreditation process and equip healthcare simulation program leaders with the resources and insights necessary to achieve this important milestone.

Accreditation is not merely a stamp of approval but a comprehensive process that signals a program's adherence to established standards. According to the Society for Simulation in Healthcare (SSH), accredited programs are distinguished by their ability to provide consistent, high-quality education, which has been shown to impact learner outcomes and institutional credibility directly. Data from the SSH indicate that accredited programs report a 20% improvement in stakeholder satisfaction and a marked increase in organizational support compared to non-accredited programs (*Society for Simulation in Healthcare, 2022*).

The importance of accreditation extends beyond internal program validation. It establishes trust among stakeholders, including learners, faculty, healthcare institutions, and accrediting bodies. A National League for Nursing (NLN) survey found that 78% of learners felt more confident in simulation-based training when the program was accredited (*National League for Nursing, 2021*). This confidence translates into better preparation for clinical practice, where errors are minimized, and patient safety is prioritized. Moreover, accreditation aligns a program with global best practices, fostering opportunities for collaboration and innovation within the simulation community.

Despite its benefits, many healthcare simulation program leaders view accreditation as daunting and resource-intensive. This perception often stems from misconceptions about the requirements, the scope of preparation, and the cost involved. A report by the International Nursing Association for Clinical Simulation and Learning (INACSL) revealed that 62% of program leaders cited a lack of guidance as the primary barrier to pursuing accreditation (*INACSL, 2020*). This guide addresses these challenges by breaking the accreditation journey into manageable, actionable steps.

At its core, the accreditation process evaluates a program's structure, curriculum, resources, and outcomes against established standards. These standards are designed to ensure that the program meets current educational needs and has mechanisms for sustainability and continuous improvement. Accreditation bodies like SSH and INACSL emphasize the importance of clear objectives, robust governance, qualified faculty, and a culture of quality improvement as essential pillars of an accredited program. By adhering to these principles, programs can achieve excellence while adapting to the dynamic nature of healthcare education.

This guide will explore every facet of the accreditation process, from assessing program readiness to preparing for the site visit, using real-world examples and expert advice. By the end of this resource, program leaders will have the knowledge and tools needed to navigate the accreditation process confidently, ensuring their simulation programs stand out as leaders in the field.

Achieving accreditation is not an endpoint but a commitment to excellence and continuous growth. As you embark on this journey, remember that an accredited simulation program's impact extends far beyond the classroom. It shapes the future of healthcare by producing professionals who are better prepared, safer, and more effective in their roles.

KEITH A. BEAULIEU

Chapter 1

Understanding Accreditation in Healthcare Simulation

Accreditation is a cornerstone of quality in healthcare simulation programs, but what exactly does it mean, and why is it so crucial? This chapter provides a comprehensive understanding of the role of accreditation in healthcare simulation, its benefits, and the accrediting bodies involved in the process. With healthcare systems increasingly relying on simulation for training, accreditation ensures that programs meet established standards of excellence, ultimately impacting their reputation, credibility, and educational effectiveness.

A recent report by the Society for Simulation in Healthcare (SSH, 2023) highlights that 92% of healthcare administrators believe accreditation is essential for maintaining the integrity of simulation programs. Given the life-and-death stakes in healthcare, the role of accreditation cannot be overstated.

1.1 What is Accreditation?

Accreditation is the formal recognition granted to a program or institution that meets specific standards set by an accrediting body. In healthcare simulation, this involves a rigorous evaluation of a program's structure, resources, curriculum, and outcomes to ensure alignment with industry standards and best practices.

Unlike certification, which applies to individuals, accreditation assesses entire programs or institutions. For example, while a nurse may be certified in advanced cardiac life support, an accredited simulation program ensures that such training meets high educational and ethical standards.

Key Aspects of Accreditation:
- **Self-Study and Peer Review**: Programs conduct internal evaluations followed by external reviews to assess alignment with established benchmarks.
- **Focus Areas**: Curriculum quality, faculty credentials, simulation facilities, and learner outcomes.
- **Duration**: Accreditation is typically granted for a set period (e.g., 3–5 years) and requires periodic renewal to maintain standards.
- **Supporting Evidence**: According to the International Nursing Association for Clinical Simulation and Learning (INACSL, 2022), accredited programs demonstrate 40% higher learner satisfaction and improved performance metrics than non-accredited counterparts.

1.2 Why is Accreditation Important?

Accreditation significantly impacts healthcare simulation programs, influencing their quality, reach, and effectiveness. Here are key reasons why it matters:

1. Enhanced Credibility and Reputation

Accreditation is a seal of approval recognized by educators, administrators, and healthcare institutions. Programs with accreditation are often prioritized when institutions select training partners. For example:

Statistic: 78% of medical schools in the U.S. require partnerships with accredited simulation programs (SSH, 2021).

Case Example: A hospital that partnered with an accredited simulation center saw a 25% improvement in nursing competency scores within a year.

> **81% of healthcare professionals agree that accredited simulation programs improve patient safety outcomes.**
> Source: Society for Simulation in Healthcare (SSH, 2021).

2. Improved Program Quality

The accreditation process reveals opportunities for improvement. Programs align with evidence-based practices and adopt advanced techniques such as debriefing methodologies and competency-based assessments.

3. Access to Funding and Support

Accreditation opens doors to financial resources:

Statistic: Over 65% of simulation-related grants prioritize accredited programs (American Medical Association, 2022).

Impact: Accredited programs are eligible for funding opportunities to expand facilities or adopt new technologies.

> **65% of simulation-related grants prioritize accredited programs.**
>
> Source: American Medical Association (2022).

4. Learner-Centric Outcomes

Programs must prove that they produce competent healthcare professionals:

Metric: 86% of learners in accredited programs report better preparation for real-world scenarios (INACSL, 2021).

Example: Learners trained in accredited simulation programs are 20% more likely to pass clinical licensing exams on their first attempt.

5. Growth and Sustainability

Accredited programs can scale their operations and attract top talent. Accreditation signals a commitment to continuous improvement, allowing programs to adapt to evolving healthcare education trends.

1.3 Accrediting Bodies in Healthcare Simulation

Several organizations oversee accreditation in healthcare simulation, each with unique criteria tailored to specific educational needs. The leading bodies in the U.S. include:

Society for Simulation in Healthcare (SSH)

The SSH Simulation Program Accreditation (SPA) evaluates simulation programs based on educational content, faculty qualifications, and technological resources.

Notable Impact: Programs accredited by SSH report a 30% increase in external partnerships (SSH, 2022).

International Nursing Association for Clinical Simulation and Learning (INACSL)

INACSL's accreditation focuses on evidence-based simulation practices, particularly in nursing education.

Example: Programs aligned with INACSL standards have seen a 15% reduction in medical errors among learners.

Association of Standardized Patient Educators (ASPE)

ASPE accreditation recognizes excellence in programs integrating standardized patients (SPs) into healthcare education. It emphasizes SP recruitment, training, and program quality.

Example: Accredited programs report a 20% improvement in learner communication skills due to enhanced SP methodologies.

American College of Surgeons (ACS)

ACS accreditation is a benchmark of excellence for surgical simulation programs. It focuses on curriculum design, learner assessment, and advanced surgical simulation technologies.

Notable Impact: ACS-accredited programs report a 25% increase in learner competency in surgical procedures (ACS, 2022).

Other influential bodies include:
National League for Nursing (NLN): Focuses on nursing education and faculty development.

Simulation Canada: Offers guidance for simulation centers in North America.

1.4 Standards and Guidelines for Accreditation

Accreditation standards and guidelines provide a comprehensive framework for building, maintaining, and continuously improving healthcare simulation programs. These standards are not just checklists but a pathway to excellence, ensuring that simulation programs meet rigorous quality benchmarks and effectively prepare learners for real-world challenges.

Each component of the accreditation standards plays a vital role in shaping the program's overall impact, guiding everything from its foundational mission to its operational practices.

Mission and Objectives: Defining the Program's Purpose

The foundation of any accredited simulation program is a clear and well-defined mission that reflects its commitment to addressing healthcare needs and aligning with global best practices. A mission statement is a compass guiding the program's goals, strategies, and daily operations. It must articulate how the program advances healthcare education, patient safety, and clinical competence.

Accrediting bodies also emphasize the importance of setting measurable objectives that translate the mission into actionable goals. For example, a mission to improve interprofessional collaboration might include specific objectives, such as incorporating team-based simulation scenarios into 80% of the curriculum within three years. These objectives ensure that the program's activities are aligned with its vision and measurable in their impact.

Example:
A nursing simulation program developed its mission to focus on equipping learners with patient-centered care skills. Its objectives included integrating debriefing techniques that encourage reflection and empathy, which resulted in improved learner engagement and measurable increases in patient safety outcomes during clinical rotations.

Faculty and Staff: The Cornerstone of Excellence

Faculty and staff are the backbone of any simulation program, and their qualifications and commitment to professional growth are critical for accreditation. Accrediting bodies require programs to employ educators with relevant clinical expertise, experience in simulation-based education, and a commitment to continuous learning.

Continuous professional development is particularly significant. Faculty must stay abreast of advances in simulation technology, pedagogical methods, and healthcare standards. Certified Healthcare Simulation Educator (CHSE) or Certified Healthcare Simulation Operations Specialist (CHSOS) are often encouraged or required. These certifications validate the educator's expertise and enhance the program's credibility.

Example:
Faculty members regularly attended conferences at one simulation center, participated in workshops, and pursued advanced certifications. Over five years, this investment in professional development translated into a 30% improvement in learner satisfaction and outcomes, earning the program special recognition during its accreditation review.

Facilities and Technology: Creating Realistic Learning Environments

Simulation facilities and technology are the physical foundation of an accredited program. Accrediting bodies set high expectations for these resources' quality, functionality, and realism, which are critical for creating engaging learning experiences.

Programs must invest in state-of-the-art simulation labs equipped with high-fidelity manikins, task trainers, and immersive technologies like virtual reality (VR) or augmented reality (AR). These tools enable learners to practice clinical skills in a risk-free environment, fostering confidence and competence. Additionally, integrated audiovisual systems are essential for recording simulations and conducting reflective debriefing sessions, a cornerstone of effective simulation education.

Example:
A small simulation program facing budget constraints secured a grant to upgrade its facilities with VR technology. This investment elevated the realism of its scenarios and increased learner confidence by 40%, as measured by post-simulation surveys.

Curriculum Integration: Bridging Theory and Practice

For accreditation, simulation must not operate in isolation but be seamlessly woven into the program's broader curriculum. Simulation activities should align with defined learning objectives and support the development of clinical and critical thinking skills that learners can transfer to real-world settings.

Accreditation standards emphasize curriculum mapping to ensure that every simulation aligns with professional competencies, such as those outlined by organizations like the Accreditation Council for Graduate Medical Education (ACGME) or the American Association of Colleges of Nursing (AACN). Scenario design, facilitation, and debriefing must also adhere to evidence-based best practices.

Example:
One medical simulation program collaborated with faculty from various disciplines to align simulation scenarios with course objectives. This integration resulted in a 50% improvement in learner retention rates and was highlighted as a best practice during accreditation.

Continuous Quality Improvement: Adapting to Evolving Needs

Accreditation is not a static achievement but a commitment to continuous growth. Programs must demonstrate robust Continuous Quality Improvement (CQI) processes that evaluate and enhance their operations, curricula, and outcomes.

CQI collects data on key performance indicators (KPIs), such as learner satisfaction, faculty performance, and clinical skill acquisition. Programs must analyze this data to identify trends, address gaps, and adapt to emerging healthcare demands, such as integrating new technologies or responding to workforce needs.

Example:
A simulation center implemented quarterly CQI reviews, incorporating learner feedback, faculty evaluations, and outcome metrics. Over two years, this process led to significant improvements, including a 25% reduction in scenario completion time without compromising learning outcomes. This adaptability was commended during the accreditation process.

The accreditation standards and guidelines provide a roadmap for simulation programs to achieve and maintain excellence. From crafting a mission statement that resonates with healthcare priorities to building cutting-edge facilities and fostering faculty expertise, each component contributes to the program's impact and credibility. Programs that embrace these standards meet accreditation requirements and set the stage for sustained innovation, learner success, and improved patient care.

1.5 Key Takeaways:

- Accreditation guarantees quality, credibility, and effectiveness in healthcare simulation.
- Accredited programs see measurable benefits, including improved learner outcomes and expanded funding opportunities.

- Understanding accrediting bodies and their standards is essential for programs aiming to achieve and maintain accreditation.

1.6 Summary

Chapter 1 establishes a foundational understanding of accreditation in healthcare simulation programs and highlights its critical role in ensuring quality, credibility, and effectiveness in simulation-based education. Accreditation is a formal recognition process in which programs adhere to established standards set by accrediting bodies such as the Society for Simulation in Healthcare (SSH) and the International Nursing Association for Clinical Simulation and Learning (INACSL). This chapter explores the distinctions between accreditation and certification, emphasizing the program-wide impact of accreditation.

Key benefits of accreditation include enhanced program credibility, improved training quality, access to funding, and a demonstrated commitment to producing competent healthcare professionals. Accredited programs are shown to align more closely with evidence-based practices and global healthcare standards, yielding better learner outcomes and improved patient safety.

The chapter also introduces the primary accrediting organizations and their respective focuses, offering insights into the standards and guidelines programs must meet. These standards encompass essential areas such as organizational mission, faculty qualifications, simulation resources, curriculum integration, and continuous quality improvement. Programs are encouraged to view accreditation as an opportunity to foster innovation, achieve sustainability, and elevate educational outcomes.

By the end of the chapter, readers gain an appreciation for the value of accreditation, not only as a benchmark of excellence but also as a transformative process that strengthens simulation programs and supports their growth. This sets the stage for subsequent chapters, which delve deeper into preparing for accreditation and achieving compliance with these rigorous standards.

KEITH A. BEAULIEU

Chapter 2

Assessing Your Program's Readiness

Before embarking on the accreditation journey, healthcare simulation programs must assess their readiness to meet rigorous accreditation standards. A comprehensive readiness assessment allows program leaders to identify gaps, prioritize improvements, and allocate resources effectively. According to the Society for Simulation in Healthcare (SSH), programs that conduct a readiness assessment improve their first-attempt success rate by 25% compared to those that skip this critical step (SSH, 2022). This chapter provides a detailed guide to evaluating your program's readiness and creating a roadmap for accreditation success.

2.1 The Importance of Assessing Readiness

Embarking on the accreditation journey without thorough preparation is akin to navigating uncharted waters without a map. It can lead to unnecessary stress, wasted resources, and application delays that derail the accreditation process. A readiness assessment is not merely a preparatory step but the foundation for a successful accreditation journey. It allows simulation programs to evaluate their current practices critically, measure their performance against established accreditation standards, and identify areas for improvement.

Reducing Unnecessary Stress

Programs that dive into the accreditation process without assessing readiness often encounter unexpected hurdles. These can range from incomplete documentation to untrained staff, creating a stressful, reactive environment. By conducting a readiness assessment, programs can anticipate challenges, develop a structured plan, and foster team confidence. The result is a smoother, more predictable accreditation process.

Optimizing Resource Allocation

Resources in simulation programs are often limited, whether funding, staffing, or time. A readiness assessment helps prioritize where these resources should be allocated for maximum impact. For instance, if the assessment reveals that faculty need training in debriefing techniques or that equipment maintenance logs are incomplete, the program can first direct its efforts to these areas.

Establishing a Culture of Quality Improvement

One of the most valuable outcomes of a readiness assessment is the opportunity to embed a culture of quality improvement within the program. This culture goes beyond meeting accreditation standards; it fosters an environment where continuous evaluation and enhancement become the norm. Programs that embrace quality improvement are better equipped to adapt to changing standards, integrate new technologies, and address emerging learner needs.

Assessing readiness is not just a preparatory step—it is the foundation for a successful accreditation process. It allows programs to proactively identify gaps, allocate resources effectively, and foster a culture of excellence and continuous improvement. By evaluating their readiness, simulation programs can confidently approach accreditation, ensuring a smoother process and a greater likelihood of success.

Statistics Supporting Readiness Assessments:
Data supports the value of readiness assessments. According to the Society for Simulation in Healthcare (SSH), programs that conduct thorough readiness assessments improve their first-attempt accreditation success rate by 25% compared to those that skip this step (SSH, 2022). This statistic underscores the importance of preparation in achieving accreditation efficiently and effectively.

Programs with readiness assessments are 33% more likely to identify deficiencies early and address them before applying for accreditation (INACSL, 2021).

Organizations that engage stakeholders early report a 20% increase in team satisfaction and collaboration during accreditation (SSH, 2022).

2.2 Gap Analysis

A gap analysis is a critical first step in preparing for healthcare simulation accreditation, serving as a roadmap to align a program's current practices with accreditation standards. By systematically identifying strengths and weaknesses, a gap analysis provides a clear picture of where a program stands and what actions are needed to achieve compliance. This process saves time and resources by preventing costly last-minute fixes and fosters a culture of accountability and continuous improvement. In healthcare simulation, where the quality of education directly impacts patient safety and learner outcomes, a gap analysis ensures that programs meet rigorous benchmarks and remain adaptable to the field's evolving needs. Programs that prioritize this analysis confidently approach accreditation, positioning themselves for success and long-term excellence.

Step 1: Conducting a Gap Analysis

A gap analysis compares a program's current practices, resources, and outcomes against the standards outlined by accrediting bodies such as SSH or INACSL.

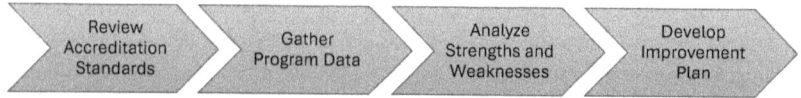

Figure 1 Steps to Perform a Gap Analysis

1. Review Accreditation Standards

Obtain and thoroughly review the accrediting body's most recent guidelines. Standards typically address mission objectives, curriculum design, faculty qualifications, infrastructure, and quality improvement.

2. Gather Program Data

Collect and organize data such as:
- Program policies and procedures
- Curriculum and learner assessments
- Faculty qualifications and training records
- Facility and resource inventories

3. Analyze Strengths and Weaknesses
Assess your program's alignment with accreditation requirements:
- Does your curriculum integrate simulation with real-world clinical objectives?
- Are faculty members adequately trained in debriefing and learner evaluation?

For example, an analysis may reveal that while your program excels in scenario design, it lacks a structured debriefing policy, a common gap identified during accreditation evaluations.

> **Accreditation Tip:**
> When reviewing the accreditation standards during the gap analysis process, write what you have completed, what is in progress, and what you must start. I recommend using a simple traffic light system or something similar to quickly see what portions of the accreditation standards you must focus on as you progress through the process.

4. Develop an Improvement Plan
Create an action plan to address deficiencies with specific goals, timelines, and responsible personnel. For example:
- Goal: Implement a formal debriefing policy.
- Timeline: 6 months.
- Responsible Team Member: Simulation Educator Lead.

Step 2: Engaging Stakeholders
Accreditation is a collaborative process that requires the support of stakeholders, including program leaders, faculty, staff, learners, and external partners.

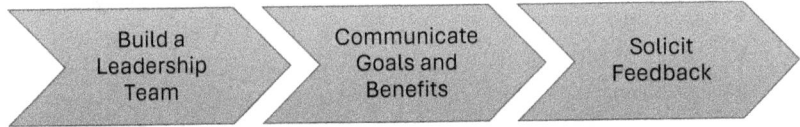

Figure 2 Steps to Engage Stakeholders

1. Build a Leadership Team
Assemble a team of representatives from critical areas, such as curriculum design, faculty training, and quality assurance.

2. Communicate Goals and Benefits
Share how accreditation will enhance:

- Program credibility and reputation
- Learner outcomes
- Access to funding and institutional partnerships

3. Solicit Feedback
Engage stakeholders in discussions about roles, responsibilities, and potential challenges. According to a 2021 SSH survey, stakeholder engagement reduces resistance to changes required for accreditation by 28%.

Step 3: Evaluating Resources and Infrastructure
Healthcare simulation programs need adequate physical, technological, and human resources to meet accreditation standards.

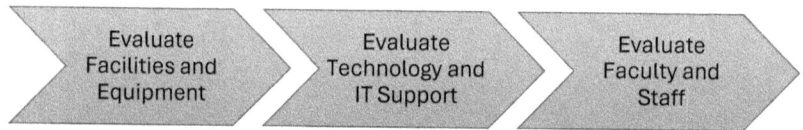

Figure 3 Steps to Evaluate Resources and Infrastructure

1. Facilities and Equipment
Ensure that simulation centers meet industry standards for safety, functionality, and realism:

2. Technology and IT Support
Evaluate your program's technology, including:
- Learning management systems
- Scenario design software
- Audiovisual equipment for debriefing

> Programs with a 1:15 ratio of simulation technicians to learners report a 95% learner satisfaction rate
>
> Source: INACSL, 2021

3. Faculty and Staff
Assess whether faculty and staff meet the required qualifications.

Step 4: Building a Timeline for Accreditation
Accreditation can take months or years. A structured timeline ensures programs remain on track.

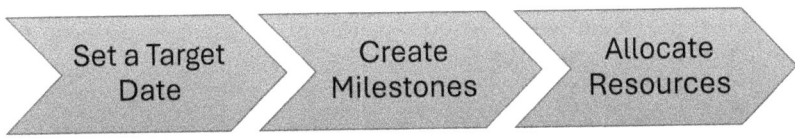

Figure 4 Steps for building a timeline

1. Set a Target Date
Choose a realistic accreditation application date, considering the time needed for preparation, implementation, and evaluation.

2. Create Milestones
Break the process into manageable tasks with deadlines:
- Faculty training completed by Month 6
- Policy updates by Month 8
- Mock review conducted by Month 12

3. Allocate Resources
Develop a budget for accreditation-related expenses, such as training workshops, facility upgrades, or new equipment.

Step 5: Assessing Organizational Readiness
Beyond technical readiness, evaluate the program's cultural and operational preparedness for accreditation.

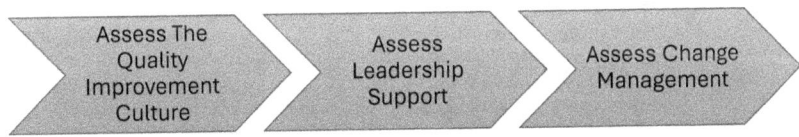

Figure 5 Steps to Assess Organizational Readiness

1. Quality Improvement Culture
Does your program regularly:
- Collect and analyze learner feedback?
- Adapt processes based on evaluation data?

2. Leadership Support
Strong leadership ensures success. Leaders must actively champion accreditation goals and allocate necessary resources.

3. Change Management
Evaluate the organization's ability to adapt to changes required for accreditation, such as policy revisions or new technologies.

A comprehensive readiness assessment lays the foundation for accreditation success. Simulation programs can address deficiencies and foster a culture of excellence by conducting a gap analysis, engaging stakeholders, evaluating resources, and building a timeline. Accreditation is not merely a checkbox; it reflects a commitment to continuous improvement and innovation. With careful planning and preparation, your program can confidently embark on the accreditation journey.

2.3 Takeaways

- **Readiness is Critical:**
  Programs conducting readiness assessments are 25% more likely to achieve accreditation on their first attempt.

- **Stakeholder Engagement Matters:**
  Early involvement reduces resistance and improves collaboration.

- **Resource Evaluation is Key:**
  Programs with adequate resources (e.g., facilities, technology, staff) consistently meet accreditation standards.

- **Build a Realistic Timeline:**
  Proper planning ensures that improvements are implemented systematically.

2.4 Summary

Chapter 2 emphasizes the importance of a comprehensive readiness assessment as the first critical step in the accreditation journey for healthcare simulation programs. It provides a detailed framework for evaluating whether a program is prepared to meet accreditation standards and outlines practical strategies for identifying gaps, prioritizing improvements, and fostering stakeholder collaboration.

The chapter concludes by emphasizing that accreditation readiness is more than meeting technical requirements; it reflects a program's commitment to excellence, innovation, and continuous improvement. Programs that invest in thorough readiness assessments position themselves for long-term success, achieving accreditation and delivering high-quality simulation-based education.

KEITH A. BEAULIEU

Chapter 3

Key Components of Accreditation Standards

Understanding and meeting accreditation standards is essential for achieving and maintaining accreditation in healthcare simulation. These standards are blueprints for program development, implementation, and continuous improvement. According to the Society for Simulation in Healthcare (SSH), accredited programs report a 30% improvement in learner outcomes and a 25% increase in operational efficiency compared to non-accredited counterparts (SSH, 2022). This chapter delves into the key components of accreditation standards and provides actionable strategies for compliance.

3.1 Overview of Accreditation Standards

Accreditation standards are the foundation of any successful healthcare simulation program, providing a structured framework to ensure consistency, quality, and alignment with industry best practices. While specifics may vary depending on the accrediting body—such as the Society for Simulation in Healthcare (SSH) or the International Nursing Association for Clinical Simulation and Learning (INACSL)—the core components of these standards share a common goal: to establish programs that are effective, learner-focused, and responsive to the demands of modern healthcare education.

A Unified Vision with Unique Approaches

Each accrediting body brings a unique perspective to accreditation, shaped by its mission and target audience. For example, SSH focuses broadly on simulation in various healthcare disciplines, offering standards that emphasize interprofessional education, simulation design, and learner assessment. INACSL, on the other hand, is renowned for its Standards of Best Practice in Simulation, which include specific guidelines for debriefing, simulation facilitation, and operations. Despite these differences, both organizations champion core values such as rigor, transparency, and continuous improvement.

The Importance of Aligning with Accreditation Standards

Adhering to accreditation standards is not merely a checkbox exercise but a commitment to excellence and accountability. These standards drive programs to implement evidence-based practices, ensure consistent quality, and prepare learners for the complexities of modern healthcare. Programs internalizing these standards are better equipped to address challenges, foster innovation, and contribute meaningfully to advancing healthcare education.

By understanding the overarching principles and specific requirements of accrediting bodies, simulation programs can navigate the accreditation process more effectively. This alignment facilitates a smoother accreditation journey and positions programs as leaders in their field, capable of shaping the future of healthcare simulation.

Statistics Supporting Accreditation Standards:

Efficiency Gains: Accredited programs save an average of 20% in resource costs due to streamlined processes and clear standards (INACSL, 2021).

Learner Preparedness: 87% of learners in accredited programs report feeling better prepared for clinical challenges (SSH, 2022).

3.2 Core Components of Accreditation Standards

Organizational Structure and Governance

The backbone of any successful simulation program lies in its organizational structure and governance. This foundation ensures accountability, promotes effective decision-making and establishes a clear framework for leadership and collaboration. Accrediting bodies emphasize governance because it reflects a program's ability to operate efficiently and achieve its educational goals while adapting to challenges. Without a robust governance structure, even the most well-resourced programs can falter under unclear roles and fragmented decision-making.

The governance of a simulation program begins with defining the roles and responsibilities of its team members. This often involves creating a documented organizational chart that outlines reporting lines, leadership positions, and areas of accountability. Delineating these roles fosters transparency and streamlines communication across the program.

Stakeholder engagement is another cornerstone of effective governance. By involving faculty, staff, learners, and even external partners in decision-making processes, programs can ensure that diverse perspectives are considered. This collaborative approach strengthens trust and commitment and promotes innovative solutions to potential challenges.

Simulation programs often maintain records such as meeting minutes, strategic plans, and policy documents to demonstrate governance in practice. These artifacts provide tangible evidence of oversight and planning, which accrediting bodies look for as indicators of a program's readiness and sustainability.

For example, one simulation center identified a gap in communication and decision-making processes. To address this, it formed a dedicated quality assurance team to oversee operational improvements. Within a year, the center reported a 15% boost in internal communication efficiency and smoother implementation of quality initiatives (INACSL, 2021).

Governance also benefits from specialized committees that tackle specific program areas, such as curriculum design, technology management, and quality improvement. These committees create a focused environment for addressing critical program components and ensure that every area receives the attention and expertise it requires.

Policies are another essential aspect of governance. Clear decision-making frameworks and conflict-resolution procedures provide a roadmap for effectively handling challenges. Without these structures, programs risk losing direction when faced with conflicts or complex decisions.

Ultimately, a strong governance framework is more than an administrative necessity—it is the driving force behind a cohesive and effective simulation program. By building a structured, inclusive, and transparent governance model, programs can set the stage for success in accreditation and beyond.

2. Program Mission, Vision, and Objectives

The mission, vision, and objectives of a simulation program are more than just words on paper—they serve as the program's guiding compass, defining its purpose, direction, and alignment with broader organizational goals. Together, these elements form a cohesive narrative that informs every decision, from curriculum development to resource allocation.

A strong **mission statement** captures the program's core purpose, answering the fundamental question: *Why does this program exist?* For simulation programs, this might mean emphasizing the enhancement of clinical competence, fostering patient safety, or addressing specific gaps in healthcare training. The mission should resonate with the organization's values while reflecting the unique role of the simulation program in advancing education and practice.

> **Accreditation Tip:** Ensure that your program's mission and vision are known to stakeholders and visible physically within your center, website, marketing materials, etc....

The **vision statement** complements the mission by describing the program's aspirations. It outlines the program's future goals and inspires stakeholders to work toward shared long-term goals. For example, a vision might emphasize becoming a regional leader in innovative simulation-based education or achieving international recognition for excellence in interprofessional training.

Objectives serve as the roadmap, translating the mission and vision into actionable steps. These objectives should be SMART: Specific, Measurable, Achievable, Relevant, and Time-bound. For instance, a program might set a measurable goal to increase learner assessment pass rates by 10% within a year or implement five new simulation scenarios addressing emerging healthcare trends.

Developing these elements requires collaboration. Engaging stakeholders—faculty, staff, learners, and organizational leaders—ensures that the mission, vision, and objectives reflect diverse perspectives and align with institutional priorities. Workshops and brainstorming sessions provide opportunities for meaningful input, fostering a sense of ownership and commitment among participants.

It is equally important to revisit these statements periodically. Healthcare education is a dynamic field constantly influenced by new technologies, practices, and societal needs. Regular updates to the mission, vision, and objectives ensure they remain relevant and aligned with current trends. A static mission that fails to evolve risks becoming disconnected from the program's activities and the needs of its stakeholders.

A compelling example comes from a nursing simulation program that revised its mission to emphasize patient-centered care. This change was more than a rebranding effort; it reoriented the program's focus toward fostering empathy and teamwork among learners. Within a year, the program saw a 25% increase in learner engagement during team-based scenarios, demonstrating the power of a clear, purpose-driven mission (SSH, 2022).

Simulation programs can create a framework for meaningful impact by defining a mission that inspires, a vision that motivates, and objectives that guide. These foundational elements set the tone for accreditation efforts and ensure that the program continually aligns with its highest aspirations and organizational priorities.

3. Curriculum Design and Delivery

Curriculum design is the cornerstone of a successful simulation program. It serves as the roadmap that guides learners toward achieving critical educational objectives. It transforms high-level goals into actionable, measurable learning experiences. For healthcare simulation, this means creating scenarios and activities that mirror the complexities of real-world clinical environments while adhering to evidence-based practices. A well-crafted curriculum doesn't just teach skills—it shapes competent, confident healthcare professionals ready to meet the demands of patient care.

A strong simulation curriculum begins with clearly defined learning objectives. Each simulation activity should have a purpose, whether it's improving clinical decision-making, refining technical skills, or fostering interprofessional communication. These objectives must align with broader programmatic goals and professional competencies. For instance, nursing simulations might integrate the AACN competencies, while medical simulations might map to ACGME (Accreditation Council for Graduate Medical Education) milestones. Simulation programs ensure learners gain relevant, transferable skills by aligning with recognized standards.

Another critical component is integration into the broader educational curriculum. Simulation should not exist in isolation; it should complement and enhance traditional learning methods, such as lectures, case studies, and clinical rotations. For example, a nursing program might use simulation to bridge the gap between pharmacology coursework and medication administration practice, allowing learners to apply theoretical knowledge in a controlled, hands-on environment.

Scenario design is where the curriculum truly comes to life. Effective scenarios are grounded in best practices and tailored to the learners' level of training. Standardized templates can ensure consistency in scenario structure, including clearly stated objectives, realistic case narratives, and defined roles for participants. These templates also streamline the scenario creation process, reducing variability and ensuring alignment with the program's goals.

Facilitation and debriefing are equally essential. Learning doesn't end when the scenario does; during debriefing, learners reflect, analyze, and internalize their experiences. Structured debriefing models scaffold meaningful discussions, such as the PEARLS (Promoting Excellence and Reflective Learning in Simulation) framework or DASH (Debriefing Assessment for Simulation in Healthcare) methodology. According to INACSL (2021), programs adopting standardized debriefing methods report 40% higher learner satisfaction scores than programs with unstructured debriefing.

> Programs adopting standardized debriefing methods report **40%** higher learner satisfaction scores than programs with unstructured debriefing.

Faculty training is pivotal to the success of curriculum delivery. Simulation educators must be skilled in scenario facilitation and guiding reflective learning during debriefing. Programs should invest in ongoing professional development for faculty, including workshops, certifications, and peer mentoring. For example, faculty trained in the PEARLS debriefing framework often report increased confidence in leading discussions, resulting in more impactful student learning experiences.

The impact of a well-designed curriculum is profound. Simulation programs with robust, evidence-based curricula see measurable improvements in learner outcomes, including higher assessment scores, increased confidence in clinical skills, and enhanced teamwork. For instance, a program that incorporated standardized scenario templates and faculty training in debriefing models saw a 20% improvement in learner performance on clinical competency exams within a single academic year.

Curriculum design is not a one-time effort—it's an ongoing process of evaluation and refinement. Programs must regularly assess the effectiveness of their simulations, gathering feedback from learners and faculty to identify areas for improvement. By continuously adapting to meet the evolving needs of healthcare education, simulation programs ensure they remain at the forefront of training innovation.

Ultimately, a well-designed and delivered curriculum does more than meet accreditation standards; it prepares learners to excel in the dynamic, high-pressure world of healthcare. Through thoughtful planning, integration, and execution, simulation programs can create transformative learning experiences that leave a lasting impact on both learners and the patients they serve.

4. Faculty and Staff Qualifications

The success of any healthcare simulation program relies heavily on the expertise, dedication, and preparedness of its faculty and staff. These individuals are the architects and facilitators of learning experiences that shape future healthcare professionals. As such, accrediting bodies emphasize ensuring faculty and staff possess the qualifications and training to deliver high-quality simulation education. Beyond meeting accreditation standards, investing in qualified personnel builds credibility, enhances learner outcomes, and drives program innovation.

<u>Faculty Qualifications</u>

The educators who bring scenarios to life are at the heart of any simulation program. Faculty should possess clinical expertise and educational experience tailored to simulation-based learning. This dual skill set ensures they can create realistic scenarios, facilitate engaging sessions, and effectively assess learner performance. Faculty with a strong clinical background can draw on real-world knowledge to design scenarios that reflect the complexities of patient care. At the same time, their educational expertise allows them to employ effective teaching strategies, such as structured debriefing and competency-based assessments.

<u>Ongoing Professional Development</u>

Simulation education is a dynamic and ever-evolving field. Technologies advance, best practices evolve, and learner needs shift over time. To keep pace, faculty and staff must engage in continuous professional development. This might include attending conferences, participating in workshops, or pursuing certifications such as the Certified Healthcare Simulation Educator (CHSE) or Certified Healthcare Simulation Operations Specialist (CHSOS). According to the Society for Simulation in Healthcare (SSH), simulation centers with certified educators report a 33% increase in learner outcomes compared to centers without certified faculty (SSH, 2022). Certification not only validates expertise but also signals a commitment to excellence.

Adequate Staffing Levels
A well-staffed simulation program is essential for smooth operations and high-quality learner experiences. Programs should ensure they have sufficient personnel to support all simulation aspects, from scenario design and facilitation to equipment maintenance and administrative tasks. For example, simulation technicians are critical in managing technology, setting up scenarios, and troubleshooting issues. A study by the International Nursing Association for Clinical Simulation and Learning (INACSL) found that programs with a ratio of at least one simulation technician per 15 learners reported higher satisfaction rates and fewer operational disruptions (INACSL, 2021).

Implementation Strategies
Programs must actively invest in their faculty and staff to meet these requirements. Encouraging certification is a key step. Certifications such as CHSE and CHSOS provide a structured pathway for educators and operations staff to gain specialized knowledge and skills. Programs should also develop comprehensive training plans that cover simulation pedagogy, scenario design, assessment methods, and emerging technologies. Faculty workshops, peer mentoring, and access to online training modules effectively support ongoing learning.

Performance evaluations are another critical component. Annual reviews provide an opportunity to assess strengths, identify areas for growth, and set professional development goals. These evaluations should be constructive and focus on how faculty and staff can enhance their contributions to the program. For instance, a faculty member might identify a need for advanced debriefing training, while a technician might seek to deepen their expertise in managing high-fidelity manikins.

Real-World Impact
The impact of qualified faculty and staff on learner outcomes cannot be overstated. For example, a simulation center that prioritized faculty

certification and implemented regular training saw a measurable improvement in learner performance. Within one year, the center reported a 20% increase in learners' clinical competency scores and a 15% reduction in errors during simulation-based assessments (SSH, 2022).

Faculty and staff are the backbone of healthcare simulation programs, and their qualifications directly influence program quality and learner success. Programs can create a culture of excellence that benefits educators and learners by hiring individuals with relevant experience, fostering professional growth, and maintaining adequate staffing levels. Investing in the people who power simulation is not just a requirement for accreditation—it's a commitment to delivering transformative educational experiences that prepare healthcare professionals for the challenges of modern practice.

5. Simulation Resources and Facilities

A simulation program's physical and technological resources are the foundation for creating immersive and effective learning experiences. A well-equipped and thoughtfully designed simulation facility provides learners with a realistic environment where they can practice, make mistakes, and grow. Accrediting bodies emphasize the importance of resources and facilities because they directly impact education quality and the scenarios' fidelity. From state-of-the-art manikins to carefully arranged debriefing spaces, every detail contributes to the learner's ability to engage deeply with the material.

Adequate Physical Space

A simulation facility must have enough space to accommodate a variety of activities, from high-fidelity scenarios in simulated operating rooms to team debriefings in comfortable, quiet settings. Well-planned physical spaces enhance the realism of simulations and the effectiveness of post-scenario discussions. For instance, debriefing areas should be private, distraction-free, and equipped with tools like audiovisual playback systems to support reflective learning. Simulation rooms, on the other hand, need to mimic real-world clinical environments as closely as possible, complete with hospital beds, medical equipment, and charting stations.

Programs that do not focus more on spatial considerations often need help to achieve their learning objectives. A crowded or poorly organized facility can hinder movement, communication, and engagement. To ensure that facilities meet the needs of learners and educators alike, many programs perform a resource audit, identifying gaps in space and functionality.

Reliable Simulation Equipment
Simulation technology has advanced significantly in recent years, offering tools like high-fidelity manikins that simulate everything from cardiac arrest to childbirth, virtual reality systems for immersive training, and task trainers for specific skills like suturing or intubation. However, even the most advanced technology is only as effective as its reliability.

Manikins and audiovisual systems require regular maintenance to function correctly. Programs implementing a preventive maintenance schedule report a 20% reduction in simulation downtime, ensuring learners have uninterrupted access to training opportunities (INACSL, 2021). This is particularly important for programs with large cohorts, where scheduling time in the simulation lab is already challenging. Equipment failures during scheduled sessions disrupt the learning process and erode confidence in the program's resources.

Policies for Equipment Maintenance and Safety
Establishing clear equipment use, maintenance, and safety policies is crucial for long-term sustainability. These policies should include guidelines for routine checks, troubleshooting, and repairs. Partnering with vendors to train faculty and staff on operating and maintaining equipment can also reduce wear and tear caused by improper handling. For instance, a program that worked with its manikin supplier to train technicians on routine maintenance extended the lifespan of its equipment by two years, saving thousands of dollars in replacement costs.

Safety policies should also address the physical and psychological well-being of learners. For example, simulation scenarios involving high-stakes emergencies can be stressful; creating a safe, supportive environment helps learners process the experience without undue anxiety. Physical safety considerations, such as ensuring that cables and equipment are securely arranged to prevent tripping hazards, are equally important.

Implementation Strategies
To address the demands of maintaining high-quality simulation facilities and resources, programs should take proactive steps:

- *Resource Audit:* Conduct a thorough review of existing resources, identifying gaps in equipment, space, or technology. This audit can help prioritize upgrades and allocate funding effectively.
- *Vendor Partnerships:* Build relationships with simulation technology providers to access the latest advancements, training, and maintenance support. Vendors often offer discounted educational institutions packages or trial periods for new technologies.
- *Preventive Maintenance:* Develop and adhere to a schedule for inspecting and maintaining equipment. Regular maintenance reduces downtime and extends the lifespan of expensive tools, maximizing return on investment.

Impact on Learner Outcomes

The quality of simulation resources and facilities directly influences learner outcomes. For example, programs equipped with high-fidelity manikins and realistic clinical environments often see higher levels of learner engagement and confidence. In one study, learners reported a 35% increase in confidence when practicing on advanced simulation equipment versus low-fidelity models (INACSL, 2021). Similarly, debriefing conducted in well-designed, distraction-free spaces leads to more meaningful reflection and retention of lessons.

Simulation resources and facilities are more than just physical assets—they are integral to the learner's experience and the program's success. By providing adequate space, reliable equipment, and robust maintenance policies, programs create an environment that fosters effective learning and supports accreditation standards. Investments in high-quality resources improve learner outcomes and demonstrate a commitment to excellence, positioning simulation programs as leaders in healthcare education.

6. Assessment and Evaluation

Assessment and evaluation lie at the heart of a high-performing healthcare simulation program. These practices are essential for measuring learner performance, ensuring educational objectives are met, and continuously improving program quality. Without robust assessment mechanisms, programs risk delivering inconsistent learning experiences and failing to identify improvement areas. Accrediting bodies prioritize assessment and evaluation as cornerstones of effective education, emphasizing their role in fostering learner competency and program accountability.

Measuring Learner Performance

The primary goal of assessment in simulation education is to evaluate whether learners have achieved the competencies necessary for safe and effective clinical practice. This requires standardized tools, such as checklists and rubrics, which provide objective and reliable performance measures. Tools like the Lasater Clinical Judgment Rubric, for example, offer a structured framework for assessing critical thinking, decision-making, and clinical judgment.

These assessments go beyond technical skills. Simulation scenarios often emphasize soft skills such as communication, teamwork, and leadership—critical components of modern healthcare practice. By assessing these attributes, programs help learners develop the well-rounded competencies required in real-world settings.

Program Effectiveness

Assessment doesn't end with learners; simulation programs must also evaluate their own effectiveness. This includes analyzing the quality of scenarios, faculty performance, and overall program outcomes. Regular scenario reviews ensure that learning activities remain relevant and aligned with current clinical standards. Faculty evaluations, meanwhile, provide opportunities for professional growth and help maintain high teaching standards.

For example, a program that conducted quarterly scenario reviews found that 20% of its scenarios needed updates to reflect recent changes in clinical guidelines. By implementing these updates, the program ensured that its curriculum remained cutting-edge and clinically relevant.

Data-Driven Improvement

Data is one of the most powerful tools in assessment and evaluation. Programs that collect, analyze, and act on data can identify trends, pinpoint weaknesses, and implement targeted improvements. Mechanisms such as learner surveys, focus groups, and performance tracking tools provide rich insights into what's working and what needs improvement.

Dashboards are particularly effective for visualizing and monitoring key performance indicators (KPIs) such as pass rates, satisfaction scores, and competency milestones. For instance, a simulation program that implemented data dashboards reported a 50% improvement in tracking learner competency milestones, enabling them to tailor support for struggling learners and celebrate those exceeding expectations (SSH, 2022).

Feedback Mechanisms

Learner feedback is a vital component of evaluation. Post-scenario surveys and focus groups allow learners to share their experiences, offering invaluable perspectives on the strengths and weaknesses of simulation activities. Faculty can use this feedback to refine their facilitation and debriefing techniques, ensuring that sessions are as impactful as possible.

For example, a program that introduced anonymous learner surveys after each simulation found that learners valued longer debriefing sessions and more opportunities for peer feedback. The program improved learner satisfaction by 30% within a single academic year by incorporating these insights.

Implementation Strategies

To establish effective assessment and evaluation practices, programs should:

- *Standardize Tools:* To ensure consistency and reliability in assessments, use validated rubrics and checklists, such as the Lasater Clinical Judgment Rubric or the Debriefing Assessment for Simulation in Healthcare (DASH).
- *Leverage Technology:* Implement dashboards to track and analyze KPIs, making data-driven decisions more accessible and actionable.
- *Engage Learners:* Collect feedback through surveys and focus groups to identify areas for improvement and adapt accordingly.

The Role of Continuous Improvement

Assessment and evaluation are not one-time activities but ongoing processes that drive continuous improvement. Programs must regularly review their assessment methods, incorporate new tools and technologies, and adapt to educational standards and clinical practice changes. This commitment to continuous evaluation demonstrates a program's dedication to excellence and ensures alignment with accreditation standards.

Robust assessment and evaluation practices elevate simulation programs from good to great. Programs create a culture of accountability and innovation by systematically measuring learner performance, evaluating program effectiveness, and using data to inform improvements. These practices satisfy accreditation requirements and ensure that learners are equipped to deliver safe, competent, and compassionate care in real-world settings. With the right tools, feedback mechanisms, and commitment to improvement, assessment and evaluation can become the engine that drives a simulation program's success.

7. Continuous Quality Improvement (CQI)

Continuous Quality Improvement (CQI) is not just a process but a mindset that drives a simulation program's commitment to excellence. CQI ensures that programs remain dynamic and responsive, continuously adapting to meet the evolving needs of healthcare education and standards. By systematically analyzing performance, identifying areas for enhancement, and implementing changes, CQI transforms challenges into opportunities for growth.

A Framework for Evolution

In healthcare simulation, CQI is the engine that propels programs forward. It emphasizes the importance of data-driven decision-making and fosters a culture of accountability and innovation. Structured processes for data collection, analysis, and planning form the foundation of CQI. These processes are necessary for programs to avoid stagnation, fail to address emerging needs, or align with industry best practices.

For example, a simulation program might notice a plateau in learner performance on clinical decision-making tasks. Through CQI, the program could analyze assessment data, identify gaps in the curriculum, and implement targeted changes, such as new scenario designs or enhanced debriefing techniques.

Key Components of CQI

- *Data Collection and Analysis.* Robust data collection is the starting point for CQI. Programs must gather information on learner outcomes, faculty performance, scenario effectiveness, and resource utilization. Analysis of this data can uncover trends, such as consistent learner struggles with specific competencies or underutilized simulation equipment.

- *Regular Reviews* Regularly reviewing policies, curricula, and outcomes ensures that programs remain relevant and effective. These reviews also allow for assessing whether current practices align with accreditation standards and organizational goals.

Documenting Improvement Activities

Documenting CQI efforts is critical for internal tracking and external validation during accreditation. Documentation should include the rationale for changes, the steps taken, and measurable outcomes to demonstrate the impact of improvement activities.

Implementing CQI: Practical Strategies

One of the most effective methods for implementing CQI is the **Plan-Do-Study-Act (PDSA) cycle**, a proven framework for iterative improvement:

- *Plan:* Identify an area for improvement, such as enhancing learner debriefing sessions. Develop a plan with clear objectives, action steps, and success metrics.
- *Do:* Implement the plan on a small scale, such as piloting a new debriefing model with a single cohort of learners.
- *Study:* Evaluate the results by collecting feedback, analyzing data, and comparing outcomes to baseline metrics.
- *Act:* Refine the approach based on findings and roll it out more broadly.

For instance, a simulation program using PDSA cycles to refine its debriefing practices reported a 30% reduction in learner assessment errors within a year (INACSL, 2021).

The Role of Leadership and Collaboration

Effective CQI requires strong leadership and collaboration. Establishing a quality improvement committee with representatives from key areas—such as curriculum development, faculty training, and technology—ensures that initiatives are well-coordinated and inclusive. This committee can oversee CQI efforts, prioritize initiatives, and ensure alignment with program goals.

Equally important is engaging stakeholders, including faculty, staff, learners, and external partners, in the CQI process. Sharing findings and celebrating successes fosters buy-in and collaboration. For example, a program that transparently shared CQI outcomes with its stakeholders saw increased support for implementing changes, such as additional funding for faculty development.

CQI in Action: A Case Study

A nursing simulation program identified that learners were consistently underperforming in team-based scenarios. By applying CQI principles, the program used PDSA cycles to address this issue. The "Plan" phase involved identifying potential causes, such as insufficient preparation or unclear scenario roles. In the "Do" phase, the program introduced pre-scenario briefings focused on teamwork strategies. During the "Study" phase, feedback and performance data showed a significant improvement in team dynamics. Finally, in the "Act" phase, the program integrated the new briefing approach into all team-based simulations.

Within one year, the program observed a 20% increase in learner satisfaction and a 15% improvement in team-based performance metrics.

<u>Building a Culture of Continuous Improvement</u>
CQI is most successful when embedded into the culture of a simulation program. This means fostering an environment where faculty and staff are encouraged to innovate, learners feel empowered to provide feedback, and leadership actively supports improvement initiatives. Tools like dashboards to visualize progress, regular CQI meetings, and recognition of successful initiatives can sustain this culture over time.

Continuous Quality Improvement is a powerful mechanism for ensuring simulation programs meet and exceed accreditation standards. Programs can evolve by adopting structured processes like PDSA cycles, conducting regular reviews, and engaging stakeholders to address new challenges and opportunities. Beyond compliance, CQI reflects a commitment to delivering the highest education standards, ultimately preparing learners to excel in the complex and ever-changing world of healthcare.

3.3 Takeaways

- *Standards Drive Excellence:* Accreditation standards improve learner outcomes and program efficiency.
- *Governance is Foundational:* Strong leadership and clear roles ensure accountability.
- *Resources Matter:* High-quality facilities and equipment are non-negotiable for success.
- *CQI is Ongoing:* Continuous improvement is essential for maintaining accreditation and adapting to healthcare trends.

3.4 Summary

Accreditation standards provide a robust framework for developing and maintaining a high-quality healthcare simulation program. By addressing key components such as governance, curriculum design, faculty qualifications, resources, assessment, and CQI, programs can align with best practices and achieve accreditation success. Beyond compliance, these standards elevate program credibility and ensure learners are prepared to meet modern healthcare challenges.

Chapter 4

Preparing Documentation and Evidence

Preparing documentation and evidence is one of the most critical aspects of achieving accreditation for a healthcare simulation program. Accrediting bodies require detailed records to assess a program's adherence to established standards. This chapter provides a comprehensive guide to preparing the necessary documentation, organizing evidence, and avoiding common pitfalls to ensure a successful accreditation submission.

4.1 The Role of Documentation in Accreditation

Documentation is the primary evidence that a simulation program meets accreditation standards. It provides a transparent view of the program's policies, practices, and outcomes. According to the Society for Simulation in Healthcare (SSH), programs with well-organized documentation reduce the risk of accreditation delays by 30% and increase their chances of first-time approval by 25% (*SSH, 2022*).

Well-prepared documentation also reflects a program's commitment to quality and professionalism. Accrediting bodies evaluate not only the content of the documents but also their clarity, organization, and alignment with accreditation criteria.

> Accrediting bodies evaluate not only the content of the documents but also their clarity, organization, and alignment with accreditation criteria.

4.2 Preparing Documentation

Preparing documentation for accreditation is not merely a bureaucratic exercise; it is a critical opportunity to showcase your program's strengths, align with best practices, and demonstrate your commitment to excellence in simulation-based education. Effective documentation provides the foundation for a successful accreditation application, illustrating how your program meets or exceeds the required standards. It is both a reflective exercise and a strategic endeavor that requires careful planning, organization, and attention to detail.

Step 1: Understanding Required Documentation

The first step in preparing for accreditation is thoroughly understanding the accrediting body's documentation requirements. These requirements serve as the blueprint for your submission, ensuring that every aspect of your program is accounted for and aligned with standards.

Accrediting bodies typically request evidence in several key categories:

- *Organizational Structure:* Programs must provide documents like organizational charts and governance policies to demonstrate clear leadership roles and decision-making processes. For example, an organizational chart might illustrate how the simulation director reports to the dean of education and collaborates with faculty leads.
- *Program Mission and Objectives:* Accrediting bodies expect mission and vision statements that articulate the program's purpose and long-term goals, along with strategic plans that translate these aspirations into actionable objectives.
- *Curriculum and Instructional Design:* Simulation scenarios, learning objectives, and instructional materials are required to showcase how your program aligns with professional standards and educational goals. These documents provide reviewers with a snapshot of the educational journey your learners experience.
- *Faculty and Staff Records:* Up-to-date résumés, certifications, and professional development records demonstrate the qualifications and growth of your team and underscore your commitment to quality education.
- *Resources and Facilities:* Maintenance logs, inventory lists, and safety policies highlight the program's investment in providing a safe, well-equipped environment for learners.

- *Assessment and Evaluation:* Learner assessment tools, grading rubrics, and data on outcomes provide measurable evidence of program effectiveness.
- *Continuous Quality Improvement (CQI):* Reports on CQI initiatives and meeting minutes illustrate the program's ongoing efforts to evolve and improve.

Understanding these categories upfront allows you to map out a strategy for collecting and organizing the necessary evidence.

Step 2: Creating a Comprehensive Self-Study Report

The self-study report is the centerpiece of your accreditation submission. It is not merely a collection of documents but a cohesive narrative that tells the story of your program's achievements, alignment with standards, and vision for the future.

- *Organize by Standards:* Structure your report to correspond directly to the accreditation standards. Each section should address a specific area, such as governance, curriculum design, or quality improvement, creating a logical flow for reviewers.
- *Craft a Clear Narrative:* Use a concise yet engaging writing style to explain how your program meets each standard. Highlight accomplishments, innovative practices, and areas where your program goes above and beyond. For instance, you might describe how your program has implemented cutting-edge simulation technology to address evolving healthcare needs.

> **Accreditation Tip:**
> Many programs will assign different faculty/staff to write parts of the self-study. It is essential that once all parts are written, the entire document is reviewed for accuracy, and one voice

- *Incorporate Evidence:* Attach relevant documents as appendices or embed links to digital files. Each piece of evidence should be referenced within the narrative, ensuring that reviewers can easily locate and verify it.
- *Visual Aids:* Enhance your report with charts, graphs, and tables. For example, a graph showing trends in learner competency scores over time can illustrate the impact of your curriculum.

Step 3: Gathering and Organizing Evidence

Collecting and organizing evidence can be overwhelming, but it becomes manageable and efficient with the right approach.

- *Create an Evidence Checklist:* Develop a detailed checklist aligned with the accreditation standards to track the status of each required document. The SSH accreditation guide provides a sample checklist that can be customized to your program's needs.
- *Centralize Document Storage:* Store all evidence in one place using a shared drive or document management system. Organize files into folders labeled by standard or category to streamline access.
- *Ensure Accuracy:* Regularly review documents to ensure they are complete, up-to-date, and error-free. For example, check that faculty CVs reflect their most recent certifications and that safety policies include the latest updates.
- *Maintain Version Control:* Track document revisions to ensure that your submission includes only the most current versions. Document changes using software or manual logs.

Step 4: Avoiding Common Pitfalls

Even with thorough preparation, certain challenges can derail the documentation process. Awareness of these pitfalls and strategies for avoiding them can save time and reduce stress.

- *Incomplete or Missing Documentation:* Submitting incomplete evidence, such as outdated policies or missing faculty records, can delay or jeopardize accreditation. Use a checklist and conduct a final review before submission.
- *Disorganization:* Poorly labeled or disorganized submissions can frustrate reviewers and reflect poorly on your program. Ensure all evidence is clearly labeled and follows a consistent format.
- *Irrelevant Information:* Including excessive or unnecessary documentation can clarify key points. Focus on evidence that directly supports accreditation standards. The reviewers will be focusing on how the answer supports meeting the standard.

> **Accreditation Tip:**
> When writing the self-study, ask yourself how your response meets the standard.
>
> Some organizations, such as SSH, offer a companion guide explaining the information reviewers need to meet the standard.

- *Inconsistent Data:* Conflicting or outdated information, such as discrepancies in learner outcomes, can raise red flags. Cross-check all data for accuracy and consistency. This occurs frequently when multiple people are writing the self-study.

Step 5: Preparing for Electronic or On-Site Submission
Most accrediting bodies require electronic submissions, on-site visits, or a combination of both. Preparation is key to ensuring a smooth review process.
- *Electronic Submission:* Share files using a secure and user-friendly platform, ensuring all documents are accessible and properly labeled. Including a navigation guide or table of contents can help reviewers quickly locate specific evidence.
- *On-Site Presentation:* Physical copies of key documents should be readily available during on-site reviews. Designate a team member to oversee document access and answer reviewer questions, ensuring a seamless and professional process.

Preparing documentation for accreditation is a meticulous but rewarding process that allows programs to showcase their strengths and align with industry standards.

Case Example: Successful Documentation Preparation
ABC University's simulation program successfully achieved accreditation by following a strategic approach to documentation. The program director began by creating an evidence checklist and assigning responsibilities to team members. They used a shared drive to centralize records and implemented a quarterly review process to ensure all documentation was current.

During their self-study, the team used visual aids to present data on learner outcomes, including a 20% improvement in clinical competency scores over three years.

This comprehensive and organized approach earned the program high praise from accrediting reviewers.

4.3 Take Aways

- **Thorough Preparation is Key**
  Preparing comprehensive and well-organized documentation is critical to the success of a simulation program's accreditation process. Accurate and complete records demonstrate alignment

with accreditation standards, commitment to quality, and professionalism.

- **Understanding Accreditation Requirements**
  Familiarize yourself with the accrediting body's documentation standards early in the process. Key categories often include organizational structure, program mission and objectives, curriculum design, faculty qualifications, resource management, learner assessments, and quality improvement efforts.

- **The Self-Study Report is Your Narrative**
  The self-study report is the central narrative for your program's accreditation application. Structure the report to align directly with accreditation standards, integrate relevant evidence, and use visuals like graphs or tables to enhance clarity and impact.

- **Centralized Organization Improves Efficiency**
  A centralized system, such as a shared drive, can store and organize documentation. Categorize files based on accreditation standards or key themes and maintain strict version control to ensure all documents are current and accurate.

- **Avoid Common Pitfalls**
  - **Incomplete Documentation:** Ensure all required evidence is included and up to date.
  - **Disorganization:** Present materials in a clear, logical format that meets reviewer expectations.
  - **Irrelevant Information:** Focus on essential documents that support accreditation standards.
  - **Inconsistent Data:** Double-check for errors or discrepancies in information from different team members.

- **Leverage Checklists and Tools**
  Develop an evidence checklist aligned with accreditation requirements to track progress. Use templates, guides, or tools provided by accrediting bodies to ensure thorough preparation.

- **Electronic and On-Site Readiness**
  For electronic submissions, use secure, user-friendly platforms with clear navigation guides. Prepare physical copies of key documents for on-site visits and designate a team member to manage document access and respond to reviewer queries.

- **Continuous Documentation Review**
  Review and update documentation regularly to reflect program developments, such as new faculty certifications, revised policies, or updated learner outcomes. Quarterly reviews can help maintain accuracy and readiness.

- **Showcase Success with Visual Aids**
  Enhance your submission with visual representations of program impact, such as trends in learner performance, CQI outcomes, or resource utilization improvements.
- **Team Collaboration is Essential**
  Engage faculty, staff, and administrators in documentation to ensure completeness and accuracy. Clear communication and collaboration foster shared ownership and accountability.

4.3 Summary

Preparing documentation and evidence is a critical step in the accreditation process. Healthcare simulation programs can demonstrate their commitment to excellence and readiness to meet accreditation standards by understanding the requirements, organizing evidence effectively, and avoiding common pitfalls. In the next chapter, we will explore how to train staff and faculty to ensure they are equipped to support the accreditation process and contribute to the program's long-term success.

Chapter 5

Governance

Effective governance forms the backbone of a successful simulation program. It ensures that the program operates with accountability, aligns with institutional goals, and meets the standards required for accreditation. This chapter provides a framework for establishing governance structures, defining roles, and fostering a culture of compliance and continuous improvement.

5.1 Establishing Governance Structures

A well-defined governance structure provides the foundation for an effective simulation program. It ensures operations' clarity, decision-making accountability, and alignment with strategic goals. Such a structure is essential for managing day-to-day activities and demonstrating the program's readiness for accreditation.

Define Leadership Roles and Responsibilities
The first step in creating a strong governance framework is clearly defining all program participants' roles and responsibilities.
- **Program Directors**: Responsible for setting the vision, strategic planning, and overall management of the simulation program. They act as the primary liaison with institutional leadership and accreditation bodies.
- **Faculty**: Tasked with curriculum development, scenario creation, and teaching. Faculty members are the foundation of the program's educational offerings and must align their work with its mission and goals.
- **Simulation Specialists**: They ensure the technical and operational aspects of simulation activities are seamless. They

maintain and operate simulation equipment, design scenarios in collaboration with faculty, and manage logistics during sessions.
- **Administrative Staff**: Provide crucial support, including scheduling, budget tracking, documentation, and stakeholder communication. Their organizational skills ensure the program runs smoothly.

Clearly defined roles eliminate ambiguity, foster accountability, and enable a coordinated approach to achieving program objectives.

Develop Governance Committees

Governance committees or advisory boards provide an additional layer of oversight, ensuring the program remains mission-driven and evolves in response to stakeholder needs.
- **Composition of Committees**: Committees should include a mix of educators, clinicians, administrators, simulation experts, and learners. This diversity brings multiple perspectives to the table, enriching decision-making processes.
- **Functions of Governance Committees**: These committees can oversee strategic planning, quality improvement initiatives, and resource allocation and serve as a sounding board for new ideas and innovations within the program.

> **Accreditation Tip:**
> Include the committee charter in your self-study materials.
>
> This will provide reviewers with the purpose and role of the committee.

- **Regular Meetings and Reports**: Committees should meet regularly to discuss progress, review performance metrics, and address challenges. Transparent communication through meeting minutes and reports ensures alignment across all program levels.

An active governance committee fosters collaboration, guides long-term planning, and provides crucial input for accreditation preparation.

Align with Institutional Policies

For a simulation program to be successful and sustainable, it must align with its parent institution's broader policies and goals.

- **Integration with Institutional Mission**: The simulation program's goals and activities should support the institution's overall mission, whether it's improving healthcare education, advancing clinical competency, or fostering research.
- **Consistency with Institutional Policies**: Governance structures and policies must adhere to institutional guidelines regarding finance, human resources, safety, and compliance. For example, simulation labs must meet the institution's safety standards and protocols.
- **Securing Institutional Support**: Alignment with institutional priorities increases the likelihood of securing funding, administrative backing, and access to shared resources such as IT support, facilities, and marketing.

> **Accreditation Tip:**
> Crosswalk the institutional mission with the simulation program mission.
>
> This is an easy way for site reviewers to make the connection.

By demonstrating that the simulation program complements the institution's strategic objectives, the program gains internal support and strengthens its case for accreditation.

The Importance of Governance in Accreditation Readiness

Effective governance structures signal to accrediting bodies that the simulation program operates with transparency, accountability, and a focus on continuous improvement. Well-defined leadership roles, active advisory committees, and alignment with institutional policies demonstrate a mature and organized approach to program management. Together, these elements lay the groundwork for a successful accreditation process and ensure the program is equipped to meet and exceed the standards set by accrediting organizations.

5.2 Creating a Mission and Vision

A clear and compelling mission, vision, and strategic plan form the guiding framework for a simulation program. These elements define the program's purpose and aspirations and serve as critical evidence of planning and intent for accreditation. They articulate the program's identity, long-term direction, and the steps it will take to achieve excellence.

Craft a Mission Statement

The mission statement serves as the foundation of the simulation program. It should succinctly articulate the program's core purpose and reflect its dedication to advancing healthcare education, research, and service through simulation.

- **Purpose and Alignment**: The mission should align with the parent institution's overarching mission while addressing the simulation's unique role in achieving educational and clinical objectives. For example, it might emphasize improving patient safety, fostering interprofessional collaboration, or enhancing learner competencies.

- **Key Elements to Include**: Highlight commitments to quality, innovation, and evidence-based practices. For instance, a mission statement might read, *"To advance healthcare education and patient outcomes through high-quality, simulation-based training, fostering innovation, collaboration, and lifelong learning."*

- **Stakeholder Involvement**: Engage key stakeholders, including faculty, administrators, and learners, in crafting the mission statement. Their input ensures the mission reflects shared values and priorities, fostering a sense of ownership and alignment.

A strong mission statement clearly answers the question: "Why does this program exist?" It also serves as a touchstone for decision-making and prioritization.

Define a Vision for the Future

The vision statement expands on the mission by articulating the program's long-term aspirations. It should be inspirational, forward-looking, and aligned with the evolving landscape of simulation-based education and healthcare.

- **Positioning the Program as a Leader**: The vision should convey the program's aim in five to ten years. For example, a vision might state, *"To be a global leader in simulation-based learning, driving innovation and excellence in healthcare education and patient care."*

- **Addressing Industry Trends**: Consider emerging trends such as integrating artificial intelligence, augmented reality, or interdisciplinary training. The vision should reflect how the program intends to adapt to and leverage these advancements.

- **Inspiring Stakeholders**: The vision should resonate with faculty, learners, and institutional leaders, inspiring them to contribute to its realization.

A compelling vision serves as a rallying point, uniting all stakeholders behind a shared future.

Connecting Mission, Vision, and Strategy to Accreditation
Accreditation bodies such as the Society for Simulation in Healthcare (SSH) require evidence of thoughtful planning and alignment with institutional and educational goals. A well-articulated mission and vision demonstrate the program's purpose and direction, while a detailed strategic plan provides a concrete framework for achieving and maintaining excellence. Together, these elements form a comprehensive narrative of commitment, progress, and readiness for accreditation.

By crafting a meaningful mission, articulating an ambitious yet achievable vision, and developing a dynamic strategic plan, the simulation program positions itself as a leader in healthcare education and sets the stage for long-term success.

Policies and Procedures for Operational Excellence

Establishing and maintaining comprehensive policies and procedures is a cornerstone of operational excellence for simulation programs. These documents provide a structured framework ensuring consistency, compliance with standards, and delivering high-quality simulation-based education. Accreditation bodies view robust policies and procedures as critical indicators of a well-managed and sustainable program.

Document Core Policies
Core policies are the foundation for the simulation program's operations, defining the principles and guidelines governing its activities. These policies address essential aspects of the program's infrastructure and educational practices.

- **Program Governance**: Outline the structure and responsibilities of leadership, advisory committees, and staff to ensure accountability and clear decision-making pathways. Governance policies should also address conflict resolution, resource allocation, and program oversight.

- **Curriculum Design**: Specify guidelines for creating simulation scenarios that align with learning objectives and competencies. Policies should address the integration of simulation into broader curricula, emphasizing standardization and relevance to educational goals.

- **Assessment Practices**: Define methods for evaluating learner performance, faculty effectiveness, and overall program success. This includes using validated tools, ensuring fairness, and maintaining confidentiality.

- **Safety Protocols**: Include policies for physical safety, such as equipment usage and emergency procedures, and psychological safety for learners and faculty during simulation debriefings and assessments.

> **Accreditation Tip:**
> Don't forget to check the accreditation standards
>
> Some organizations, such as SSH, require specific policies to be included in the policies and procedure manual.

- **Resource Management**: Address the acquisition, maintenance, and disposal of simulation equipment. Policies should ensure the efficient use of resources while maintaining high quality and safety standards.

Well-documented policies ensure operational consistency and provide evidence of compliance with accreditation standards.

Organizations that are not allowed to have official policies
Using the terminology "Guideline" instead of policies is okay if your institution restricts the term "Policy." Demonstrate to the site review team that the program uses the guidelines for guiding documents. Ensure that "official" policies are also tied to these guidelines for the review team.

Standardize Operational Procedures
Operational procedures translate policies into actionable steps, providing a practical guide for the daily activities of faculty, staff, and learners.

- **Scenario Development**: Develop clear, step-by-step protocols for creating simulation scenarios, from defining learning objectives to incorporating technical elements and briefing participants. Procedures should include guidelines for scripting, timing, and managing variability.

- **Equipment Maintenance**: Establish schedules and checklists for the regular maintenance and calibration of simulation tools, such as manikins, task trainers, and audiovisual systems. Include instructions for troubleshooting and documenting issues to minimize downtime.

- **Learner Evaluation**: Standardize processes for assessing learner performance, including the use of rubrics, objective structured clinical examinations (OSCEs), and feedback mechanisms. Ensure alignment with competency frameworks and accreditation requirements.

- **Faculty Training**: Provide procedural guidance for onboarding new faculty and conducting ongoing professional development in simulation-based education and debriefing methodologies.

By standardizing procedures, the program ensures consistency, reduces variability, and enhances efficiency, all contributing to a high-quality learning experience.

Ensure Accessibility and Transparency

Making policies and procedures accessible and transparent is critical for fostering a culture of collaboration, trust, and accountability within the program.

- **Centralized Documentation**: Store all policies and procedures in a centralized location, such as a shared digital repository or program handbook, where they can be easily accessed by faculty, staff, and stakeholders.

- **Regular Updates**: Schedule periodic documentation reviews to ensure it remains relevant and reflects current best practices, Accreditation standards and institutional priorities. Assign responsibility for updates to specific individuals or committees.

> **Accreditation Tip:** Ensure all staff know where to find a copy of the policies and procedures and when they were last revised.

- **Training and Communication**: Educate faculty and staff on the program's policies and procedures through regular training sessions, onboarding programs, and communication channels. Encourage questions and feedback to ensure understanding and engagement.

- **Transparency with Stakeholders**: Share key policies with external stakeholders, such as institutional leaders, accrediting bodies, and clinical partners. This transparency builds trust and demonstrates the program's commitment to excellence.

Accessibility and transparency in policies and procedures help embed them into the program's culture, ensuring they are consistently followed and easily adapted to meet changing needs.

Connecting Policies and Procedures to Accreditation

Comprehensive policies and standardized procedures are critical for accreditation readiness. Accrediting bodies require evidence that the simulation program operates with consistency, efficiency, and a commitment to quality. Documenting and implementing policies and procedures demonstrates to reviewers that the program is well-organized, compliant with industry standards, and proactive in addressing challenges.

Moreover, robust policies and procedures provide a framework for continuous improvement, ensuring that the program evolves alongside advancements in simulation technology and educational methodologies. By emphasizing documentation, standardization, and accessibility, simulation programs can achieve operational excellence and meet the rigorous demands of accreditation.

5.4 Financial and Resource Planning

Financial and resource planning are vital to a sustainable and well-governed simulation program. Effective planning ensures that the program can meet its operational needs, maintain high-quality standards, and remain adaptable to future challenges. It also demonstrates the program's fiscal responsibility and long-term viability, essential for accreditation readiness.

Develop a Sustainable Budget

A comprehensive and forward-looking budget is the cornerstone of financial planning. It must address both current needs and future growth, ensuring the program operates without financial disruptions.

- **Operational Costs**: Include recurring expenses such as staffing salaries, simulation consumables, and utilities. Anticipate costs related to program delivery, including learner materials and technical support.
- **Equipment Updates**: Account for acquiring, maintaining, and eventually replacing simulation tools. High-fidelity manikins, task trainers, and audiovisual systems require regular updates to stay relevant and functional.
- **Faculty and Staff Training**: Allocate funds for professional development, such as workshops, certifications (e.g., CHSE or CHSOS), and attendance at simulation conferences. Investing in the expertise of faculty and staff enhances program quality.
- **Contingency Planning**: Set aside a portion of the budget for unforeseen expenses, such as urgent equipment repairs or unexpected enrollment increases. A contingency fund ensures that the program can respond to challenges without disrupting operations.
- A well-prepared budget provides a roadmap for financial stability, ensuring that resources are available to achieve the program's goals and objectives.

> **Accreditation Tip:**
> When describing finance and budget in your self-study, don't forget to identify:
> - The process of drafting the budget
> - Who drafts the budget?
> - Who reviews the budget?
> - Who approves the budget?

Secure Funding and Support

Funding is critical for sustaining and growing the program. Exploring diverse funding sources helps reduce reliance on a single revenue stream and increases financial resilience.

- **Grants**: Pursue local, national, and international grants that support healthcare education and simulation. Many organizations and government bodies fund initiatives to improve patient safety, healthcare innovation, and workforce development.

- **Institutional Backing**: Work closely with institutional leaders to secure financial support, demonstrating how the simulation program aligns with the institution's strategic goals. Showcase the program's potential to enhance learner outcomes, improve institutional reputation, and attract external funding.
- **Partnerships**: Build partnerships with healthcare organizations, industry leaders, and community stakeholders. These relationships can lead to financial contributions, in-kind donations, or access to additional resources such as shared facilities and equipment.
- **Revenue Generation**: Consider offering fee-based services, such as customized training for healthcare professionals, CPR certifications, or facility rentals for external organizations. These activities can provide supplementary income while expanding the program's reach.
- Securing diverse funding sources strengthens the program's financial position and demonstrates its value and impact to a wide range of stakeholders.

> **Accreditation Tip:**
> The site reviewers will examine the program's funding model to determine whether it is sustainable in the long term.
>
> Accrediting agencies, such as SSH, do not ask for specific budgets; however, within reason, be as transparent with the reviewers about the funding sources.

Resource Allocation

Efficient resource allocation ensures that the program's priorities are met without overspending or underutilizing available assets.

- **Prioritizing Needs**: Use data and stakeholder input to identify critical needs and allocate resources accordingly. For example, prioritize replacing aging equipment that directly impacts the quality of learner experiences.

> **From the Reviewer's Perspective:**
> Reviewers will examine how the program prioritizes resources based on its mission and funding sources.

- **Aligning with Strategic Goals**: Ensure that resource allocation decisions are guided by the program's mission, vision, and strategic plan. For example, if the program's vision includes expanding interprofessional

education, resources should be directed toward tools and facilities that support collaborative learning.
- **Tracking and Optimization**: Implement systems to monitor resource usage, such as software for tracking equipment utilization or financial management tools. Use this data to identify areas where efficiency can be improved, such as reducing waste or streamlining processes.
- **Building Sustainability**: Allocate resources with an eye toward long-term sustainability. For instance, invest in durable equipment, energy-efficient facilities, and scalable technologies that adapt to future needs.

Strategic resource allocation ensures that every dollar spent, and every asset utilized contributes meaningfully to the program's success.

Connecting Financial and Resource Planning to Accreditation

Accreditation bodies evaluate a program's financial health and resource management as sustainability and organizational capacity indicators. A simulation program with a well-constructed budget, diverse funding sources, and efficient resource allocation demonstrates its ability to meet current demands while preparing for future growth.

In addition, strong financial and resource planning supports the program's ability to deliver consistent, high-quality educational experiences. It ensures learners have access to state-of-the-art tools and well-trained faculty, positioning the program as a leader in simulation-based education. The simulation program builds a foundation for long-term success and accreditation readiness by prioritizing financial stability and strategic investment.

5.5 Stakeholder Engagement and Communication

Governance is most effective when it fosters collaboration and transparency among all stakeholders.
- **Engage Key Stakeholders**: Include faculty, learners, institutional leaders, and community partners in program planning and decision-making processes.
- **Implement Regular Communication Channels**: Use meetings, newsletters, and reports to keep stakeholders informed about program developments, outcomes, and opportunities for involvement.
- **Cultivate a Culture of Feedback**: Encourage open dialogue and feedback to identify strengths, address challenges, and drive continuous improvement.

5.6 Governance for Continuous Quality Improvement (CQI)

Accreditation standards emphasize CQI as a cornerstone of effective governance.

- **Establish Metrics for Success**: Define measurable program performance indicators, such as learner outcomes, faculty satisfaction, and resource utilization.
- **Conduct Regular Program Reviews**: Schedule routine evaluations of program operations, policies, and outcomes to ensure alignment with accreditation standards.
- **Integrate Improvement Cycles**: Use data-driven insights to implement targeted improvements and document these efforts as evidence of a commitment to CQI.

5.7 Preparing for Accreditation

Preparing for accreditation requires a comprehensive approach to demonstrating that the simulation program meets the high standards of excellence established by accrediting bodies such as the Society for Simulation in Healthcare (SSH). Strong governance plays a pivotal role in this preparation, ensuring that the program operates efficiently, aligns with institutional and accreditation goals, and is positioned for long-term success.

Accreditation Readiness Checklist

A detailed accreditation readiness checklist is an invaluable tool for ensuring that all governance-related elements are addressed and documented.

- ☐ **Governance Policies and Procedures**: Verify that policies related to program governance, leadership roles, advisory committees, and decision-making processes are clearly defined and accessible.
- ☐ **Mission, Vision, and Strategic Plan**: Ensure that the program's mission and vision statements are concise, impactful, and aligned with the strategic plan. Demonstrate that these documents guide the program's operations and future growth.
- ☐ **Documentation of Core Activities**: Compile records of governance activities, such as committee meeting minutes, leadership decisions, and stakeholder engagement efforts. This

documentation provides evidence of transparency and accountability.
- ☐ **Continuous Quality Improvement (CQI)**: Prepare reports and data demonstrating how CQI processes are integrated into governance. Highlight examples of how data has been used to make meaningful improvements.
- ☐ **Resource Management and Financial Planning**: Include budgets, funding reports, and resource allocation plans that demonstrate the program's sustainability and capacity for growth.
- ☐ **Accreditation-Specific Requirements**: Address specific accreditation standards related to governance, ensuring all criteria are met and supported by evidence.

This checklist helps track progress and serves as a structured guide for organizing the accreditation submission and preparing for site visits.

Governance in Accreditation Reporting

Governance is a critical component of accreditation applications and site visits. Highlighting the program's governance structures and processes demonstrates a commitment to excellence, accountability, and strategic alignment.

- **Describe Leadership and Oversight**: Explain the roles and responsibilities of program leaders, committees, and advisory boards. Highlight how these entities contribute to decision-making and strategic planning.
- **Showcase Strategic Planning**: Provide examples of how the program's strategic plan has been implemented, emphasizing alignment with the mission and vision. Detail measurable goals and outcomes that reflect the program's progress.
- **Emphasize CQI Processes**: Demonstrate how CQI processes are integrated into governance. For instance, share examples of data-driven decisions, such as implementing new training protocols or upgrading equipment based on performance metrics.

> **From the Reviewer's Perspective:**
> The site reviewers will be looking to see:
> - Who oversees the program, and how are decisions made at the operational level?
> - Methods of communicating in the program from leadership to staff and leadership to faculty.

- **Highlight Stakeholder Engagement**: Include evidence of how the program involves stakeholders—faculty, learners, administrators, and external partners—in governance and decision-making. This reflects a collaborative and inclusive approach to program management.

During site visits, be prepared to provide documentation and articulate how governance processes contribute to the program's success and adherence to accreditation standards.

Leadership Role in Accreditation

Program leaders are critical in guiding the program through the accreditation process. Their ability to advocate for the program and articulate its governance framework is essential for building confidence with accreditation reviewers.

- **Leadership Advocacy**: Leaders should confidently describe how governance supports the program's mission, ensures operational efficiency, and aligns with accreditation standards. Their ability to connect governance processes to program outcomes can make a significant impression.
- **Engagement with Accreditation Teams**: Leaders should be prepared to interact directly with accreditation teams, answering questions about governance structures, strategic planning, and resource allocation. This will demonstrate transparency and readiness.
- **Training for Leadership and Staff**: Ensure that all leadership and staff involved in the accreditation process are well-versed in the program's governance framework and standards. Conduct mock interviews and rehearsals to build confidence and consistency in responses.
- **Visionary Leadership**: Leaders should present a forward-looking perspective, showing how the program is positioned to adapt to emerging trends and maintain excellence post-accreditation.

Effective leadership showcases the program as well-organized, future-ready, and committed to quality.

The Role of Governance in Accreditation Success

Strong governance serves as the backbone of accreditation readiness. It ensures that the program operates efficiently, aligns with strategic priorities, and continuously improves to meet evolving standards.

Accrediting bodies recognize governance as a key factor in sustaining program quality and achieving long-term success.

- **Operational Efficiency**: Governance structures streamline decision-making and resource allocation, ensuring that the program runs smoothly and consistently.
- **Strategic Alignment**: Governance ensures that the program's goals and activities align with its mission, vision, and institutional priorities. This alignment strengthens the program's case for accreditation.
- **Model of Excellence**: A robust governance framework positions the simulation program as a leader in its field, exemplifying best practices in simulation-based education and healthcare innovation.

5.8 Take Ways

- **Strong Governance is Foundational**
  Effective governance provides the structure and accountability necessary for simulation programs to operate efficiently, align with institutional goals, and meet accreditation standards. Clear roles, responsibilities, and decision-making pathways are essential.
- **Defined Roles Enhance Accountability**
  Clearly defining leadership roles (e.g., program directors, faculty, simulation specialists, and administrative staff) eliminates ambiguity, fosters accountability, and ensures a coordinated approach to achieving program objectives.
- **Governance Committees Add Value**
  Establishing governance committees or advisory boards with diverse stakeholders enhances oversight, guides strategic planning, and fosters innovation. Regular meetings and transparent reporting ensure alignment and stakeholder engagement.
- **Alignment with Institutional Policies is Critical**
  Successful simulation programs align their mission and policies with the parent institution's goals, securing administrative support, resources, and integration into broader strategic objectives.
- **Mission and Vision Guide the Program**
  A clear mission defines the program's purpose, while an inspiring vision sets long-term aspirations. Together, they

provide a strategic framework for decision-making, stakeholder engagement, and accreditation readiness.

- **Policies and Procedures Drive Operational Excellence**
Comprehensive policies and standardized operational procedures ensure consistency, compliance with accreditation standards, and high-quality simulation-based education. Accessibility and regular updates reinforce their effectiveness.

- **Financial and Resource Planning Ensures Sustainability**
A forward-looking budget, diverse funding sources, and strategic resource allocation are critical for meeting operational needs, supporting growth, and demonstrating fiscal responsibility to accrediting bodies.

- **Stakeholder Engagement is Key**
Engaging faculty, learners, institutional leaders, and external partners fosters collaboration, trust, and shared ownership of the program's success. Open communication and feedback mechanisms drive continuous improvement.

- **Continuous Quality Improvement (CQI) is Central to Governance**
Governance structures should integrate CQI processes, using measurable metrics and data-driven decisions to identify areas for improvement, implement changes, and document progress.

- **Accreditation Success Relies on Governance**
Accrediting bodies emphasize governance as a critical factor in program sustainability and excellence. Strong governance demonstrates transparency, accountability, and a commitment to continuous improvement, positioning the program for long-term success.

- **Leadership is Crucial in Accreditation**
Effective leadership advocates for the program connects governance to outcomes and engages confidently with accreditation teams. Visionary leaders position the program as adaptable and future ready.

5.9 Summary

By establishing and maintaining effective governance, simulation programs can confidently navigate the accreditation process, demonstrating their commitment to operational excellence, strategic foresight, and the continuous pursuit of quality. This not only enhances the program's credibility but also secures its position as a trusted and impactful contributor to healthcare education.

KEITH A. BEAULIEU

Chapter 6

Strategic Planning and Plan

Strategic planning is a critical process for simulation programs seeking accreditation. A comprehensive strategic plan serves as a roadmap, outlining the program's mission, vision, objectives, and actionable steps. It ensures that the program is focused on achieving accreditation standards while fostering growth, sustainability, and innovation.

This chapter will explore the importance of strategic planning, key components of a strategic plan, and strategies for developing and implementing an effective plan tailored to simulation programs.

6.1 The Importance of Strategic Planning in Simulation Programs

Strategic planning ensures that a simulation program operates effectively and aligns with institutional and accreditation goals.

- **Alignment with Accreditation Standards**: Accrediting bodies, such as the Society for Simulation in Healthcare (SSH), require evidence of strategic planning as part of their evaluation process. A robust plan demonstrates the program's readiness and long-term sustainability.
- **Focused Resource Allocation**: Strategic planning helps prioritize resource use, ensuring that funding, equipment, and personnel are directed toward initiatives that align with the program's mission and objectives.
- **Proactive Adaptation**: A strategic plan enables the program to anticipate and respond to changes in healthcare education, technology, and accreditation requirements.

- **Engagement and Collaboration**: The planning process fosters stakeholder collaboration, creating a shared vision and commitment to the program's success.

Strategic planning articulates clear goals and actionable steps, ensuring that the program remains mission-driven, adaptable, and prepared to meet the highest standards of excellence.

6.2 Key Components of a Strategic Plan

A strategic plan for a simulation program seeking accreditation should include the following key components:

1. **Mission and Vision Statements**
   - **Mission**: Define the program's purpose, such as advancing healthcare education, improving patient safety, or fostering interprofessional collaboration through simulation-based learning.
   - **Vision**: Articulate the program's long-term aspirations, such as becoming a leader in simulation education or setting benchmarks for innovative practices.

   > **Accreditation Tip:** The strategic plan should be separate and specific to the simulation program, not an institutional strategic plan with simulation-specific objectives.

2. **Core Values**
   - Identify the program's principles, such as integrity, collaboration, innovation, and excellence.
3. **SWOT Analysis**
   - Analyze the program's **Strengths**, **Weaknesses**, **Opportunities**, and **Threats**. This assessment provides a foundation for strategic decision-making.
4. **Strategic Goals**
   - Establish measurable, time-bound goals addressing accreditation readiness, learner outcomes, faculty development, research initiatives, and resource management.
5. **Actionable Objectives**
   - Break down strategic goals into specific, actionable steps. For example, "Develop five new simulation scenarios focused on interprofessional teamwork by the end of the academic year."

6. **Key Performance Indicators (KPIs)**
    o Define metrics to evaluate progress, such as the number of learners trained, faculty certifications achieved, equipment uptime, or stakeholder satisfaction levels.
7. **Resource Allocation**
    o Identify the resources needed to achieve strategic goals, including personnel, funding, technology, and facilities.
8. **Timeline and Milestones**
    o Create a timeline that includes key milestones, such as the completion of accreditation-related documentation or the implementation of new simulation technologies.
9. **Continuous Quality Improvement (CQI)**
    o Incorporate mechanisms for regular evaluation and revision of the strategic plan based on performance data and feedback.

6.3 Developing the Strategic Plan

An effective strategic plan involves a structured, collaborative process that engages key stakeholders and aligns with institutional priorities.

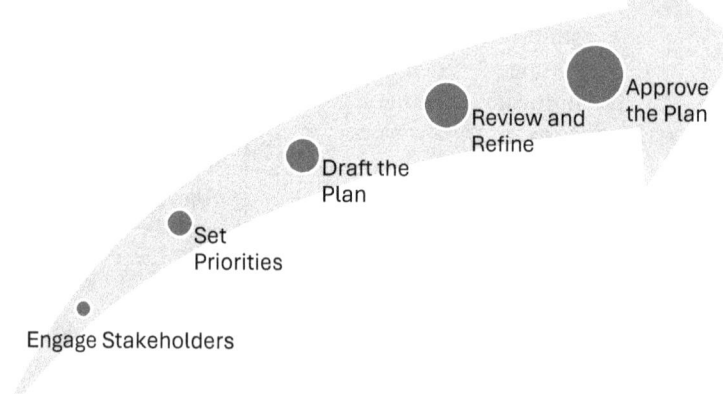

Figure 6 Developing a Strategic Plan

1. **Engage Stakeholders**
    o Involve faculty, staff, learners, institutional leaders, and external partners in planning. Their input ensures the plan is comprehensive and reflects diverse perspectives.
2. **Set Priorities**

- Use data from the SWOT analysis to identify high-priority areas that align with accreditation standards and institutional goals.

3. **Draft the Plan**
   - Organize the plan into clear sections, starting with the mission and vision, followed by strategic goals, actionable objectives, and resource requirements.

4. **Review and Refine**
   - Share the draft with stakeholders for feedback. Incorporate suggestions to ensure clarity, feasibility, and alignment with institutional and accreditation expectations.

5. **Approve the Plan**
   - Obtain formal approval from institutional leadership or governing committees to ensure alignment and support.

6.4 Implementing the Strategic Plan

Successful strategic plan implementation requires consistent effort, accountability, and monitoring.

1. **Assign Roles and Responsibilities**
   - Designate individuals or teams to lead specific objectives. Clearly define their responsibilities and provide the resources they need to succeed.

2. **Communicate the Plan**
   - Share the plan with all stakeholders, ensuring everyone understands their role in achieving its objectives. Use meetings, newsletters, or dashboards to provide updates on progress.

3. **Monitor Progress**
   - Regularly track KPIs and compare results against milestones. Use this data to identify successes, challenges, and areas for improvement.

4. **Adapt as Needed**
   - Be prepared to revise the plan based on feedback, changing priorities, or unexpected challenges. Flexibility is essential for long-term success.

6.5 Sample Strategic Goals for Simulation Programs

To illustrate the strategic planning process, here are examples of goals that a simulation program might include in its plan:

1. **Accreditation Readiness**
   - Complete all documentation and prepare for a mock accreditation review by the end of the next fiscal year.
2. **Faculty Development**
   - Ensure 50% of faculty achieve CHSE or CHSOS certification within two years.
3. **Program Expansion**
   - Increase the number of simulation scenarios offered by 25% within the next academic year.
4. **Resource Optimization**
   - Upgrade simulation equipment to include augmented reality capabilities by the next budget cycle.
5. **Learner Outcomes**
   - Improve learner performance metrics in teamwork and communication by 15% based on simulation assessments over the next two years.

6.6 Strategic Planning and Accreditation Success

Accrediting bodies view a strategic plan as a reflection of the program's commitment to excellence and its ability to sustain high-quality operations. A well-crafted plan demonstrates:

- **Accountability**: Clearly defined goals and KPIs show the program's focus on achieving measurable outcomes.
- **Alignment**: The plan illustrates how the program's mission, vision, and activities align with accreditation standards and institutional priorities.
- **Continuous Improvement**: The inclusion of CQI processes highlights the program's dedication to evolving and maintaining excellence.

6.7 Take Aways

- **Strategic Planning is Essential for Accreditation Success**
  A comprehensive strategic plan demonstrates the program's readiness, sustainability, and commitment to excellence. It aligns the program's mission, vision, and activities with institutional goals and accreditation standards.

- **Key Components of an Effective Strategic Plan**
  A well-structured strategic plan should include:
  - **Mission and Vision Statements:** Define the program's purpose and long-term aspirations.
  - **Core Values:** Establish guiding principles such as collaboration, innovation, and excellence.
  - **SWOT Analysis:** Identify strengths, weaknesses, opportunities, and threats to inform priorities.
  - **Strategic Goals and Objectives:** Set measurable, time-bound goals and actionable steps to achieve them.
  - **Key Performance Indicators (KPIs):** Use metrics to monitor progress and evaluate success.
  - **Resource Allocation:** Ensure personnel, funding, and facilities are aligned with objectives.
  - **Timeline and Milestones:** Provide clear deadlines for achieving critical goals.
  - **Continuous Quality Improvement (CQI):** Incorporate mechanisms for regular evaluation and updates.
- **Collaboration Drives Strategic Planning**
  Engaging stakeholders—including faculty, staff, learners, institutional leaders, and external partners—ensures the plan reflects diverse perspectives and aligns with institutional priorities. Collaboration fosters shared ownership and commitment.
- **Implementation Requires Accountability**
  - **Role Assignment:** Assign clear responsibilities to individuals or teams for each strategic objective.
  - **Communication:** Share the plan with all stakeholders to ensure clarity and alignment.
  - **Monitoring and Flexibility:** Regularly track progress against KPIs and adapt the plan as needed based on feedback and changing priorities.
- **Strategic Plans Enhance Resource Allocation**
  Focused resource allocation ensures funding, staffing, and facilities are prioritized effectively to support program growth and accreditation standards. Strategic decisions optimize limited resources for maximum impact.
- **CQI Ensures Plan Relevance and Evolution**
  Continuous Quality Improvement (CQI) processes are integral to strategic planning. They enable programs to evaluate

performance regularly, incorporate feedback, and make data-driven adjustments.
- **Accreditation Bodies Value Strategic Planning**
  Accrediting organizations view strategic plans as evidence of accountability, alignment, and a commitment to maintaining high standards. Programs that demonstrate thoughtful planning and measurable outcomes position themselves for success.

6.8 Summary

By developing and implementing a strategic plan, simulation programs prepare for accreditation and position themselves as leaders in healthcare education. A robust plan fosters confidence among stakeholders, strengthens the program's operational framework, and ensures its long-term impact and success.

Chapter 7

Staff and Faculty Development

Accreditation standards for healthcare simulation programs strongly emphasize the qualifications, training, and ongoing development of staff and faculty. A well-trained and motivated team is essential for creating a high-quality learning environment and meeting accreditation requirements. This chapter explores the key aspects of staff and faculty development, including qualifications, training opportunities, and strategies for fostering a culture of continuous improvement.

7.1 The Role of Faculty and Staff in Accreditation

Faculty and staff are the lifeblood of any healthcare simulation program, serving as the architects of transformative learning experiences and the stewards of operational excellence. Their qualifications, dedication, and professional growth directly influence the quality of simulation-based education and the success of accreditation efforts. Accrediting bodies such as the Society for Simulation in Healthcare (SSH) and the International Nursing Association for Clinical Simulation and Learning (INACSL) place significant emphasis on the role of personnel, recognizing that the expertise and professionalism of faculty and staff are key drivers of program credibility and effectiveness.

<u>The Importance of Qualified Personnel</u>
Qualified faculty and staff bring a depth of knowledge and experience that elevates the learning environment. Faculty with strong clinical backgrounds can design realistic scenarios that mirror the complexities of real-world healthcare, while those with educational expertise can facilitate impactful debriefings and assessments. For staff, technical

proficiency ensures the seamless operation of simulation technologies, from high-fidelity manikins to audiovisual systems.

Beyond technical skills, faculty and staff serve as mentors and role models, guiding learners in acquiring competencies and developing critical thinking, teamwork, and communication skills. Programs with highly skilled educators foster an environment of trust and engagement, where learners feel supported in taking risks and learning from mistakes.

The Impact of Professional Development

Ongoing professional development is a cornerstone of accreditation and program improvement. Faculty and staff must stay abreast of advancements in simulation technology, educational methodologies, and healthcare practices. This can be achieved through certifications, workshops, conferences, and peer learning opportunities.

Certifications such as the Certified Healthcare Simulation Educator (CHSE) or Certified Healthcare Simulation Operations Specialist (CHSOS) provide a formal framework for building and validating expertise. According to a study published in the *Journal of Clinical Simulation in Healthcare* (2021), programs with certified faculty report 30% higher learner satisfaction and a 25% improvement in learner outcomes than programs without certified educators. These statistics underscore the value of investing in professional development to enhance both program quality and learner success.

Faculty and Staff as Accreditation Champions

Faculty and staff play a critical role in the accreditation process itself. They are often tasked with aligning curriculum, scenarios, and assessments with accreditation standards. Their intimate knowledge of program operations makes them invaluable in identifying gaps, proposing solutions, and implementing changes. For example, a faculty member with expertise in debriefing may lead the development of standardized debriefing protocols, addressing a common gap identified during readiness assessments.

Staff, particularly those in technical and administrative roles, ensure that resources and documentation are well-organized and accessible for review. From maintaining equipment logs to preparing evidence for self-study reports, their contributions are integral to presenting a program that meets and exceeds accreditation standards.

Building a Collaborative Culture

The role of faculty and staff extends beyond individual contributions to fostering a culture of collaboration and excellence. Accreditation is not a solo endeavor; it requires a cohesive team working toward shared goals. Faculty and staff must communicate effectively, share knowledge, and support one another in addressing challenges. Programs that prioritize teamwork and open dialogue are better equipped to navigate the complexities of accreditation and sustain long-term success.

> **Case Example: The Power of Certification and Teamwork**
> Consider a simulation program that significantly improved learner outcomes after prioritizing faculty certification and team development. By supporting three educators in obtaining CHSE credentials and organizing regular interdisciplinary meetings, the program achieved a 20% increase in clinical competency scores among learners within a year. Additionally, the faculty reported higher confidence in scenario facilitation and debriefing, translating into more engaging and effective learner experiences.

Faculty and staff are not merely contributors to a simulation program; they are its foundation. Their expertise, continuous learning, and teamwork drive the program's ability to deliver high-quality education and achieve accreditation. Accrediting bodies recognize this by strongly emphasizing qualified personnel in their standards. Investing in faculty and staff is not just a requirement for programs seeking accreditation—it is a strategic imperative that enhances program credibility, learner success, and long-term impact.

7.2 Faculty and Staff Qualifications

Meeting accreditation standards requires simulation programs to demonstrate that faculty and staff possess the qualifications and competencies to deliver exceptional education. The expertise of these individuals directly impacts the quality of learner experiences and the program's ability to meet its goals. Accrediting bodies, such as SSH and INACSL, prioritize faculty and staff qualifications, recognizing their pivotal role in driving program excellence.

Minimum Qualifications: A Foundation of Expertise

At a baseline, faculty and staff should have clinical expertise in their respective fields, nursing, medicine, or allied health. This ensures they have real-world knowledge to create realistic and relevant simulation scenarios. Clinical expertise allows educators to incorporate practical insights into scenarios, bridging the gap between theoretical knowledge and hands-on practice. For example, a nurse educator with critical care experience can design high-stakes scenarios, such as cardiac arrest simulations, that accurately reflect learners' challenges in clinical settings.

Faculty should have clinical expertise and experience in simulation-based education. This includes skills such as scenario design, facilitation, and debriefing—key components of effective simulation pedagogy. Understanding adult learning theories and instructional design principles is equally important, as it enables educators to tailor learning activities to the needs and preferences of adult learners.

Staff members, such as simulation technicians and operations specialists, also need a solid foundation in the technical aspects of simulation, including operating and maintaining equipment, troubleshooting, and ensuring seamless session delivery.

> **From the Reviewer's Perspective:**
> The reviewers will look for basic qualifications and who within the simulation program determines that they are qualified.

Preferred Qualifications: Elevating Program Quality

While minimum qualifications are essential, preferred qualifications enhance the program's credibility and effectiveness. Faculty with advanced degrees in healthcare, education, or related fields bring a deeper understanding of both clinical practice and educational methodologies. Their ability to integrate these perspectives enhances the depth and rigor of simulation activities.

Certification in simulation education is particularly valuable. Credentials such as Certified Healthcare Simulation Educator (CHSE) or Certified Healthcare Simulation Operations Specialist (CHSOS) validate an individual's expertise in simulation and ensure that they adhere to industry best practices. According to the Society for Simulation in Healthcare (SSH, 2021), programs with certified faculty report significantly higher learner satisfaction and improved outcomes, as certified educators are better equipped to implement evidence-based practices and innovative teaching strategies.

Building a Team: Implementation Strategies

To attract and retain qualified faculty and staff, programs should develop clear job descriptions that outline required and preferred qualifications. Job postings should emphasize the program's commitment to excellence and professional growth, highlighting opportunities for training, certification, and leadership development.

Thorough vetting is crucial during the hiring process. Interviews should include practical assessments, such as having candidates facilitate a mock simulation or troubleshoot equipment, to evaluate their hands-on skills and problem-solving abilities. This ensures that candidates align with the program's needs and standards.

Once hired, programs should invest in their faculty and staff through ongoing professional development. Providing access to certification programs, workshops, and conferences enhances their skills and fosters a culture of continuous learning. For example, a program that supported its staff in obtaining CHSOS certifications saw a 25% improvement in simulation session efficiency and learner satisfaction within a year.

The Impact of Qualified Faculty and Staff
Faculty and staff qualifications exceed accreditation standards; they directly influence learner outcomes. For instance, an educator certified in the PEARLS debriefing framework will more likely facilitate reflective discussions that enhance critical thinking and decision-making skills. Similarly, a technician with CHSOS certification can ensure that simulations run smoothly, minimizing technical disruptions that could detract from the learning experience.

In addition, well-qualified faculty and staff elevate the program's reputation, attracting learners, partners, and funding opportunities. Healthcare institutions are more likely to collaborate with or invest in programs known for their expertise and professionalism.

Case Study: Certification as a Catalyst for Success
A healthcare simulation program faced inconsistent learner outcomes and high session variability. Recognizing the need for improvement, the program supported three faculty members in obtaining CHSE certification and one technician in achieving CHSOS certification. Within six months, the program reported a 20% increase in learner satisfaction scores and a 15% improvement in clinical competency assessments. Faculty confidence also improved, resulting in more innovative and engaging scenario designs.

Faculty and staff qualifications are a cornerstone of successful simulation programs and accreditation. By ensuring that personnel meet both minimum and preferred qualifications, programs can deliver high-quality education that prepares learners for the complexities of modern healthcare. Investing in certification, professional development, and strategic hiring practices strengthens the team's capabilities and enhances the program's overall impact. In the journey toward accreditation, qualified faculty and staff are not just participants but leaders and catalysts for success.

7.3 Onboarding and Initial Training

Effective onboarding and initial training are critical for ensuring that new faculty and staff are well-prepared to contribute to the success of a simulation program. Beyond familiarizing new team members with daily operations, a robust onboarding process establishes a shared understanding of the program's goals, standards, and expectations. Accrediting bodies like SSH and INACSL emphasize this process, recognizing its role in maintaining consistency, quality, and alignment with accreditation standards.

The Purpose of Onboarding

Onboarding goes beyond welcoming new hires—it is an opportunity to immerse them in the program's mission, vision, and objectives. Understanding these guiding principles allows new team members to align their contributions with the program's goals. A well-structured onboarding process also helps new hires integrate into the team more quickly, fostering a sense of belonging and collaboration.

For example, when a new simulation educator joins a program, onboarding provides insight into how their role fits within the broader context of learner education and program accreditation. This understanding enables them to approach their responsibilities with clarity and purpose.

Key Components of Onboarding

- *Program Orientation.* A comprehensive orientation introduces new team members to the program's mission, vision, and objectives, ensuring they understand its purpose and goals. This foundational knowledge helps staff see how their individual roles contribute to the program's success.

- *Training on Simulation Technologies.* Simulation programs often utilize complex technologies, such as high-fidelity manikins, audiovisual systems, and software for scenario design and learner assessment. New hires need hands-on training to operate these tools confidently and troubleshoot issues effectively.

  For example, a newly hired simulation technician might receive training on setting up and calibrating manikins for various clinical scenarios and using audiovisual systems to record and playback simulation sessions.

  > **From the Reviewer's Perspective:**
  > The reviewers will seek evidence of a formal orientation to the simulation program beyond the institutional program. They will look for standardization in the process tailored specifically for the job. They will also seek or request evidence that each staff member completed orientation.

- *Familiarization with Policies and Standards.* New staff must be educated on program policies, accreditation standards, and industry best practices. This includes understanding documentation protocols, safety guidelines, and quality improvement processes. Familiarity with these areas ensures new team members can adhere to operational and accreditation requirements from day one.

Implementation Strategies for Onboarding

- *Onboarding Checklist.* A standardized checklist ensures that all new hires receive consistent training and information. The checklist might include reviewing program policies, completing equipment training, and attending an introductory meeting with the leadership team.
- *Mentorship Programs* Pairing new hires with experienced mentors provides ongoing support during the onboarding process. Mentors can offer practical advice, answer questions, and model best practices. For example, a senior faculty member might guide a new educator through designing and facilitating a simulation scenario.
- *Hands-On Training Sessions* Simulation is inherently experiential, and onboarding should reflect this by incorporating hands-on training. New hires should practice using equipment, facilitating

scenarios, and conducting debriefings in a supportive environment. For instance, a new simulation educator might co-facilitate a session with a mentor before leading one independently.

The Impact of Effective Onboarding
A well-executed onboarding process prepares new team members to meet the demands of their roles' demands and sets the tone for their long-term success and engagement. Faculty and staff who feel supported and equipped during their early days are more likely to become confident, collaborative, and innovative contributors to the program.

For example, a program implementing a mentorship-based onboarding process saw a 30% reduction in errors during simulation setup and a 20% increase in faculty confidence within the first three months of hire. Additionally, learner feedback highlighted improved consistency and quality in simulation delivery, demonstrating the downstream impact of effective onboarding.

Onboarding ensures that new faculty and staff are prepared to meet the high standards required in simulation-based education and accreditation. By providing a comprehensive orientation, hands-on training, and mentorship, programs can empower new hires to contribute effectively from the outset. This investment in onboarding strengthens the team and reinforces the program's commitment to excellence and continuous improvement, key pillars of accreditation success.

7.4 Specific Training

Faculty play a pivotal role in the success of simulation programs, particularly in assessment and evaluation. These processes are critical for measuring learner performance, ensuring the effectiveness of simulation-based education, and aligning with accreditation standards. Specific training for faculty in assessment and evaluation equips them with the skills and knowledge to deliver consistent, fair, and impactful learning experiences.

Why Faculty Training in Assessment and Evaluation Matters

Ensuring Consistency and Reliability

Faculty trained in standardized assessment methodologies are better equipped to ensure consistency across evaluations. This reduces variability caused by subjective judgment and enhances the reliability of performance assessments.

Consistent evaluation practices are crucial for meeting accreditation standards, as they demonstrate that learner assessments are equitable and aligned with defined competencies.

> **From the Reviewer's Perspective:**
> Site reviewers will look for specific education and training in assessment topics/practices for faculty who assess and evaluate students.

Measuring Learner Competency
Accurate assessment is essential for evaluating learners' knowledge, skills, and attitudes. Faculty who are well-versed in competency-based assessment frameworks can effectively identify whether learners meet required standards and identify areas for improvement.

Training helps faculty design and implement tools such as checklists, rubrics, and Objective Structured Clinical Examinations (OSCEs) that provide measurable, objective results.

Facilitating Meaningful Feedback
Faculty with training in evaluation techniques are more skilled at providing constructive, actionable feedback.

Feedback grounded in structured evaluation frameworks helps learners understand their performance, address gaps, and achieve learning goals.

Supporting Accreditation Requirements
Accreditation bodies like the Society for Simulation in Healthcare (SSH) require programs to demonstrate robust assessment and evaluation processes. Faculty training ensures that assessments are aligned with learning objectives and accreditation standards, strengthening the program's case for accreditation.

Promoting Learner Growth and Development
Effective evaluation methods go beyond grading; they serve as tools for guiding learners toward mastery. Trained faculty can create a safe and supportive environment where learners feel encouraged to reflect on their performance and strive for continuous improvement.

Key Areas of Faculty Training in Assessment and Evaluation

Understanding Assessment Frameworks

Faculty should be trained in established frameworks, such as Kirkpatrick's Levels of Evaluation or Miller's Pyramid of Clinical Competence. These frameworks guide the development of assessments that measure learning outcomes at different levels, from knowledge acquisition to real-world application.

Developing Effective Assessment Tools

Training should focus on creating valid and reliable tools, such as:

- **Checklists**: Step-by-step guides to ensure specific tasks or competencies are completed.

- **Rubrics**: Detailed scoring guides that outline performance expectations across various proficiency levels.

- **Simulation-Specific Tools**: Instruments tailored to measure performance in simulation scenarios, such as teamwork, decision-making, and procedural skills.

- **Conducting Objective Evaluations**
  Faculty must learn techniques to minimize bias and ensure fair evaluations. Training in calibration exercises, where faculty practice scoring and align their evaluations, enhances objectivity.

- **Debriefing Skills and Formative Assessment**
  Faculty should be skilled in integrating assessment into debriefing sessions. Training in structured debriefing models, such as PEARLS or the Debriefing with Good Judgment approach, enables faculty to use simulation outcomes as teaching moments.

- **Data Analysis and Reporting**
  Faculty training should include interpreting assessment data to identify trends, measure program effectiveness, and inform decisions. Understanding how to report findings in a meaningful way is essential for both internal CQI efforts and meeting accreditation documentation requirements.

- **Cultural Competence in Assessment**

Simulation faculty should be trained to recognize and mitigate the impact of cultural biases in assessment and feedback. This ensures evaluations are fair and supportive of diverse learner populations.

Benefits of Faculty Training in Assessment and Evaluation

- **Improved Learner Outcomes**: Faculty who are confident and skilled in evaluation can more effectively guide learners to meet and exceed competency standards.

- **Enhanced Program Credibility**: Consistent, reliable assessment practices build trust among learners, stakeholders, and accrediting bodies

- **Support for Accreditation**: Faculty expertise in assessment strengthens the program's alignment with accreditation standards, showcasing its commitment to excellence.

- **Professional Development**: Training in assessment and evaluation contributes to faculty growth, encouraging them to pursue certifications like the Certified Healthcare Simulation Educator (CHSE).

Specific training for faculty in assessment and evaluation is a cornerstone of successful simulation programs. It ensures that learner performance is measured accurately and fairly, fosters meaningful feedback and growth, and aligns with accreditation requirements. Investing in this training not only enhances the quality of simulation-based education but also positions the program as a leader in healthcare education and innovation.

7.5 Ongoing Professional Development

Ongoing professional development is not just a recommendation for accredited simulation programs—it is an expectation and a strategic investment in maintaining excellence. The healthcare simulation field constantly evolves, driven by technological advancements, emerging educational methodologies, and shifting healthcare priorities. Faculty and staff must avoid these changes to deliver high-quality, impactful learning experiences. Accrediting bodies such as SSH and INACSL highlight continuous professional development as a core element of successful simulation programs, emphasizing its role in fostering innovation, adaptability, and credibility.

The Importance of Lifelong Learning
Continuous learning enables faculty and staff to enhance their skills, explore emerging trends, and adopt evidence-based practices. Simulation educators who stay current with developments in pedagogy and technology are better equipped to design engaging scenarios, facilitate reflective debriefings, and assess learner outcomes effectively. Similarly, simulation technicians who keep up with the latest equipment and software advancements can ensure smooth operations and introduce learners to cutting-edge tools.

For instance, a faculty member attending a virtual reality (VR) integration workshop in healthcare education may return equipped to incorporate immersive VR scenarios into the program, providing learners with innovative and realistic training experiences.

Opportunities for Professional Development
Accredited programs should provide diverse opportunities for faculty and staff to grow professionally. These opportunities include:
- *Conferences and Events:* Conferences like the International Meeting on Simulation in Healthcare (IMSH) offer a platform to explore the latest innovations, network with peers, and gain insights from industry leaders. Attending these events helps staff stay informed about global trends and best practices.
- *Workshops and Webinars:* Focused training sessions on debriefing techniques, scenario design, or cultural humility in simulation can deepen expertise. Webinars provide accessible, cost-effective learning opportunities that can be integrated into busy schedules.
- *Advanced Certifications*: Certified Healthcare Simulation Educator (CHSE) or Certified Healthcare Simulation Operations Specialist (CHSOS) validate expertise and demonstrate a commitment to professional growth. According to SSH, programs with certified educators report 30% higher learner satisfaction and a measurable improvement in learner outcomes (SSH, 2021).
- *Research and Publications:* Engaging in peer-reviewed research or publishing in simulation journals allows faculty and staff to contribute to the body of knowledge in healthcare simulation.

Research involvement enhances critical thinking and problem-solving skills while raising the program's profile.

Implementation Strategies for Professional Development
- *Budget Allocation:* Investing in professional development requires financial support. Programs should allocate a portion of their budget specifically for activities such as conference attendance, certification fees, and training sessions. This investment signals the program's commitment to faculty and staff growth.
- *Knowledge Sharing:* Encourage staff who attend conferences or workshops to share their insights through in-service training sessions or team meetings. This not only multiplies the value of professional development activities but also fosters a culture of collaborative learning.
- *Individual Development Plans:* Create personalized professional development plans for each team member, outlining short-term and long-term goals. For instance, a faculty member might aim to achieve CHSE certification within two years, while a technician might aim to attend an advanced workshop on manikin troubleshooting. These plans provide structure and accountability for ongoing growth.

The Ripple Effect of Professional Development

The impact of professional development extends far beyond individual growth. A team that continually develops its skills enhances the overall quality and reputation of the simulation program. Learners benefit from improved scenarios, more effective debriefings, and exposure to the latest technologies. Faculty and staff, in turn, experience greater job satisfaction, increased confidence, and stronger professional networks.

For example, a simulation program that supported its team in earning advanced certifications and attending annual conferences saw a 25% improvement in learner competency scores and a 20% increase in faculty retention rates within two years.

Ongoing professional development is a hallmark of excellence in healthcare simulation programs. By staying current with advancements in simulation technology, pedagogy, and healthcare practices, faculty and staff can continuously elevate the quality of their programs. Programs prioritizing professional development meet accreditation standards and create a dynamic, forward-thinking environment where educators and learners thrive. Through strategic investments in conferences, certifications, workshops, and research, simulation programs can position themselves as leaders in the ever-evolving field of healthcare education.

> **Accreditation Tip:**
> The program should describe or list any internal training or workshops provided by the program and describe how the program supports professional development via conferences and other educational opportunities.
>
> The Program should address professional development opportunities for faculty and facilitators who may facilitate in the program but are not necessarily attached to it and how they would be funded.

7.6 Building a Culture of Collaboration

A culture of collaboration is the glue that binds a simulation program together, enabling faculty, staff, and stakeholders to work cohesively toward common goals. In the complex, interdisciplinary world of healthcare simulation, collaboration isn't just a "nice-to-have"—it is essential for meeting accreditation standards, fostering innovation, and achieving program excellence. Simulation programs can enhance their effectiveness and sustainability by creating an environment where diverse voices are heard, ideas are freely exchanged, and challenges are tackled collectively.

<u>The Importance of Collaboration</u>
Healthcare simulation inherently involves interdisciplinary engagement. Faculty may bring clinical expertise, staff may contribute technical know-how, and administrators may offer strategic guidance. When these roles collaborate effectively, the results are greater than the sum of their parts. For example, a nurse educator designing a critical care scenario might collaborate with a simulation technician to ensure the manikin's programming aligns with the learning objectives and with an administrator to secure the necessary resources.

Collaboration fosters a shared sense of ownership and accountability, motivating team members to invest in the program's success. It promotes innovation by bringing diverse perspectives to problem-solving, ensuring the program evolves to meet the dynamic needs of healthcare education.

Strategies to Foster Collaboration
- *Regular Team Meetings:* Regularly scheduled meetings allow team members to discuss program updates, share challenges, and celebrate successes. These meetings encourage open communication, ensuring that all voices are heard and that everyone stays informed about program priorities.

  For example, a weekly meeting might include an update on the program's progress toward accreditation milestones, followed by a brainstorming session to address gaps identified during a readiness assessment.

- *Interdisciplinary Collaboration:* Bringing together clinicians, educators, administrators, and other stakeholders enhances the quality and relevance of simulation activities. Interdisciplinary teams can design scenarios that reflect real-world healthcare dynamics, integrating perspectives from various disciplines to improve learner outcomes.

  For instance, an interprofessional team might create a simulation scenario that trains learners to collaborate effectively during a complex surgical procedure, mirroring the teamwork required in actual operating rooms.

- *Networking and Team-Building Activities:* Informal networking and team-building activities strengthen relationships among team members, fostering trust and camaraderie. These connections can make formal collaborations more productive, as team members are more likely to share ideas and seek input when they feel a sense of mutual respect and support.

Implementation Tips
- *Collaborative Tools:* Technology can streamline communication and project management, especially in large or geographically dispersed teams. Shared calendars, project management software (e.g., Trello, Asana), and cloud-based document-sharing platforms (e.g., Google Drive) help ensure everyone stays on the same page. For example, a shared task board can track progress on accreditation documentation, making responsibilities clear and deadlines visible.

- *Recognition and Celebration:* Recognizing and celebrating team achievements boosts morale and motivation. Whether a formal award for a faculty member who earned CHSE certification or a simple thank-you note to a technician who resolved a challenging technical issue, acknowledging contributions reinforces a culture of collaboration and appreciation.
- *Inclusive Decision-Making:* Inviting input from team members at all levels fosters a sense of inclusion and empowerment. For example, asking simulation technicians for feedback on optimizing equipment usage or involving faculty in curriculum revisions ensures that diverse perspectives inform decisions.

<u>The Impact of Collaboration</u>
A collaborative culture improves team dynamics and directly impacts program outcomes. Programs prioritizing collaboration often see higher learner satisfaction, more innovative scenario designs, and smoother operational workflows. Additionally, accreditation processes benefit from strong collaboration, as team members work together to align with standards, gather evidence, and address feedback from accrediting bodies.

For instance, a simulation program that implemented regular interdisciplinary meetings saw a 20% improvement in scenario design efficiency and a 15% increase in learner satisfaction scores. Faculty reported feeling more connected to the program's mission, and technicians expressed greater confidence in their roles.

Building a culture of collaboration is not a one-time effort but an ongoing commitment to creating a positive and productive work environment. Simulation programs can harness the collective expertise of their teams to achieve excellence by fostering open communication, encouraging interdisciplinary engagement, and recognizing contributions. Collaboration is not just about working together—it's about thriving together and ensuring that faculty, staff, and stakeholders are united in pursuing high-quality education and accreditation success.

7.7 Faculty and Staff Evaluation

Regular performance evaluations for faculty and staff are essential for maintaining the quality and consistency of a simulation program. Accrediting bodies require these evaluations to ensure compliance with professional standards and foster an environment of continuous improvement. Evaluations identify strengths, address areas for growth, and align individual performance with the program's goals and accreditation requirements.

The Importance of Evaluation

Evaluating faculty and staff is more than a compliance measure or an administrative task; it is a strategic opportunity to nurture talent, recognize accomplishments, and foster continuous improvement. Evaluations provide a structured framework for celebrating achievements, identifying areas for growth, and aligning individual contributions with program goals. They allow simulation programs to create an environment where team members feel valued, supported, and inspired to excel.

Celebrating achievements during evaluations highlights the positive impact of faculty and staff on the program and its learners. Recognizing accomplishments—whether a faculty member designs an innovative scenario or a technician resolves a challenging equipment issue—boosts morale and reinforces a sense of purpose. Such acknowledgment fosters a culture of appreciation, motivating team members to continue striving for excellence.

Constructive feedback is equally essential. It transforms evaluations from a simple review process into a developmental tool. For instance, an educator who excels in scenario facilitation but struggles with debriefing can benefit from tailored recommendations, such as attending a debriefing workshop or pairing with a mentor skilled in reflective dialogue. This approach reframes weaknesses as opportunities for professional growth, demonstrating that the program is invested in the individual's success.

Beyond individual development, evaluations are pivotal in reinforcing a culture of excellence within the program. Encouraging faculty and staff to reflect on their contributions promotes self-awareness and accountability. Reflection allows team members to assess their strengths, recognize areas for improvement, and align their personal goals with the program's mission. This process enhances individual performance and strengthens team cohesion by fostering a shared commitment to quality and innovation.

When thoughtfully designed and implemented, evaluations' impact extends beyond the individual. They become a mechanism for driving program-wide improvements, cultivating a team of motivated, engaged, and equipped professionals to deliver exceptional simulation-based education. Ultimately, evaluations help simulation programs achieve their broader goals, ensuring they remain leaders in healthcare education and accreditation.

Components of Performance Evaluation

Teaching Effectiveness: Teaching is at the heart of any simulation program, and evaluating teaching effectiveness is critical to faculty assessments. This includes reviewing skills in:

- *Scenario facilitation:* Are educators engaging learners and effectively managing scenarios?
- *Debriefing techniques:* Are debriefings structured, reflective, and aligned with best practices such as the PEARLS or DASH framework?

Feedback from learners often plays a vital role in assessing teaching effectiveness. For instance, anonymous post-session surveys can provide valuable insights into how learners perceive an educator's ability to foster critical thinking and communication.

Contributions Beyond Teaching: Faculty and staff contribute to simulation programs in many ways beyond direct teaching. Evaluations should also consider:

- *Curriculum development:* Are team members involved in creating innovative and evidence-based scenarios?
- *Research and scholarship:* Are faculty contributing to the advancement of simulation through publications or conference presentations?
- *Quality improvement:* Are staff actively participating in initiatives to enhance program operations or learner outcomes?

Multi-Source Feedback: Incorporating feedback from various sources—learners, colleagues, and supervisors—provides a comprehensive view of performance. Peer reviews can offer unique perspectives on teaching style, teamwork, and professional behavior.

Implementation Strategies for Effective Evaluations

Standardized Evaluation Tools: Validated tools, such as the Debriefing Assessment for Simulation in Healthcare (DASH), ensure consistency and objectivity in evaluations. The DASH tool provides specific criteria for evaluating debriefing skills, allowing educators to receive detailed feedback on areas like communication, analysis, and learner engagement.

Constructive Feedback: Evaluations should provide more than just a performance score—they should include actionable recommendations that guide improvement. Constructive feedback delivered in a supportive manner helps team members feel valued and motivated to enhance their skills.

For example, instead of saying, "Your debriefings need work," feedback might include, "Your debriefings are engaging, but consider incorporating more learner-driven discussions to enhance critical thinking."

Self-Assessment: Encouraging faculty and staff to complete self-assessments fosters self-reflection and accountability. These assessments help individuals identify their strengths and areas for growth, making them more receptive to external feedback.

Ongoing Support and Resources: Evaluations should be paired with opportunities for professional development. If educators receive feedback to improve their debriefing skills, the program should provide access to relevant training, such as workshops or peer mentorship programs.

> **Case Example: Improving Debriefing Skills Through Evaluation**
> A simulation program noticed inconsistent debriefing practices among its educators, leading to uneven learner experiences. Implementing regular performance evaluations using the DASH tool identified specific gaps in debriefing techniques. The program also supported its faculty in refining their skills through tailored feedback and a peer mentorship initiative. Within a year, learner feedback indicated a 25% increase in satisfaction with debriefing sessions, and faculty reported greater confidence in facilitating reflective discussions.

The Benefits of Evaluation

Regular evaluations extend their impact beyond individual performance reviews—essential to a program's overall success and sustainability. When faculty and staff feel supported, valued, and actively engaged in their professional development, their commitment to the program's mission deepens. This sense of purpose and belonging enhances morale and strengthens retention, creating a stable and cohesive team dedicated to delivering high-quality simulation-based education.

Evaluations also provide actionable insights into the program's strengths and areas for improvement. The systematic collection and analysis of performance data create a roadmap for aligning individual efforts with broader program objectives. For instance, a trend showing that faculty consistently seek more training in scenario design could prompt the program to offer targeted workshops or invite experts to lead professional development sessions. Similarly, if data highlights a need for advanced technologies to improve learner outcomes, the program can prioritize investments in equipment upgrades or software enhancements. The program remains agile, responsive, and future-focused by addressing these insights proactively.

Moreover, evaluations reinforce a culture of accountability and continuous improvement. They establish clear expectations for excellence while encouraging open dialogue between faculty, staff, and leadership. This two-way communication ensures team members understand their roles and feel empowered to provide feedback on the program's processes and priorities. Such an environment fosters innovation, as individuals are more likely to share creative ideas and collaborate on solutions when they feel their input is valued.

When evaluations are conducted thoughtfully and consistently, they become more than a measure of individual or team performance—they become a tool for transformative growth. Evaluations ensure that faculty and staff meet the high accreditation standards by assessing critical elements such as teaching effectiveness, contributions to curriculum development, and professional behavior. Paired with constructive feedback, self-assessment, and ongoing support, these evaluations inspire confidence, foster professional pride, and drive a collective commitment to excellence.

The ripple effect of effective evaluations extends to learners and stakeholders as well. Engaged, well-supported faculty and staff deliver more impactful simulations, resulting in better-prepared learners who are confident and competent in real-world healthcare environments. These outcomes enhance the program's reputation, attracting partnerships, funding, and recognition as a leader in healthcare education.

Ultimately, faculty and staff evaluations are a regulatory requirement and a strategic tool for empowering teams, advancing program quality, and ensuring long-term success. Simulation programs can continuously raise the bar by embracing evaluations as a catalyst for growth and innovation, achieving and sustaining excellence in an ever-evolving field.

7.8 Addressing Faculty and Staff Challenges

Simulation programs often face challenges in recruiting and retaining qualified faculty and staff and managing workload demands. If left unaddressed, these challenges can compromise program quality, hinder the achievement of accreditation standards, and negatively affect team morale. Identifying these issues and implementing proactive solutions is critical to ensuring long-term success and sustainability of simulation programs.

Challenge 1: Limited Pool of Qualified Candidates

Many programs need help attracting highly qualified candidates with clinical expertise and simulation education experience. The niche nature of simulation education and the specialized skills required, such as scenario design and debriefing techniques, often limit the candidate pool.

Solution:

To attract top talent, simulation programs must position themselves as desirable workplaces. Competitive salaries are a baseline, but offering professional development opportunities is equally important. Programs that support faculty in pursuing certifications, attending conferences, or engaging in research enhance their appeal to candidates and demonstrate a commitment to excellence. Building partnerships with academic institutions can also create a pipeline of qualified graduates trained in simulation-based education. For instance, programs might collaborate with universities to offer internships or fellowships in simulation, cultivating talent from within the field.

Challenge 2: High Workload and Burnout

Simulation programs often operate with lean teams, requiring faculty and staff to juggle multiple responsibilities, from designing and facilitating scenarios to managing equipment and documentation. This heavy workload can lead to burnout, reduced job satisfaction, and high turnover rates.

> **From the Reviewer's Perspective**
>
> Site reviewers will look for staff workload overloading and potential signs of burnout regarding *adequate staffing* and *sustainability standards*.

Solution:

Adequate staffing levels are critical to mitigating burnout. Programs should assess workload distribution regularly and hire additional staff as needed to ensure manageable responsibilities. Cross-training team members can also provide flexibility, allowing tasks to be shared and reducing the burden on any individual. Additionally, fostering a culture that prioritizes work-life balance is essential. Offering flexible scheduling, mental health resources, and opportunities for downtime can help staff recharge and remain engaged. For example, scheduling regular team retreats or "wellness days" can provide much-needed relief and strengthen team morale.

Challenge 3: Resistance to Change or New Technologies
The rapid pace of technological advancements in simulation can be daunting for some faculty and staff, particularly those less familiar with emerging tools and practices. Resistance to change can stall progress and hinder the adoption of innovative solutions that improve learner outcomes.

Solution:
Overcoming resistance requires a thoughtful approach that combines education, support, and involvement. Providing hands-on training sessions and access to user-friendly resources can help staff feel more confident in adopting new technologies. Peer mentorship programs can also ease the transition by pairing less tech-savvy staff with colleagues skilled in new tools. Importantly, involving team members in decision-making processes—such as selecting new simulation technologies—can foster buy-in and reduce apprehension. When staff feel they have a voice in changes affecting their work, they are more likely to embrace and adapt.

Creating a Supportive Environment

Addressing recruitment, retention, and workload challenges is not a one-size-fits-all endeavor. It requires a strategic and holistic approach to creating a workplace culture where faculty and staff feel valued, supported, and empowered to thrive. This involves more than just addressing immediate concerns; it demands a long-term commitment to fostering an environment where employees can grow professionally, collaborate effectively, and find fulfillment in their roles.

Simulation programs prioritizing their teams' well-being and professional development reap tangible benefits, including higher levels of engagement, better collaboration, and improved program outcomes. A supported team is more likely to contribute innovative ideas, remain dedicated to the program's mission, and deliver high-quality educational experiences to learners. This, in turn, elevates the program's reputation and positions it as a leader in healthcare simulation.

Creating such an environment begins with active listening and open communication. Leadership must proactively seek feedback from faculty and staff to understand their challenges and aspirations. For example, implementing regular one-on-one check-ins provides an opportunity to discuss workload concerns, career goals, and resource needs. These conversations signal to team members that their voices are heard and their well-being matters.

For instance, a high turnover simulation program recognized signs of burnout among its staff, including decreased morale and inconsistent performance. Leadership responded by organizing monthly check-ins where team members could share concerns and suggest improvements. Based on this feedback, the program hired an additional technician to alleviate workload pressures, introduced flexible scheduling to accommodate work-life balance, and offered optional wellness workshops focusing on stress management and self-care. Within a year, staff satisfaction increased by 25%, and learner feedback reflected a noticeable improvement in the consistency and quality of simulation sessions.

Investment in professional development is another key pillar of a supportive environment. Providing opportunities for faculty and staff to attend conferences, earn certifications, or participate in workshops fosters a sense of growth and progression. When team members see that their organization values their professional journey, they are likelier to stay engaged and committed. For example, supporting a faculty member in achieving CHSE certification enhances their skills and boosts their confidence and satisfaction, creating positivity throughout the program.

Cultivating a culture of collaboration and mutual respect is equally important. Encouraging teamwork and interdisciplinary engagement strengthens relationships among staff and promotes innovative problem-solving. Informal networking events, team-building activities, and recognition of contributions reinforce this unity and shared purpose.

Addressing recruitment, retention, and workload challenges is about building a resilient, motivated team that feels empowered to excel. Simulation programs can create an environment where staff and learners thrive by focusing on long-term strategies prioritizing well-being, professional growth, and collaboration. Such efforts enhance program quality and contribute to a sustainable culture of excellence that supports the program's mission and goals well into the future.

The Role of Accreditation in Addressing Challenges

Accreditation is not just a benchmark for quality but also a guiding framework that helps simulation programs address core staffing, professional development, and resource management challenges. By emphasizing these areas as essential to program success, accreditation standards encourage programs to prioritize strategies that build strong, sustainable teams. This alignment between accreditation goals and organizational practices creates a dual benefit: meeting external expectations while fostering an internal culture of excellence and resilience.

Emphasizing Adequate Staffing

Accreditation standards often underscore the necessity of adequate staffing levels to support program operations and learner outcomes. This requirement highlights the need for strategic recruitment and retention practices that attract qualified individuals and provide an environment where they can thrive. For example, a program preparing for accreditation might assess its current staffing levels against anticipated learner demand, identifying areas where additional hires are needed to maintain quality.

Accrediting bodies also encourage programs to consider workload distribution. Overburdened staff can lead to burnout, diminished morale, and higher turnover rates, jeopardizing a program's ability to deliver consistent, high-quality simulation experiences. By aligning with accreditation standards, programs are incentivized to implement workload management strategies, such as hiring additional personnel, cross-training staff, or adopting tools that streamline operations.

Prioritizing Professional Development

Accreditation standards often include criteria for ongoing professional development, recognizing its importance in maintaining a skilled, confident, and innovative team. Programs that align with these standards are encouraged to invest in their staff through certifications, workshops, and conferences, ensuring that team members stay current with advancements in

The focus on professional growth meets accreditation requirements and enhances staff satisfaction and retention.

simulation technology, pedagogy, and healthcare practices.

This focus on professional growth meets accreditation requirements and enhances staff satisfaction and retention. Faculty and staff who feel supported in their career development will likely remain engaged and committed to the program's mission. For example, a program that sponsors CHSE or CHSOS certification for its team members strengthens its compliance with accreditation standards and signals its commitment to excellence and innovation.

Resource Management as a Foundation

Accreditation standards also address resource management, a critical area where programs must demonstrate that they have the facilities, equipment, and budgetary resources needed to support their operations and achieve their goals. By aligning resource management practices with accreditation standards, programs can address challenges related to outdated equipment, insufficient space, or inadequate funding.

For instance, a program seeking accreditation might conduct a resource audit to ensure it meets facility and equipment requirements. If gaps are identified, such as insufficient manikins for high-fidelity scenarios, the program can use this information to advocate for additional funding or vendor partnerships. Accreditation provides both the motivation and the framework for making these improvements, ensuring that programs are equipped to deliver high-quality education.

Accreditation as a Catalyst for Cultural Change

Beyond addressing operational challenges, accreditation can catalyze cultural change within a program. Preparing for accreditation often requires a program to evaluate its values, priorities, and practices, fostering a culture of reflection and continuous improvement. By aligning recruitment, retention, and workload strategies with accreditation standards, programs meet external expectations and build internal systems that promote long-term success.

For example, a program preparing for accreditation might implement regular staff evaluations and feedback sessions, ensuring team members feel heard and valued. These practices support accreditation goals and create a work environment prioritizing collaboration, innovation, and professional growth.

The Dual Impact of Accreditation

Accreditation provides a clear roadmap for addressing challenges that might otherwise seem insurmountable. By embedding practices like adequate staffing, professional development, and resource management into accreditation standards, accrediting bodies help programs establish systems supporting compliance and operational excellence. The result is a thriving team that is not only capable of meeting accreditation requirements but also poised to drive innovation, improve learner outcomes, and achieve long-term success.

Accreditation's role in addressing challenges extends far beyond meeting regulatory requirements. It provides a structured framework that guides simulation programs in building strong, resilient teams and sustainable operations. By aligning recruitment, retention, professional development, and resource management strategies with accreditation standards, programs can create an environment where staff are empowered, learners benefit from high-quality education, and the program thrives as a leader in healthcare simulation.

Faculty and staff are the cornerstone of any simulation program, and addressing recruitment, retention, and workload challenges is essential for maintaining program quality and meeting accreditation standards. By offering competitive compensation, fostering professional growth, managing workload effectively, and facilitating adaptation to change, programs can build resilient teams ready to tackle the complexities of simulation-based education. These efforts not only enhance the day-to-day experience of staff but also ensure the program's long-term success and reputation for excellence.

Case Example: Faculty Development at ABC Simulation Center

The ABC Simulation Center provides a powerful example of how a strategic focus on faculty development can meet accreditation standards and elevate a program's overall quality and reputation. Recognizing the critical role of faculty in delivering high-quality simulation-based education, the center made faculty development a cornerstone of its accreditation preparation and ongoing operations.

Establishing Certification Requirements

To ensure consistency and excellence in teaching, the center implemented a policy requiring all faculty members to earn the Certified Healthcare Simulation Educator (CHSE) certification within two years of hire. This requirement underscored the center's commitment to maintaining a team of highly skilled and knowledgeable educators. The program allocated funding for certification courses and examination fees to support faculty in achieving this goal. Faculty were also encouraged to participate in study groups and mentorship programs designed to prepare them for the certification process.

The emphasis on CHSE certification met accreditation standards for faculty qualifications and empowered educators with advanced simulation techniques and pedagogical strategies. Faculty reported increased confidence in designing engaging scenarios, facilitating reflective debriefings, and effectively assessing learner outcomes.

Fostering Ongoing Professional Growth
Beyond certification, the center prioritized ongoing professional development to keep faculty abreast of emerging trends and best practices in simulation education. Faculty attended annual conferences, such as the International Meeting on Simulation in Healthcare (IMSH), where they gained exposure to innovative technologies, methodologies, and research. Upon returning, attendees shared their insights during monthly professional development workshops, fostering a culture of collaborative learning and continuous improvement.

These workshops became valuable platforms for faculty to exchange ideas, address challenges, and explore new teaching approaches. For example, one faculty member who attended a virtual reality (VR) integration session at IMSH led a workshop on incorporating VR into high-fidelity scenarios. This initiative successfully implemented VR training modules, enhancing the realism and engagement of the center's simulations.

Incorporating Feedback and Peer Reviews
ABC Simulation Center also leveraged performance evaluations for growth and improvement. Evaluations included learner feedback, peer reviews, and self-assessments, providing a comprehensive view of each faculty member's strengths and areas for development. Learner feedback, collected through post-simulation surveys, offered insights into teaching effectiveness, scenario facilitation, and debriefing quality. Peer reviews added another layer of evaluation, enabling faculty to receive constructive input from colleagues who understood the nuances of simulation education.

For instance, one faculty member received feedback indicating a need to enhance their debriefing techniques. The center responded by arranging one-on-one mentorship sessions with a senior educator experienced in the PEARLS framework. Within a few months, the faculty member demonstrated marked improvement in leading structured and impactful debriefings, as reflected in subsequent learner feedback.

The Impact on Accreditation and Beyond
These faculty development efforts fulfilled accreditation standards and solidified ABC Simulation Center's reputation as a leader in simulation education. Accrediting bodies commended the program for its robust faculty training initiatives and commitment to continuous improvement. Moreover, the center experienced tangible benefits beyond accreditation:

- **Enhanced Learner Outcomes**: Learners consistently reported high satisfaction with the quality of instruction and felt better prepared to apply their skills in real-world clinical settings.
- **Increased Faculty Engagement**: Faculty expressed greater job satisfaction and a stronger professional identity, contributing to higher retention rates.
- **Program Growth**: The center's reputation for excellence attracted partnerships, funding opportunities, and increased program enrollment.

Conclusion
The ABC Simulation Center's faculty development program demonstrates how a strategic investment in professional growth can drive success in accreditation and beyond. The center created a team of confident, competent, and innovative educators by requiring CHSE certification, fostering ongoing learning, and incorporating feedback into performance evaluations. This case illustrates that when simulation programs prioritize faculty development, they meet accreditation standards and create a culture of excellence that benefits learners, staff, and the broader healthcare community.

7.9 Take Aways

- **Faculty and Staff Are the Foundation of Accreditation Success**
  - Faculty and staff qualifications, training, and engagement are critical to delivering high-quality simulation education and meeting accreditation standards.
  - Their expertise in clinical practice, simulation pedagogy, and technical operations directly impacts learner outcomes and program credibility.
- **Qualified Personnel Enhance Program Quality**

- Minimum qualifications, such as clinical expertise and experience in simulation-based education, ensure the delivery of realistic and relevant scenarios.
- Advanced qualifications, including certifications like CHSE and CHSOS, validate expertise and align programs with best practices, improving learner satisfaction and outcomes.
- **Onboarding Is Critical for New Team Members**
  - Comprehensive onboarding ensures new hires understand the program's mission, goals, and operations.
  - Key components include orientation, hands-on training, and mentorship to build confidence and competence.
- **Ongoing Professional Development Fosters Excellence**
  - Continuous learning through conferences, certifications, workshops, and research keeps faculty and staff up-to-date with the latest technologies and pedagogies.
  - Programs that prioritize professional development see higher learner outcomes, staff retention, and alignment with accreditation standards.
- **Faculty Training in Assessment and Evaluation Is Vital**
  - Effective training ensures faculty can measure learner performance accurately and provide meaningful feedback.
  - Using validated tools, such as rubrics and the DASH framework, promotes consistent and reliable evaluations.
- **Building a Collaborative Culture Drives Success**
  - Open communication, interdisciplinary teamwork, and shared decision-making enhance the program's ability to innovate and achieve goals.
  - Collaboration fosters trust, mutual respect, and a sense of ownership among team members.
- **Evaluations Are a Catalyst for Growth**
  - Regular performance evaluations identify strengths and areas for improvement, offering actionable feedback and fostering self-reflection.
  - Evaluations ensure alignment with accreditation standards and support a culture of accountability and excellence.
- **Addressing Faculty and Staff Challenges Is Essential**
  - Programs must tackle challenges such as limited candidate pools, high workloads, and resistance to new technologies.
  - Solutions include competitive compensation, professional growth opportunities, workload management, and inclusive change strategies.

- **Accreditation Supports Sustainable Practices**
  - Accreditation standards encourage programs to prioritize adequate staffing, professional development, and resource management.
  - These requirements help programs build resilient teams and align with long-term operational goals.
- **Staff and Faculty Investment Benefits Everyone**
  - A well-supported team fosters learner confidence, program innovation, and stakeholder trust.
  - Programs that invest in their people achieve higher learner outcomes, stronger team retention, and greater program reputation.

7.10 Summary

Developing and maintaining a skilled, motivated, and collaborative team is essential for achieving accreditation and delivering high-quality simulation education. Programs can meet accreditation standards and foster a culture of excellence by investing in faculty and staff qualifications, onboarding, professional development, and performance evaluation. In the next chapter, we will discuss how to conduct a mock accreditation review to assess readiness and identify areas for final adjustments before the official accreditation visit.

Chapter 8

Conducting a Mock Accreditation Review

A mock accreditation review is vital in preparing your healthcare simulation program for a successful accreditation visit. By simulating the accreditation process, programs can identify gaps, test their preparedness, and gain valuable insights for improvement. This chapter provides a detailed guide to planning, executing, and utilizing the results of a mock accreditation review to ensure your program is ready for the official site visit.

8.1 The Importance of a Mock Accreditation Review

A **mock review** is a critical rehearsal for the official accreditation process, serving as a diagnostic tool and a confidence-building exercise. This practice allows simulation programs to assess their preparedness rigorously by simulating the accreditation experience. By replicating the review process, mock reviews provide invaluable insights into potential weaknesses, highlight gaps in documentation, and ensure that faculty and staff are ready to engage effectively with accreditation reviewers.

Strengthening Preparedness
One of the most significant advantages of a mock review is its ability to identify weaknesses that might otherwise go unnoticed until the official site visit. Programs can test the robustness of their documentation, evaluate the clarity of their processes, and ensure that all materials are well-organized and accessible. For example, a mock review might reveal inconsistencies in learner assessment data or outdated faculty résumés.

These findings allow the program to address these issues proactively before the formal review.

Mock reviews also allow programs to evaluate how well their operational procedures align with accreditation standards. From scenario development workflows to equipment maintenance protocols, every aspect of the program is scrutinized. This level of preparation not only strengthens the program's overall readiness but also demonstrates a commitment to continuous improvement—a value highly regarded by accrediting bodies.

Building Team Confidence
The accreditation process can be stressful for faculty and staff, particularly if they are unsure what to expect. Mock reviews alleviate much of this anxiety by familiarizing the team with the process. Staff members gain clarity on their roles, understand the types of questions they might be asked, and learn how to confidently present their contributions to the program.

For instance, during a mock review, faculty might practice explaining how their debriefing techniques align with best practices, such as the PEARLS framework, while technicians might demonstrate how they maintain and troubleshoot simulation equipment. This rehearsal helps team members feel more prepared and reduces the likelihood of miscommunication during the actual site visit.

Refining Procedures and Documentation
Mock reviews also provide a structured opportunity to refine procedures and documentation. Reviewers conducting the mock evaluation can offer feedback on areas that require improvement, such as the organization of policies, clarity of mission statements, or alignment of learning objectives with professional standards. Programs can use this feedback to make targeted adjustments, ensuring that all materials meet or exceed accreditation expectations.

For example, a mock reviewer might note that the program's quality improvement documentation lacks specific outcome data. In response, the program could enhance its CQI reports by incorporating measurable metrics, such as learner satisfaction scores or improvements in clinical competency assessments.

Quantifiable Impact

The value of mock reviews is well-documented. According to the Society for Simulation in Healthcare (SSH, 2022), programs that conducted a mock review before their official site visit were 40% more likely to pass on their first attempt than those that did not. This statistic underscores mock reviews' critical role in ensuring a smooth and successful accreditation process. Programs that invest the time and resources into a thorough mock review often experience fewer surprises during the actual review and are better equipped to demonstrate compliance with standards.

> Programs that conducted a mock review before their official site visit were **40%** more likely to pass on their first attempt than those that did not.

Reducing Anxiety and Promoting Team Cohesion
Beyond logistical preparation, mock reviews contribute to team cohesion and morale. The process encourages faculty, staff, and leadership collaboration as team members work together to address feedback and strengthen the program. This collective effort fosters a sense of shared ownership and pride in the program's achievements.

For instance, a program that conducted a mock review found that the exercise improved readiness and enhanced communication among team members. Faculty gained a deeper appreciation for technicians' contributions, while leadership better understood the day-to-day challenges faced by staff. This shared understanding and respect strengthened the team's unity and confidence heading into the formal review.

A mock review is more than a rehearsal; it is an essential step in the accreditation process that enhances preparedness, reduces anxiety, and fosters continuous improvement. By identifying weaknesses, refining documentation, and building team confidence, mock reviews position simulation programs for success. Programs that embrace this practice increase their likelihood of passing accreditation on the first attempt and cultivate a culture of excellence and collaboration beyond the review process.

8.2 Conducting a Mock Review

A mock review is invaluable for preparing simulation programs for the official accreditation process. This structured rehearsal replicates the accreditation visit, offering an opportunity to identify and address weaknesses, refine processes, and ensure that faculty, staff, and facilities are fully prepared. A well-executed mock review increases the likelihood of success during the official visit and fosters confidence and collaboration among team members.

Figure 7 Steps for Conducting a Mock Review

Step 1: Planning the Mock Review

Effective planning is essential for a successful mock review. This phase involves setting clear objectives, selecting qualified reviewers, and creating a realistic schedule.

- *Set Clear Objectives:* A focused mock review begins with defining specific goals. Programs should determine whether they aim to test compliance with accreditation standards, evaluate documentation quality, or prepare staff for reviewer interactions. For example, a program might prioritize assessing the organization of policies and procedures while simultaneously preparing staff for interviews.
- *Choose Reviewers:* It is critical to select the right reviewers. Internal reviewers who understand the program's intricacies can provide practical, constructive feedback, while external reviewers from other simulation programs or professional organizations bring objectivity and fresh perspectives. External reviewers, such as faculty from accredited programs, can also offer insights into industry best practices and potential gaps.
- *Create a Schedule:* A detailed schedule ensures that all aspects of the program are thoroughly evaluated. This schedule should mirror the structure of an official accreditation visit, including time for document review, facility tours, and interviews. Incorporating a realistic timeline ensures that the mock review feels authentic and comprehensive.

Step 2: Preparing for the Mock Review

Preparation ensures that documentation, facilities, and staff are ready for scrutiny. This step maximizes the effectiveness of the review and minimizes last-minute stress.

Organize Documentation
- Centralize all required documents in a shared digital repository.

- Create a user-friendly table of contents or navigation guide to help reviewers locate evidence quickly.
- Perform a final review of documents to ensure they are up-to-date, accurate, and aligned with accreditation standards. For instance, double-check faculty résumés for recent certifications or confirm that policies reflect current practices.

Prepare Facilities
- Ensure that simulation labs, debriefing rooms, and other spaces are clean, organized, and fully operational.
- Verify that all equipment is functional and maintenance logs are readily available. Reviewers will expect to see evidence of routine equipment care and adherence to safety protocols.

Train Staff
- Provide staff with an overview of the mock review process and clarify their roles.
- Conduct mock interviews to help staff practice answering reviewer questions confidently.
- Emphasize professionalism, clear communication, and consistency in responses.

Step 3: Executing the Mock Review

The execution phase replicates the actual accreditation visit, providing a realistic assessment of the program's readiness.

- *Kickoff Meeting:* Begin with a welcoming session to introduce reviewers, outline the process, and set a constructive tone. This meeting sets expectations and ensures that the review proceeds smoothly.
- *Document Review:* Provide reviewers with access to all required documentation. Allow them time to evaluate critical elements such as curricula, quality improvement reports, and learner assessment tools. Encourage reviewers to flag inconsistencies or gaps.
- *Facility Tour:* Guide reviewers through the simulation facilities, showcasing key resources and features. Highlight areas demonstrating excellence, such as advanced technology or innovative scenario designs. Be prepared to answer detailed questions about facility design, safety measures, and equipment maintenance.
- *Staff and Faculty Interviews:* Arrange interviews with key personnel, including program leaders, faculty, and support staff. Encourage interviewees to articulate their roles, contributions, and

alignment with program goals. Practice responses to common questions about curriculum integration, learner outcomes, and quality improvement initiatives.
- *Learner Feedback:* Incorporate learners into the process by conducting interviews or surveys about their experiences. Highlight how the program uses learner feedback to drive continuous improvement. For example, share specific examples of changes made based on learner input, such as scenario adjustments or enhanced debriefing practices.

> The sample site review questions at the end of the book can help you prepare your faculty, students, and staff.

Step 4: Analyzing the Results

After the mock review, a thorough analysis of findings helps identify areas for improvement and solidify strengths.
- *Review Feedback:* Gather written and verbal feedback from reviewers, focusing on areas where the program may not meet accreditation standards. Ensure detailed and actionable feedback addresses major deficiencies and minor adjustments.
- *Identify Trends:* Look for recurring themes in the feedback. For example, if multiple reviewers note inconsistencies in CQI documentation, prioritize standardizing these reports across the program.
- *Prioritize Actions:* Based on the findings, develop an action plan that addresses high-impact areas first. Focus on critical elements most relevant to accreditation success, such as curriculum alignment, documentation quality, or resource availability.

Step 5: Implementing Improvements

Using the results of the mock review, programs can make targeted improvements to strengthen their accreditation readiness.
- *Update Documentation:* Revise documents to address gaps or inconsistencies identified during the review. Conduct a final quality check to ensure all evidence is accurate and comprehensive.
- *Enhance Facilities and Resources:* Address physical spaces, equipment, or other resource deficiencies. For example, repair or replace malfunctioning equipment and document these updates to demonstrate a commitment to quality.
- *Conduct Follow-Up Training:* Provide additional training for faculty and staff on improvement areas, such as interview techniques or

scenario facilitation. Reinforce the importance of teamwork, professionalism, and alignment with accreditation standards.

Conducting a mock review is a strategic and impactful step in preparing for accreditation. It provides programs with a realistic simulation of the accreditation process, helping to identify weaknesses, refine operations, and build team confidence. By following a structured approach—planning carefully, preparing thoroughly, executing effectively, and analyzing results—simulation programs can use the mock review as a powerful tool for improvement. A well-conducted mock review sets the stage for a successful accreditation visit and positions the program for sustained excellence.

Case Example: Mock Review Success at ABC Simulation Center
The ABC Simulation Center's approach to their mock review serves as a model for how programs can effectively use this preparatory step to identify weaknesses, implement meaningful changes, and achieve success in the accreditation process. Recognizing the importance of rigorous preparation, the center scheduled its mock review six months before the official accreditation visit, allowing ample time to address deficiencies and refine its operations.

To ensure the review was as objective and comprehensive as possible, the center invited external reviewers, including two simulation experts from neighboring institutions with experience in accreditation processes. This decision proved instrumental in providing fresh perspectives and actionable insights. The external reviewers meticulously examined the center's documentation, toured its facilities, and observed simulation activities. Their feedback highlighted several areas for improvement, including gaps in maintenance logs, outdated faculty résumés, and the need for a more structured approach to debriefing.

One critical finding was the lack of a standardized debriefing framework. While the center's educators demonstrated strong facilitation skills, the absence of a consistent method across sessions led to variability in learner experiences. The reviewers recommended adopting the PEARLS debriefing framework, a well-regarded model emphasizing structured, learner-centered discussions to maximize reflection and retention.

The mock review also uncovered issues with documentation. Maintenance logs for simulation equipment were incomplete, raising concerns about the program's ability to demonstrate compliance with safety and functionality standards. Additionally, several faculty résumés had not been updated to include recent certifications and professional development activities, a key requirement for accreditation.

Implementing the Recommendations
The ABC Simulation Center wasted no time in addressing these findings. They formed a task force to prioritize the recommendations and implement changes systematically:
- **Documentation Overhaul**: The team reviewed and updated all maintenance logs, ensuring that each piece of equipment had a documented history of servicing and repairs. Faculty were also encouraged to update their résumés, highlighting recent accomplishments such as certifications and conference presentations. To prevent future lapses, the center introduced a centralized digital repository for all documentation, accessible to staff and regularly audited for accuracy.
- **Debriefing Training**: The center recognized the importance of consistency in learner experiences and organized a series of workshops to train faculty on the PEARLS debriefing framework. These sessions included role-playing scenarios, peer feedback, and integrating the framework into existing simulation activities. Within three months, all educators were proficient in using PEARLS, resulting in more structured and impactful debriefings.
- **Quality Improvement Enhancements**: The center refined its quality improvement processes by introducing regular data reviews and stakeholder meetings. It also began tracking key performance indicators (KPIs) such as learner satisfaction, competency scores, and scenario completion rates. These metrics informed decisions and demonstrated the program's commitment to continuous improvement.

Accreditation Success
When the official accreditation visit arrived, the ABC Simulation Center was well-prepared and confident. Reviewers commended the center for its meticulous preparation, professional staff, and commitment to excellence. The updated documentation demonstrated clear adherence to standards, while the adoption of the PEARLS framework showcased the center's dedication to improving learner outcomes. The enhanced quality improvement process further solidified the program's reputation as a leader in simulation education.

The center achieved full accreditation, earning special commendation for their preparation and professionalism. Faculty and staff celebrated the accomplishment, recognizing that the mock review had been a pivotal step in their success. Beyond accreditation, the changes implemented during the preparation process left the program stronger and more resilient, ensuring continued excellence in simulation-based education.

Key Takeaways
The ABC Simulation Center's experience highlights the value of a well-executed mock review. The center transformed potential weaknesses into strengths by inviting external reviewers, proactively addressing gaps, and committing to continuous improvement. Their journey demonstrates that mock reviews are not just a practice run but a strategic tool for achieving accreditation and fostering a culture of excellence.

8.3 Take Aways

- **Mock Reviews Are Essential for Accreditation Readiness**
    - Mock accreditation reviews act as a rehearsal for the official visit, helping programs identify weaknesses, refine operations, and increase their likelihood of success.
    - Programs that conduct a mock review are 40% more likely to pass accreditation on their first attempt, according to SSH data.
- **Strengthening Preparedness Through Practice**
    - Mock reviews provide an opportunity to evaluate documentation, policies, and operational alignment with accreditation standards.
    - Programs can proactively address gaps in areas such as CQI reports, learner assessments, and equipment maintenance.
- **Reducing Anxiety and Building Team Confidence**
    - By familiarizing staff and faculty with the accreditation process, mock reviews reduce stress and build confidence.
    - Practicing responses to potential reviewer questions ensures clarity and professionalism during the official visit.
- **Refining Procedures and Documentation**
    - Feedback from mock reviewers helps programs fine-tune documentation, ensuring accuracy and alignment with accreditation standards.
    - Enhancing CQI reports, updating faculty résumés, and organizing policies are examples of actionable improvements.
- **Planning Is Key to Effective Mock Reviews**
    - Clear objectives, the selection of qualified reviewers, and a realistic schedule are essential for a successful mock review.

- External reviewers bring valuable objectivity and industry insights, while internal reviewers can provide practical, program-specific feedback.
- **Preparing Documentation, Facilities, and Staff**
  - Centralizing documents in a shared repository and ensuring they are up to date minimizes stress during the review process.
  - Clean, organized facilities and well-maintained equipment reflect program professionalism and commitment to quality.
  - Staff and faculty should be trained to confidently articulate their roles and contributions.
- **Analyzing Feedback to Drive Improvement**
  - Detailed feedback from the mock review should be analyzed for recurring themes, such as documentation inconsistencies or curriculum gaps.
  - Action plans should prioritize high-impact areas to strengthen accreditation readiness.
- **Implementing Targeted Improvements**
  - Programs should address deficiencies in documentation, facilities, and staff training identified during the mock review.
  - Demonstrating a commitment to quality through measurable improvements, such as equipment upgrades or enhanced debriefing protocols, is key.
- **Fostering Team Collaboration and Cohesion**
  - Mock reviews promote teamwork by engaging faculty, staff, and leadership in a shared effort to achieve accreditation.
  - Enhanced communication and collaboration contribute to a stronger, more unified team.
- **Mock Reviews Enhance Long-Term Program Excellence**
  - Beyond preparing for accreditation, mock reviews establish a culture of continuous improvement and accountability.
  - They serve as a strategic tool to maintain high standards and foster program growth, innovation, and sustainability.

8.4 Summary

Chapter 6 emphasizes the critical role of a mock accreditation review in preparing healthcare simulation programs for a successful accreditation process. This chapter provides a comprehensive guide to planning, executing, and analyzing a mock review, highlighting its value in identifying gaps, refining procedures, and building team confidence. A well-executed mock review ensures compliance with accreditation standards and fosters a culture of continuous improvement and collaboration.

By following a structured approach to planning, executing, and analyzing a mock review, programs can transform potential weaknesses into strengths, ensuring readiness for the official accreditation visit and long-term program success.

KEITH A. BEAULIEU

Chapter 9

The Accreditation Site Visit

The accreditation site visit is the culminating event in the accreditation process, where accrediting bodies assess whether a healthcare simulation program meets the required standards. This chapter provides a detailed guide to preparing for, navigating, and completing the site visit. By understanding what to expect and taking proactive steps, programs can demonstrate their commitment to excellence and achieve their accreditation goals.

9.1 The Purpose of the Site Visit

The site visit allows accreditation reviewers to verify the information in the self-study report, evaluate the program's facilities and resources, and engage directly with faculty, staff, and stakeholders. According to the *Society for Simulation in Healthcare (SSH)*, the site visit typically accounts for 20–30% of the final accreditation decision (*SSH, 2022*). Reviewers assess compliance with standards and the overall culture of quality, collaboration, and continuous improvement.

> **From the Reviewer's Perspective**
>
> Site reviewers will visit the site to verify the information you provided in the self-study, evaluate the facilities and resources, and verify operations with key stakeholders.

9.2 The Site Visit

The site visit is the culmination of the accreditation process, offering the accrediting body an opportunity to evaluate your simulation program in person. It is a moment of accountability and an opportunity to showcase the program's strengths, commitment to quality, and alignment with accreditation standards. Careful preparation, confident engagement with reviewers, and adaptability during the visit are essential for success.

Step 1: Preparing for the Site Visit

Thorough preparation sets the stage for a successful site visit. Starting early ensures that every aspect of the program is ready for scrutiny and that faculty and staff feel confident in their roles.

- *Review the Accreditation Standards*: Revisiting the accreditation standards to confirm that all program elements align with the requirements. Then, review all documentation, policies, and procedures to ensure consistency, accuracy, and clarity. For example, verify that quality improvement reports include measurable outcomes and that faculty résumés reflect current certifications and training.
- *Prepare the Facilities:* Simulation labs, debriefing rooms, and other program spaces must be clean, organized, and fully functional. Check that all equipment is in good working order and that maintenance logs are up-to-date and accessible. A well-maintained facility meets accreditation standards and demonstrates professionalism and a commitment to quality.
- *Train Faculty and Staff:* Provide a detailed briefing to faculty and staff about what to expect during the site visit. Conduct mock interviews to help them practice answering potential reviewer questions. Focus on ensuring that they can confidently and professionally articulate their roles, contributions, and the program's mission.
- *Organize Documentation:* Create a centralized repository for all required digital or physical documents and ensure it is well-organized and easy to navigate. Prepare key materials, such as policies, curricula, and quality improvement reports, in a format that reviewers can easily access and understand.
- *Develop a Schedule:* Work with the accrediting body to create a detailed site visit schedule that includes time for facility tours, document reviews, interviews, and closing meetings. Share this schedule with your team to ensure everyone is prepared and aware of their roles.

Step 2: Engaging with Reviewers During the Visit

Interactions with accreditation reviewers are critical and can significantly influence the outcome of the site visit. Professionalism, transparency, and collaboration are key.

- *Facility Tour:* Guide reviewers through the simulation facilities, showcasing key resources, technologies, and spaces. Highlight how these features support learning objectives and program goals. For example, demonstrate how a debriefing room's design facilitates reflection and discussion.
- *Documentation Review:* Ensure reviewers have easy access to all documentation and provide a designated staff member to assist with navigation and respond to questions. Anticipate questions about how documentation demonstrates adherence to standards, such as equipment maintenance policies or quality improvement initiatives.
- *Interviews with Faculty and Staff:* Interviews are an opportunity to highlight your team's expertise and dedication. Encourage open and honest communication and ensure faculty and staff can confidently articulate their roles and contributions. Discuss challenges openly, focusing on how the program addresses them.
- *Learner Engagement:* Arrange for reviewers to meet with learners to hear firsthand their experiences. Use this opportunity to showcase how learner feedback informs program improvements, such as adapting scenarios or refining debriefing techniques.
- *Responding to Questions:* Answer reviewers' questions confidently and honestly. If you don't know the answer, acknowledge it and offer to follow up with additional information after the visit. Demonstrating transparency builds trust and credibility.

> **Accreditation Tip:**
> Be prepared to explain processes in detail to the site reviewers, even if you have described them in the self-study. The reviewers are not trying to trick you.
>
> Reviewers may verify the information that leads to other questions or seek clarification of the process.
>
> Visual aids help!

Step 3: Managing Challenges

Even with thorough preparation, unexpected challenges may arise. Staying proactive and adaptable is essential.

- *Addressing Unexpected Questions:* If reviewers ask about areas not covered in your self-study, respond transparently and provide context. This will highlight the program's adaptability and problem-solving capabilities.

- *Handling Facility Issues:* If equipment malfunctions or other issues occur during the visit, explain how your program effectively handles such challenges. For example, describe your protocol for addressing technical difficulties and ensuring continuity in learner experiences.
- *Dealing with Critical Feedback:* Listen respectfully to reviewers' concerns. Acknowledge areas for improvement and describe your plans to address them. Demonstrating a commitment to continuous improvement can turn a critique into an opportunity to showcase your program's adaptability.

Step 4: The Closing Meeting

The closing meeting is a critical and formal conclusion to the accreditation site visit. It provides a structured opportunity for reviewers to share their preliminary findings and for the program to gain insight into its performance during the visit. This meeting is not only about receiving feedback but also about reinforcing professionalism and commitment to continuous improvement.

What to Expect

During the closing meeting, reviewers will summarize their observations, emphasizing strengths and areas for improvement. These observations are based on their evaluations of documentation, facilities, faculty and staff interviews, and learner engagement. Reviewers may also identify deficiencies that require attention before accreditation is granted.

For example, strengths might include innovative teaching practices, robust quality improvement processes, or effective learner engagement strategies. Areas for improvement could involve incomplete maintenance logs, inconsistencies in assessment documentation, or gaps in faculty development plans.

The meeting's tone is typically constructive and collaborative, aimed at guiding the program toward excellence. However, it is important to remember that the feedback provided during this meeting is preliminary and subject to further review.

> **Accreditation Tip:**
> The closing meeting will vary depending on the accrediting organization.
>
> Some organizations will provide a summary of the day; others will not indicate how you did.
>
> The important part of the closing meeting is to get *information on the next steps of the process.*

How to Respond
Your response during the closing meeting can significantly influence how reviewers perceive your program's adaptability and commitment to improvement. It is essential to approach this meeting with a professional and open mindset.

- *Express Gratitude:* Thank the reviewers for their time, insights, and thorough evaluation. Acknowledging their efforts sets a positive and respectful tone for the discussion.
- *Listen Actively:* Pay close attention to the feedback, noting strengths and areas for improvement. Listening without interruption demonstrates professionalism and a willingness to learn from the process.
- *Avoid Defensiveness:* Feeling protective of your program is natural but avoid debating or becoming defensive about critical feedback. Instead, view this feedback as an opportunity to refine and enhance your operations.
- *Ask Clarifying Questions:* If any feedback needs to be clarified or clarified, ask thoughtful questions to gain a better understanding. For example, if a deficiency in quality improvement documentation is noted, inquire about specific elements that must be addressed.
- *Take Notes for Follow-Up:* Document key points raised by reviewers, especially areas requiring further action. These notes will be invaluable when preparing your response to the formal feedback report.
- *Emphasize Your Commitment to Improvement:* Use this opportunity to reinforce your program's dedication to quality and continuous improvement. If reviewers identify gaps in equipment maintenance logs, outline the steps you plan to take to address the issue promptly.

Post-Meeting Follow-Up
Once you receive the feedback report, you will have an opportunity to review the findings in detail and address any factual errors or inaccuracies. This follow-up phase is crucial for clarifying misunderstandings and demonstrating responsiveness to reviewer concerns.

Example: A Constructive Closing Meeting
During the closing meeting for a healthcare simulation program, reviewers commended the program's innovative use of virtual reality in

high-fidelity scenarios but noted inconsistencies in faculty training documentation. The program director responded by thanking the reviewers for their detailed observations and asking for clarification on the specific training records in question. The reviewers provided examples, and the director outlined a plan to update the records and implement a more consistent tracking system. This collaborative exchange reassured reviewers of the program's commitment to addressing concerns effectively.

The closing meeting is more than a formality; it is an opportunity to engage constructively with reviewers, gain valuable insights, and demonstrate your program's professionalism and dedication to improvement. By approaching this meeting with gratitude, openness, and a proactive mindset, your program can turn feedback into actionable steps that strengthen its case for accreditation and pave the way for future success.

Step 5: Post-Site Visit Follow-Up

The post-site visit phase is the final stretch of the accreditation journey and plays a critical role in securing a successful outcome. This phase involves addressing deficiencies, responding to feedback, and maintaining stakeholder transparency. It is a wrap-up process and an opportunity to reinforce the program's commitment to continuous improvement and professionalism.

<u>Review the Feedback Report</u>
The first step in the post-visit phase is to review the formal feedback report the accrediting body provides thoroughly. This document summarizes the reviewers' observations during the site visit and highlights strengths, areas for improvement, and deficiencies that must be addressed.
- *Analyze Carefully*: Read the report multiple times to ensure a full understanding of its contents. Highlight specific areas that require attention and note any deadlines for follow-up actions.
- *Develop a Plan*: Create a detailed plan to address deficiencies based on the feedback. For instance, if the report cites inconsistencies in quality improvement documentation, identify the specific reports that need updates and assign responsibilities for revisions.
- *Focus on Actionable Solutions*: Ensure that your plan includes measurable steps. For example, if reviewers noted a gap in faculty training, outline a schedule for professional development sessions and track attendance to demonstrate progress.

Taking swift and organized action demonstrates responsiveness and reinforces the program's commitment to meeting accreditation standards.

Submit Additional Documentation
If the accrediting body requests additional materials to address concerns, ensure these follow-up submissions are thorough, accurate, and professional. This step demonstrates the program's ability to respond constructively to feedback.

- *Thoroughness Matters:* Double-check all submitted materials to meet the reviewers' expectations. Incomplete or poorly prepared documentation can delay the final accreditation decision.
- *Be Timely:* Follow the deadlines specified in the feedback report. Late submissions can negatively reflect on the program's organizational capabilities.
- *Demonstrate Professionalism:* Include a concise cover letter with follow-up materials summarizing the actions taken to address each concern. This extra step provides clarity and demonstrates a proactive approach.

> **Accreditation Tip:** When responding to the feedback report, identify the finding or discrepancy you are responding to so that the review team knows what finding to review before the final report

For example, if reviewers requested updated equipment maintenance logs, submit a revised document that includes detailed records and attach a policy outlining your new maintenance tracking procedures.

Communicate with Stakeholders
Transparency is key to maintaining trust and fostering a culture of collaboration. Sharing the site visit results with faculty, staff, and learners is an important step in celebrating successes and addressing areas for improvement.

- *Celebrate Achievements:* As noted in the feedback report, highlight the program's strengths. Recognize and thank team members for their contributions, which builds morale and reinforces a sense of accomplishment.
- *Outline Improvement Plans:* Share your action plan for addressing deficiencies, ensuring stakeholders understand their role in implementing changes. Transparency in this process fosters trust and promotes collective accountability.

- *Engage Stakeholders:* Encourage open dialogue about the site visit results. Provide opportunities for faculty, staff, and learners to share their perspectives and contribute ideas for program enhancement.

For instance, if the report commended the program's innovative simulation scenarios but noted gaps in learner assessment tools, involve faculty in developing new rubrics or surveys that align with accreditation standards.

The Final Steps Toward Accreditation
The post-visit phase is not just about meeting requirements; it is about demonstrating resilience, adaptability, and a commitment to excellence. Each action taken during this phase should reflect the program's dedication to continuous improvement. By addressing feedback with care and precision, the program strengthens its foundation and solidifies its readiness for the final accreditation decision.

A Successful Outcome
The efforts made during the post-visit phase often determine the accreditation outcome. Programs that approach this phase professionally and with attention to detail increase their chances of achieving accreditation and leave a lasting impression of their commitment to quality and innovation.

For example, a simulation program that promptly addressed reviewers' concerns about faculty training by scheduling workshops and submitting attendance records demonstrated its ability to implement changes quickly and effectively. The accrediting body recognized this effort, granting the program full accreditation with commendation.

The post-site visit follow-up is a crucial and dynamic phase of the accreditation process. By carefully reviewing the feedback report, submitting high-quality follow-up materials, and maintaining transparent communication with stakeholders, programs can turn challenges into opportunities for growth. This phase reinforces a culture of excellence and continuous improvement, ensuring the program is well-positioned for immediate accreditation success and long-term sustainability.

Case Example: Successful Site Visit at ABC Simulation Center
The ABC Simulation Center's approach to the site visit exemplifies how thorough preparation, strategic adjustments, and confident engagement can lead to a successful accreditation outcome. By treating the site visit

as an opportunity to showcase the program's strengths and address any lingering gaps, the center achieved full accreditation and earned commendation for its professionalism and readiness.

Meticulous Preparation: Laying the Groundwork
ABC Simulation Center conducted a comprehensive mock review three months before its scheduled site visit, inviting external reviewers with expertise in simulation education and accreditation standards. This preparatory step allowed the center to identify and address critical gaps, such as minor inconsistencies in its quality improvement documentation and outdated maintenance logs for simulation equipment. The team created a prioritized action plan and implemented changes systematically, ensuring its program aligned fully with accreditation requirements.

The mock review also allowed faculty and staff to rehearse interactions with reviewers, refining their ability to articulate their roles, highlight program strengths, and address potential questions. This preparation builds team confidence and reinforces a shared sense of purpose before the site visit.

Excellence on Display: The Site Visit Experience
The ABC Simulation Center's faculty and staff demonstrated exceptional readiness and professionalism during the official site visit. The team was organized, welcoming, and transparent from when reviewers arrived. Key elements of their success included:
- *Facility Tour:* The team guided reviewers through their state-of-the-art simulation labs, debriefing rooms, and administrative spaces, showcasing how these facilities supported the program's learning objectives. They emphasized innovative features, such as a recently implemented virtual reality (VR) module, which reviewers noted as a forward-thinking addition to their curriculum.
- *Documentation Review:* Thanks to a well-organized digital repository, reviewers had seamless access to all required documentation. A designated staff member was available to assist with navigation and answer questions, ensuring a smooth and efficient review process. This level of preparedness demonstrated the center's attention to detail and commitment to transparency.
- *Faculty and Staff Interviews:* During interviews, faculty and staff confidently described their contributions to the program, including scenario design, facilitation, and quality improvement initiatives. The reviewers were particularly impressed by their ability to explain the program's use of the PEARLS debriefing framework to standardize and enhance post-simulation discussions.

- *Learner Engagement:* During the site visit, learners shared their experiences, emphasizing how the program's innovative simulation activities improved their clinical skills and confidence. Reviewers appreciated how learner feedback was integrated into the center's continuous improvement processes, reflecting a learner-centered approach.

Addressing Challenges: A Transparent Approach
Despite their preparation, ABC Simulation Center faced a minor challenge during the site visit related to incomplete equipment maintenance logs. When reviewers raised concerns, the center's leadership acknowledged the oversight, explained the corrective steps they had initiated, and committed to submitting updated logs promptly after the visit. Their transparency and proactive response reassured the reviewers of the center's commitment to quality and accountability.

Commendation and Accreditation Success
The site visit concluded with a closing meeting, during which reviewers highlighted the center's strengths, including its innovative debriefing techniques, comprehensive quality improvement processes, and strong faculty collaboration. While the minor issue with equipment maintenance logs was noted, the center's swift response demonstrated its ability to address deficiencies effectively.

The ABC Simulation Center submitted the updated maintenance logs shortly after the visit, meeting the reviewers' expectations. The accrediting body awarded the center full accreditation and commended its professionalism, readiness, and commitment to excellence.

The XYZ Simulation Center's successful site visit demonstrates how meticulous preparation, confident engagement, and a transparent approach to challenges can lead to a positive accreditation outcome. By addressing gaps, emphasizing teamwork, and showcasing their program's innovations, the center achieved full accreditation and established a foundation for continued excellence in simulation-based education. Their experience underscores that the site visit is not just a checkpoint but a powerful opportunity to highlight a program's strengths and commitment to quality.

9.3 Take Aways

- **Purpose and Impact of the Site Visit**

- o The site visit is a pivotal moment where accrediting bodies evaluate compliance with standards, program culture, and operational excellence.
- o Site visits account for 20–30% of the final accreditation decision, emphasizing their importance.

- **Thorough Preparation is Key**
  - o Begin early to ensure readiness in all aspects, including documentation, facilities, and staff training.
  - o Review accreditation standards and ensure all documentation is consistent, accurate, and accessible.
  - o Maintain organized and fully functional facilities, showcasing professionalism and a commitment to quality.

- **Engaging Reviewers Effectively**
  - o Professionalism, transparency, and confidence are critical during interactions with reviewers.
  - o Conduct comprehensive facility tours, providing context on how resources support learning objectives and program goals.
  - o Prepare faculty, staff, and learners to articulate their roles and contributions effectively, fostering a positive impression.

- **Handling Documentation Review and Interviews**
  - o Organize all required documentation for easy access and assign a knowledgeable staff member to assist reviewers.
  - o During interviews, emphasize the expertise and dedication of team members, highlighting how challenges are addressed collaboratively.

- **Addressing Challenges During the Visit**
  - o Respond transparently to unexpected questions or issues, demonstrating adaptability and problem-solving capabilities.
  - o Use challenges as opportunities to showcase the program's commitment to continuous improvement.

- **The Closing Meeting: A Crucial Opportunity**
  - o The closing meeting offers preliminary feedback from reviewers, outlining strengths, areas for improvement, and potential deficiencies.
  - o Listen actively, take notes, and avoid defensiveness. Instead, focus on understanding the feedback and clarifying any points as needed.

- o Reinforce the program's commitment to quality and adaptability during this discussion.
- **Post-Site Visit Follow-Up**
  - o Carefully review the feedback report and develop a detailed action plan to address deficiencies.
  - o Submit thorough, accurate, and timely follow-up documentation, demonstrating professionalism and responsiveness.
  - o Use the post-visit phase to reinforce a culture of continuous improvement, involving stakeholders in refining processes.
- **Communicating with Stakeholders**
  - o Share site visit results with faculty, staff, and learners, celebrating successes and outlining improvement plans.
  - o Foster open dialogue to encourage collaboration and collective ownership of the program's quality initiatives.
- **Turning Feedback into Growth**
  - o The post-visit phase is an opportunity to strengthen program operations, address deficiencies, and demonstrate resilience.
  - o Programs that act promptly and effectively on feedback leave a lasting impression of commitment to excellence.
- **Achieving Accreditation and Long-Term Success**
  - o Programs that approach the site visit and follow-up with professionalism, transparency, and collaboration are more likely to achieve accreditation.
  - o The process reinforces a foundation of quality and sustainability, positioning the program for continued growth and innovation.

The accreditation site visit is both a challenge and an opportunity. With meticulous preparation, confident engagement, and thoughtful follow-up, programs can successfully navigate this phase, achieve accreditation, and build a culture of excellence that endures.

9.4 Summary

The accreditation site visit is the culmination of the accreditation process and represents a pivotal opportunity for simulation programs to demonstrate their commitment to excellence and alignment with accreditation standards. This chapter provides a comprehensive guide to preparing for, navigating, and following up on the site visit, ensuring that programs are ready for review and able to showcase their strengths effectively.

Chapter 7 underscores the significance of the accreditation site visit as both a moment of accountability and an opportunity to showcase a program's strengths. Simulation programs can navigate the site visit successfully by preparing thoroughly, engaging confidently, managing challenges transparently, and following up effectively. This pivotal step brings programs closer to accreditation while reinforcing a foundation of quality, innovation, and continuous improvement.

Chapter 10

Post-Accreditation: Maintaining Standards

Achieving accreditation is a significant milestone, but it is not the journey's end. Maintaining accreditation requires a commitment to continuous improvement, adherence to standards, and preparation for future re-accreditation cycles. This chapter explores strategies for sustaining accreditation, ensuring program quality, and fostering a culture of excellence in healthcare simulation.

10.1 The Importance of Maintaining Accreditation

Accreditation is more than a milestone; it is an ongoing commitment to excellence in quality and effectiveness. While achieving accreditation is significant, maintaining it requires consistent effort and a proactive approach. Accrediting bodies, such as the Society for Simulation in Healthcare (SSH), typically grant accreditation for a limited period—often three to five years—after which programs must re-accredit to demonstrate continued adherence to standards. Maintaining accreditation is critical for safeguarding a program's reputation, ensuring the quality of learner experiences, and fostering growth and sustainability.

A Continuous Commitment

Accreditation signifies that a simulation program meets rigorous industry standards in curriculum design, faculty qualifications, resource management, and quality improvement. However, maintaining these standards is an ongoing process, not a one-time achievement. Programs must continuously monitor and evaluate their operations, ensuring they remain aligned with best practices and evolving accreditation requirements.

For example, a program accredited for its innovative simulation scenarios must regularly review and update them to incorporate the latest evidence-based practices, emerging technologies, and learner feedback. This continuous improvement reflects the program's dedication to maintaining the high standards that earned its accreditation.

Benefits of Maintaining Accreditation

The benefits of maintaining accreditation extend far beyond compliance. Accreditation is the foundation for sustaining a simulation program's quality, reputation, and growth. It signals to stakeholders that a program has met and continues to uphold rigorous standards of excellence, ensuring its long-term success in a competitive and evolving educational landscape.

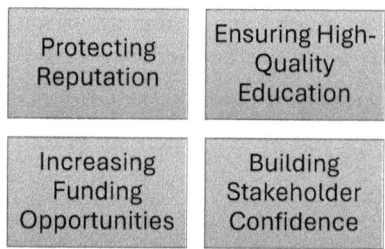

Figure 8 Benefits of Maintaining Accreditation

Protecting Reputation
Accreditation is regarded as a mark of distinction, validating that a program meets industry benchmarks for quality and effectiveness. Maintaining this status solidifies a program's reputation as a leader in simulation-based education. A lapse in accreditation, however, can severely damage credibility, leading to a loss of trust from learners, faculty, and partners.

For example, an accredited simulation center may become a preferred training partner for local healthcare institutions that recognize the program's commitment to excellence. Conversely, if accreditation is lost, the program might struggle to attract learners and partnerships, undermining its standing in the community.

Maintaining accreditation ensures that a program's reputation remains intact and is seen as a trusted provider of high-quality education.

Ensuring High-Quality Education
The cornerstone of accreditation is the delivery of consistent, high-quality education. By maintaining accreditation, programs demonstrate their dedication to preparing learners for the challenges of real-world clinical settings. This commitment enhances learner outcomes and directly contributes to patient safety and care.
Accreditation standards require regular evaluation and improvement of curriculum design, simulation scenarios, and learner assessments. Programs that uphold these standards create an environment where learners can develop critical thinking, teamwork, and technical skills that translate to better clinical performance.

For example, a simulation program that continuously aligns its scenarios with the latest evidence-based practices ensures learners are equipped with relevant knowledge. This emphasis on quality reassures stakeholders—employers, learners, and faculty—that the program delivers a superior educational experience.

Attracting Talented Faculty and Staff
Accredited programs attract talented educators and staff. Accreditation reflects a program's dedication to excellence and professional development. Talented faculty are drawn to environments where quality is prioritized, resources are available for growth, and professional achievements are recognized and celebrated.

For instance, a program that maintains its accreditation status might offer funding for faculty certifications, conference attendance, or research opportunities—making it an attractive workplace for top educators. This influx of talent further enhances the quality of education, creating a virtuous cycle of improvement.

Additionally, maintaining accreditation helps retain existing faculty and staff by fostering a sense of pride and confidence in the program. When educators know they are part of an accredited, high-performing team, they are more likely to stay engaged and committed to the program's success.

Increasing Funding Opportunities
Accreditation opens doors to critical funding opportunities. Many grant-making organizations and government agencies prioritize accredited programs for partnerships and financial support. Maintaining accreditation ensures continued eligibility for these resources, enabling programs to invest in the tools and infrastructure necessary for growth and innovation.

For example, an accredited program might receive a grant to integrate virtual reality into its simulation scenarios, enhancing the realism and effectiveness of its training. Without accreditation, securing such funding could become significantly more challenging, limiting the program's ability to innovate or expand.

This access to funding supports day-to-day operations and allows programs to develop cutting-edge capabilities that further distinguish them from competitors.

Building Stakeholder Confidence
Accreditation is a powerful signal of a program's integrity and effectiveness, inspiring confidence among stakeholders, including learners, faculty, employers, and community partners. Maintaining accreditation demonstrates a commitment to accountability, transparency, and continuous improvement, qualities stakeholders value deeply.

Learners are reassured that their education meets high standards, increasing their satisfaction and engagement. Faculty and staff feel secure knowing they are part of a program recognized for excellence. Employers trust that graduates of accredited programs are well-prepared for clinical challenges, and community partners view accreditation as evidence of the program's broader contributions to healthcare education. For example, a program that involves local healthcare leaders in its quality improvement initiatives might strengthen its community ties while enhancing its curriculum. This collaborative approach, coupled with accreditation, builds lasting trust and reinforces the program's reputation as a pillar of the healthcare education ecosystem.

The benefits of maintaining accreditation are multifaceted, touching every aspect of a simulation program's operations and impact. Accreditation is a cornerstone of success, safeguarding a program's reputation and delivering high-quality education to attracting top talent and securing funding. By upholding the standards required for accreditation, programs meet external expectations and foster a culture of excellence, collaboration, and innovation. Maintaining accreditation is an investment in the program's future, ensuring it remains a leader in simulation-based education and a trusted partner in advancing healthcare outcomes.

10.2 Strategies for Maintaining Accreditation

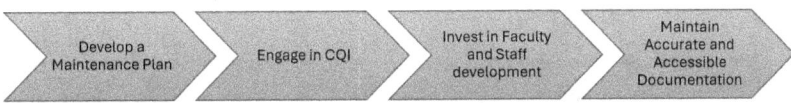

Figure 9 Strategies for Maintaining Accreditation

Maintaining accreditation requires a proactive, structured approach to ensure ongoing compliance with standards and continuous improvement. Programs that implement effective strategies safeguard their accreditation status and position themselves for growth, innovation, and enhanced learner outcomes. This section explores key strategies for maintaining accreditation and highlights their quantifiable impact.

Develop a Maintenance Plan

A well-structured maintenance plan is essential for systematically monitoring compliance with accreditation standards. This plan provides a roadmap for staying organized and ensuring no critical elements are overlooked. Key components include:

- *Regular Documentation Audits*: Conduct periodic reviews of policies, procedures, and records to ensure they are up-to-date and accurate. For example, auditing equipment maintenance logs every quarter helps identify gaps and demonstrates a commitment to safety and reliability.
- *Annual Curriculum Reviews*: Evaluate whether the curriculum aligns with current healthcare standards and best practices. Incorporate emerging technologies or methodologies to stay ahead of industry trends.
- *Scheduled Policy Updates:* Set a timeline for reviewing and revising policies to reflect changes in accreditation requirements or internal processes.

By establishing a maintenance plan, programs can avoid the pitfalls of last-minute scrambling during re-accreditation and demonstrate a consistent commitment to excellence.

Engage in Continuous Quality Improvement (CQI)

Continuous Quality Improvement (CQI) ensures that programs remain dynamic, responsive, and forward-thinking. This process involves collecting data, analyzing trends, and implementing changes to enhance program effectiveness. Examples of CQI in action include:

- *Learner Feedback:* Gathering post-simulation surveys or focus group insights helps identify areas for improvement. For instance, if learners report difficulty with specific scenarios, faculty can adjust them to better match their learning objectives.
- *Performance Metrics:* Track key indicators such as learner competency scores, faculty performance, and scenario completion rates to pinpoint opportunities for enhancement.
- *Stakeholder Collaboration:* Involve faculty, learners, and external partners in CQI initiatives to foster a culture of collaboration and shared accountability.

Programs that embed CQI into their operations demonstrate their ability to adapt to evolving needs, a quality highly valued by accrediting bodies.

Invest in Faculty and Staff Development

Faculty and staff are the backbone of any simulation program, and their growth directly impacts the program's quality and accreditation status. Prioritizing professional development ensures that educators and staff stay current with advances in simulation technology, pedagogy, and healthcare practices.

- *Certifications and Training:* Encourage faculty to pursue certifications such as Certified Healthcare Simulation Educator (CHSE) or Certified Healthcare Simulation Operations Specialist (CHSOS). These credentials enhance individual expertise and strengthen the program's overall credibility.
- *Conference Attendance:* Allocate funds for staff to attend conferences like the International Meeting on Simulation in Healthcare (IMSH) to learn about the latest trends and innovations.
- *In-Service Training:* Schedule regular workshops or peer-led training sessions to build team skills and knowledge.

Investing in faculty and staff development fosters engagement, reduces turnover, and positions the program as a leader in simulation education.

Maintain Accurate and Accessible Documentation

Clear, accurate, and well-organized documentation is the foundation of accreditation. Programs should prioritize maintaining a centralized repository for storing key records, such as:

- *Equipment Maintenance Logs:* Ensure these logs are detailed, regularly updated, and accessible for review.
- *Faculty Training Histories:* Track certifications, professional development activities, and performance evaluations.
- *Quality Improvement Reports:* Document CQI initiatives, including goals, actions taken, and measurable outcomes.

Centralized documentation streamlines audits and re-accreditation reviews and instills confidence in reviewers, stakeholders, and team members.

10.3 Prepare for Re-Accreditation

Re-accreditation is not just a formality but a reaffirmation of a program's commitment to excellence, continuous improvement, and adherence to high standards. Treating re-accreditation as an ongoing process rather than a one-time event ensures that programs remain organized, proactive, and prepared. By adopting a strategic and structured approach, programs can avoid last-minute stress and seamlessly transition through re-accreditation cycles.

The Mindset of Ongoing Preparation

Viewing accreditation as a continuous journey rather than a one-time achievement fosters a mindset of ongoing growth, improvement, and accountability. Programs that adopt this perspective are better equipped to meet the evolving standards of accrediting bodies and are more likely to thrive as leaders in simulation education. This approach transforms accreditation from a periodic challenge into an integral part of the program's culture, encouraging proactive management and long-term excellence.

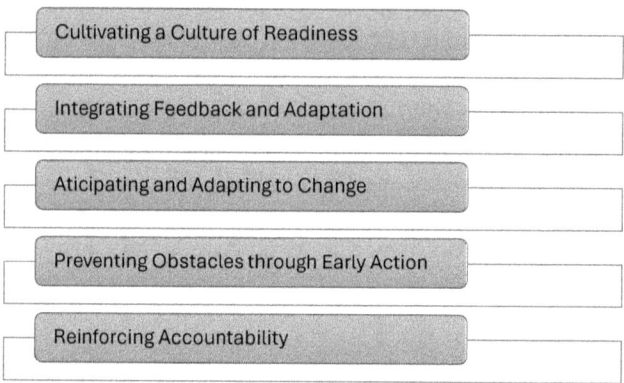

Figure 10 The Mindset of Ongoing Preparation

Cultivating a Culture of Readiness
Treating accreditation as an ongoing process emphasizes the importance of consistent monitoring and regular updates. This mindset helps programs stay organized, address issues promptly, and avoid the stress and inefficiencies of last-minute preparations. Improvements become embedded in daily operations rather than rushed in response to looming deadlines.

For instance, a program incorporating annual reviews of its policies, curriculum, and resources into its standard operations will likely catch potential issues early. This proactive approach enables the program to adapt seamlessly to new accreditation requirements or industry shifts, such as adopting advanced simulation technologies or changes in healthcare competencies.

Integrating Feedback and Adaptation
Programs that maintain a mindset of ongoing preparation actively seek and use feedback to enhance their operations. Collecting regular input

from learners, faculty, and stakeholders ensures that real needs and experiences drive improvements.

For example, if a program consistently gathers learner feedback after each simulation session, it can identify trends and areas for improvement. Learners may indicate that certain scenarios lack sufficient realism or clarity. By promptly addressing these concerns, the program improves the learner experience and aligns more closely with accreditation standards requiring high-quality, evidence-based education.

<u>Anticipating and Adapting to Change</u>
The dynamic nature of healthcare and education means that accreditation standards often evolve to reflect new practices, technologies, and challenges. Programs with an ongoing preparation mindset are better positioned to adapt to these changes without disruption.

For example, consider an accrediting body introducing a new standard requiring programs to demonstrate the integration of interprofessional education into their simulations. A program that regularly reviews its curriculum and tracks emerging trends would already have a process to identify gaps and implement interprofessional scenarios. This adaptability minimizes the risk of falling behind and demonstrates the program's commitment to continuous improvement.

<u>Preventing Obstacles Through Early Action</u>
By identifying and addressing gaps early, programs can prevent minor issues from escalating into significant obstacles during re-accreditation. Regular reviews and proactive planning ensure the program remains aligned with accreditation standards throughout the cycle.

For instance, a program that reviews its faculty training documentation annually might notice that some staff certifications have lapsed. By catching this early, the program can schedule renewal courses or professional development opportunities well before the accreditation deadline. This early action reduces stress and ensures compliance with standards requiring up-to-date qualifications.

<u>Reinforcing Accountability</u>
A culture of ongoing preparation fosters accountability among all stakeholders—faculty, staff, learners, and administrators. When accreditation is seen as a shared responsibility, team members are likelier to take ownership of their roles and contribute actively to the program's success.

For example, faculty might update scenario designs to reflect current best practices, while administrative staff ensure that documentation is consistently organized and accessible. This collective effort strengthens the program's readiness and demonstrates its commitment to excellence.

The mindset of ongoing preparation transforms accreditation from a periodic hurdle into a continuous opportunity for growth and innovation. By integrating monitoring, feedback, and adaptation into daily operations, programs ensure that they remain aligned with standards, meet stakeholder expectations, and thrive in an ever-evolving educational landscape. This proactive approach simplifies re-accreditation and solidifies the program's reputation as a leader in simulation-based education. Programs can confidently navigate the path to long-term success through consistent effort and a culture of readiness.

10.4 Key Practices for Preparing for Re-Accreditation

Annual Accreditation Requirement Reviews

Accrediting standards must be regularly revisited to ensure ongoing compliance and adaptability to change. Accrediting bodies may update their criteria to reflect industry trends, emerging technologies, or new educational practices.

- *Conduct Internal Audits:* Schedule annual review of documentation, policies, and procedures to ensure they align with accreditation requirements.
- *Monitor Changes in Standards:* Stay informed about updates from the accrediting body and adjust operations accordingly. For example, if a new standard requires data on learner progression, implement systems to track and report this information.

Regular reviews ensure that programs are always aware of compliance and that compliance is a consistent priority.

Mock Re-Accreditation Reviews

Internal mock reviews simulate the re-accreditation process, providing a practical way to identify weaknesses, refine strategies, and build confidence.

- *Simulate the Accreditation Visit:* Invite internal or external reviewers to assess the program using the accrediting body's criteria. The visit should include reviewing documentation, touring the facility, and interviewing faculty and learners.
- *Identify Gaps:* Use feedback from the mock review to address deficiencies in areas such as curriculum alignment, resource management, or learner assessment.
- *Refine Strategies:* Develop actionable plans to strengthen weaker areas. For instance, schedule a professional development review and update tracking systems if faculty training records are incomplete.

Mock reviews enhance readiness and familiarize faculty and staff with the accreditation process.

Stakeholder Engagement

Engaging faculty, staff, and learners in the re-accreditation process ensures that the entire program collaborates to maintain excellence.

- *Inform and Involve:* Regularly update stakeholders about the re-accreditation timeline, goals, and expectations. Transparency fosters a sense of shared responsibility and trust.
- *Reinforce Roles:* Clarify how each team member contributes to the program's success. For example, faculty may focus on scenario development and documentation while learners provide feedback on their educational experiences.
- *Celebrate Contributions:* Acknowledge and celebrate milestones achieved during the preparation process. Recognizing efforts boosts morale and strengthens team cohesion.

A program that actively involves its stakeholders is more likely to maintain a culture of accountability and collaboration, key factors in successful re-accreditation.

Proactive Preparation: A Case in Point

Proactive preparation for re-accreditation transforms a stressful, time-intensive process into a seamless reaffirmation of a program's commitment to quality and excellence. A prime example is a simulation program that embedded accreditation readiness into its annual operational routine, ensuring continuous improvement and alignment with standards.

Annual Reviews for Continuous Alignment
Each year, the program comprehensively reviews its policies, procedures, and practices. This includes evaluating the curriculum to ensure alignment with current healthcare standards and emerging simulation methodologies. For example, faculty analyze whether their scenarios incorporate the latest evidence-based practices and ensure consistency with accreditation requirements. This annual review also includes revisiting quality improvement documentation to ensure it reflects measurable outcomes and demonstrates the program's impact on learner success.

By routinely reviewing updates from the accrediting body, the program proactively adjusted its operations to stay ahead of new requirements. When an accrediting body introduced a standard emphasizing interprofessional education, the program had already begun integrating interprofessional scenarios into its curriculum, ensuring seamless compliance.

Mock Reviews for Readiness Assessment
Mock reviews became a cornerstone of the program's proactive strategy. These simulated accreditation visits involved internal and external reviewers who assessed documentation, facilities, and team readiness. Faculty and staff practiced articulating their roles and showcasing their contributions to the program's success, while learners were invited to provide real-time feedback on their educational experiences.

During one mock review, the program identified gaps in its equipment maintenance logs. The team implemented a new digital tracking system to streamline record-keeping, recognizing the importance of complete and accurate documentation. This improvement addressed the immediate gap and enhanced long-term operational efficiency.

Faculty and Staff Development as a Priority
The program recognized that its success hinged on the expertise and engagement of its team. Faculty and staff participated in regular professional development sessions, ensuring they stayed current with best practices in simulation education. Certifications such as the Certified Healthcare Simulation Educator (CHSE) and Certified Healthcare Simulation Operations Specialist (CHSOS) were strongly encouraged, with funding provided to support certification efforts.

In addition to technical training, faculty attended workshops on emerging pedagogical frameworks, such as the PEARLS debriefing model, which they integrated into their simulation activities. This dedication to professional growth ensured the team was prepared for re-accreditation and equipped to deliver high-quality education consistently.

Learner Feedback as a Catalyst for Improvement
Learners actively shaped the program's evolution through surveys, focus groups, and post-simulation evaluations. This feedback informed curriculum updates, highlighted areas for refinement, and demonstrated the program's commitment to meeting learners' needs.

For example, learners suggested that some scenarios needed clearer instructions and more opportunities for reflection. The program responded by revising scenario templates and incorporating additional debriefing sessions, enhancing learner satisfaction and educational outcomes.

Seamless Re-Accreditation and Enhanced Reputation
The program's proactive approach paid off when it came time for re-accreditation. Its organized documentation, well-maintained facilities, and confident, cohesive team impressed the reviewers. The site visit ran smoothly, and the accrediting body highlighted the program's strengths in quality improvement, faculty expertise, and learner engagement.

The program achieved seamless re-accreditation without deficiencies, reinforcing its reputation as a leader in simulation education. Beyond the accreditation, the program's proactive efforts positioned it as a model of excellence, attracting new partnerships, increased enrollment, and additional funding opportunities.

The Impact of Proactive Preparation

This case illustrates that re-accreditation can be a smooth process. By embedding readiness into its daily operations, the program transformed accreditation from a periodic challenge into an integral component of its culture. Proactive preparation:

- **Reduces Stress**: Annual reviews and mock assessments ensure readiness, eliminating last-minute scrambling.
- **Enhances Quality**: Continuous improvement driven by feedback and professional development ensures high standards.
- **Builds Confidence**: Faculty, staff, and learners feel prepared and supported, fostering a cohesive, high-performing team.

- **Strengthens Reputation**: Successful re-accreditation underscores the program's credibility, attracting new learners and partners.

This simulation program's proactive approach demonstrates that re-accreditation is not merely a checkpoint but an opportunity to showcase growth, innovation, and commitment to quality. By prioritizing regular reviews, engaging stakeholders, and fostering a culture of continuous improvement, the program achieved seamless re-accreditation and long-term success as a trusted leader in healthcare simulation education.

Quantifiable Impact

The impact of maintaining accreditation can be measured through qualitative and quantitative outcomes. According to the Society for Simulation in Healthcare (SSH, 2022):

Programs with robust maintenance plans are 50% more likely to achieve seamless re-accreditation than those without structured processes.

Learners from accredited programs report a 30% higher satisfaction rate, citing more consistent and effective simulation experiences.

For example, a nursing simulation program that prioritized regular curriculum updates and faculty training maintained its accreditation without deficiencies during re-accreditation. These efforts resulted in a 15% increase in enrollment, the acquisition of a major grant for facility expansion, and stronger partnerships with local healthcare institutions.

Maintaining accreditation requires dedication, organization, and a forward-thinking mindset. By developing a maintenance plan, engaging in CQI, investing in faculty development, ensuring meticulous documentation, and treating re-accreditation as an ongoing process, programs can sustain their accreditation status and thrive as leaders in simulation education. The benefits—ranging from increased learner satisfaction to enhanced reputation and funding opportunities—underscore the value of these strategies, making accreditation maintenance an investment in long-term success.

Maintaining accreditation is an essential component of a simulation program's long-term success. It ensures that the program meets high standards, delivers exceptional education to learners, and attracts the resources and talent necessary for growth. By treating accreditation as an ongoing process and implementing strategies for continuous improvement, programs protect their reputations and position themselves as leaders in simulation-based education. Maintaining accreditation is not just about compliance—it reflects a program's commitment to quality, innovation, and excellence in healthcare education.

Maintaining Continuous Quality Improvement

Maintaining accreditation requires an ongoing commitment to Continuous Quality Improvement (CQI). CQI ensures that programs meet accreditation standards and evolve to address new challenges, technologies, and learner needs. It is a structured, dynamic process that fosters a culture of excellence, enabling simulation programs to deliver high-quality education consistently.

Figure 11 Steps for Maintaining CQI

Step 1: Developing a Continuous Quality Improvement (CQI) Plan
A robust CQI plan is the foundation for sustained improvement and accreditation maintenance. It provides a clear roadmap for evaluating performance, implementing changes, and achieving measurable outcomes.

Establish CQI Processes
- Develop a structured CQI plan with specific goals, timelines, and assigned responsibilities.
- Utilize proven methodologies like the Plan-Do-Study-Act (PDSA) cycle to test changes incrementally and evaluate their impact.
- Example: A program aiming to improve learner satisfaction might pilot a revised debriefing framework in one cohort before implementing it across all scenarios.

Collect and Analyze Data
- Gather data on Key Performance Indicators (KPIs) such as learner outcomes, faculty performance, and simulation utilization rates.

- Use dashboards and visualization tools to track progress and make data-driven decisions.
- Example: A program that analyzes satisfaction scores may identify a need for additional faculty training in advanced simulation technologies.

<u>Engage Stakeholders</u>
- Involve faculty, staff, and learners in the CQI process to foster collaboration and shared accountability.
- Solicit feedback through surveys, focus groups, and interviews to identify strengths and areas for improvement.

<u>Document CQI Activities</u>
- Maintain detailed records of all CQI initiatives, including their objectives, actions taken, and results achieved.

Use these records to demonstrate alignment with accreditation standards during audits or reviews.

Step 2: Adhering to Accreditation Standards

Regularly revisiting accreditation standards ensures ongoing compliance and readiness for re-accreditation.

<u>Conduct Regular Internal Audits</u>
- Schedule self-assessments to evaluate how well the program aligns with current accreditation requirements.
- Example: A quarterly review of equipment maintenance logs ensures consistency and addresses gaps before external reviews.

<u>Update Policies and Procedures</u>
- Revise program policies to reflect accreditation standards, educational practices, or technologies changes.
- Communicate updates clearly to faculty, staff, and learners to ensure adherence.

<u>Monitor Industry Trends</u>
- Participate in professional organizations, webinars, and conferences to stay informed about developments in healthcare simulation and accreditation requirements.

Step 3: Maintaining Documentation and Records

Organized and up-to-date documentation simplifies accreditation reporting and supports quality assurance.

Use a Centralized Documentation System
- Store all policies, curricula, quality improvement reports, and faculty records in a secure, centralized repository.
- Example: A digital document management system allows easy access and prevents loss of critical information.

Keep Records Current
- Regularly update documentation to reflect new initiatives, faculty training, and learner outcomes.
- Example: Maintaining updated faculty résumés with recent certifications demonstrates ongoing professional development.

Prepare for Re-Accreditation
- Begin collecting evidence for re-accreditation at least a year before the deadline.
- Retain documentation from the initial accreditation process for reference and comparison.

Step 4: Supporting Faculty and Staff Development

Faculty and staff are essential to maintaining program quality and meeting accreditation standards.

Encourage Certification
- Support team members in pursuing certifications such as Certified Healthcare Simulation Educator (CHSE) or Certified Healthcare Simulation Operations Specialist (CHSOS) by funding courses and exams.

Offer Professional Development Opportunities
- Host regular workshops on simulation technology, pedagogy, and assessment methods.
- Encourage attendance at conferences like the International Meeting on Simulation in Healthcare (IMSH) to stay current with industry trends.

Foster a Culture of Learning
- Promote collaboration and knowledge-sharing among team members.

- Recognize and reward achievements in professional development, such as completing certifications or publishing research.

Step 5: Preparing for Re-Accreditation
Re-accreditation is an opportunity to demonstrate growth, innovation, and continued compliance.

<u>Conduct a Pre-Re-Accreditation Review</u>
- Perform an internal audit to assess readiness and identify areas requiring improvement.

<u>Highlight Achievements</u>
- Showcase accomplishments since the last accreditation cycle, such as new facilities, improved curricula, or increased learner outcomes.
- Example: Documenting the integration of virtual reality technology into simulation activities demonstrates innovation and adaptability.

<u>Engage Stakeholders</u>
- Involve faculty, staff, and learners in preparation efforts to build a unified, motivated team.
- Communicate the value of re-accreditation to emphasize its importance to the program's success.

Step 6: Addressing Challenges
Programs must be prepared to navigate resource constraints, staff turnover, or evolving standards.

<u>Ensure Adequate Resources</u>
- Advocate for funding supporting accreditation-related activities, including training, equipment upgrades, and maintenance.

<u>Manage Faculty Turnover</u>
- Develop a succession plan to ensure leadership continuity and expertise retention.
- Provide mentorship and onboarding for new faculty to integrate them quickly into the program's culture.

<u>Adapt to Changes</u>

- Stay flexible and responsive to new accreditation requirements or industry trends.
- Use feedback from accrediting bodies to guide strategic improvements.

Maintaining Continuous Quality Improvement is central to sustaining accreditation and advancing program excellence. Programs can foster a culture of resilience, adaptability, and continuous learning by developing structured CQI plans, adhering to evolving standards, keeping documentation current, supporting faculty development, and preparing strategically for re-accreditation. These efforts ensure compliance and position simulation programs as leaders in healthcare education capable of meeting the dynamic challenges of the field.

Case Example

Achieving accreditation is a significant milestone, but sustaining it requires a deliberate and ongoing effort. The ABC Simulation Center exemplifies how a proactive and structured approach to Continuous Quality Improvement (CQI) can maintain accreditation and enhance program quality and reputation.

Building a Foundation of Excellence

After achieving accreditation, ABC Simulation Center recognized the importance of embedding quality improvement into its daily operations. The center's leadership developed a robust CQI plan to ensure ongoing compliance with accreditation standards while fostering innovation and adaptability. Key elements of the plan included:

- *Quarterly Performance Reviews:* The center conducted quarterly reviews to monitor progress on Key Performance Indicators (KPIs) such as learner competency scores, faculty performance, and equipment functionality. For example, these reviews highlighted opportunities to enhance scenario fidelity by incorporating updated clinical guidelines, which the team quickly implemented.

- *Annual Faculty Training:* The center recognized that a well-trained team and mandated annual faculty development sessions are essential to program success. Topics ranged from advances in simulation technology to best practices in debriefing techniques, such as the PEARLS framework. Faculty were also encouraged to pursue certifications like CHSE and CHSOS, and the center provided financial support for exams and training.

- *Regular Updates to Policies and Curricula:* The center established a process for reviewing and revising policies and curricula annually, ensuring alignment with evolving accreditation standards and industry trends. For instance, when interprofessional education became a priority in healthcare simulation, ABC Simulation Center updated its curriculum to include collaborative scenarios featuring nursing, pharmacy, and medical learners.

Streamlined Documentation for Seamless Compliance

One of the center's standout strategies was creating a dedicated documentation team to maintain organized, up-to-date records. This team implemented a centralized digital repository to store critical documents, including:

- Faculty training logs.
- Equipment maintenance records.
- Learner feedback reports.
- Quality improvement plans and outcomes.

This system ensured compliance with accreditation requirements and simplified the re-accreditation process by providing easy access to comprehensive, well-organized documentation.

Reaping the Rewards During Re-Accreditation

When it came time for re-accreditation, ABC Simulation Center's preparation and commitment to CQI paid off. The accrediting body's reviewers noted several strengths:

- *Commitment to Continuous Improvement:* The center's quarterly performance reviews and annual training sessions demonstrated a culture of proactive growth and adaptability. Reviewers highlighted these efforts as evidence of a program deeply invested in maintaining excellence.
- *Innovative Curriculum Enhancements:* Integrating interprofessional education and advanced simulation technologies, such as virtual reality scenarios, showcased the center's dedication to staying at the forefront of healthcare simulation.
- *Flawless Documentation:* The documentation team's meticulous organization impressed reviewers, who commended the center for its seamless access to up-to-date policies, performance data, and quality improvement records.

Recognition and Re-Accreditation

As a result of these efforts, ABC Simulation Center achieved full re-accreditation without any deficiencies. Reviewers praised the program for not only meeting but exceeding accreditation standards. The center's success reinforced its reputation as a leader in healthcare simulation education and attracted new opportunities, including partnerships with local hospitals and increased enrollment in its programs.

Lessons Learned
The experience of ABC Simulation Center highlights several key takeaways for sustaining accreditation:

- *CQI is Essential:* Regular performance reviews, faculty training, and policy updates ensure a program remains dynamic and aligned with standards.
- *Teamwork Matters:* Creating a dedicated documentation team fosters accountability and streamlines compliance.
- Proactive Preparation is Key: Treating accreditation as an ongoing process rather than a periodic event minimizes stress and enhances readiness.

Conclusion
ABC Simulation Center's proactive approach to CQI and re-accreditation exemplifies how simulation programs can sustain accreditation while continuously improving their quality and impact. The center retained its accreditation status by embedding improvement into its culture and solidified its role as a trailblazer in healthcare simulation education.

10.5 Key Takeaways

CQI is Essential: Programs must continuously monitor and improve their operations to align with accreditation standards.

Stakeholder Engagement is Crucial: Faculty, staff, and learners play vital roles in maintaining accreditation and fostering a culture of collaboration.

Proactive Preparation Minimizes Stress: Integrating accreditation readiness into daily operations ensures smooth re-accreditation cycles.

10.6 Summary

Chapter 8 emphasizes that achieving accreditation is not the endpoint of a program's journey but the foundation for a continuous commitment to excellence. Maintaining accreditation requires proactive efforts, adherence to high standards, and preparation for future re-accreditation cycles. Through strategies like continuous quality improvement (CQI), faculty development, and robust documentation, simulation programs can sustain accreditation, foster a culture of excellence, and solidify their role as leaders in healthcare education.

Maintaining accreditation is an investment in a program's future, enabling it to deliver high-quality education, foster innovation, and sustain stakeholder trust. By embedding strategies like CQI, faculty development, and proactive preparation into their culture, simulation programs can confidently navigate the path to re-accreditation, ensuring long-term success as leaders in healthcare education. Accreditation is not just about meeting standards—it reflects a program's unwavering commitment to quality, integrity, and excellence.

Chapter 11

INACSL Endorsement

The International Nursing Association for Clinical Simulation and Learning (INACSL) is a globally recognized organization dedicated to advancing excellence in clinical simulation. Its Standards of Best Practice: Simulation^{SM}(SOBP) is a gold standard for simulation-based education and operations. INACSL endorsement is a prestigious recognition that signifies a program's alignment with these best practices, validating its commitment to quality and innovation in healthcare simulation.

Achieving INACSL endorsement elevates a program's reputation and ensures it provides consistent, evidence-based learning experiences that enhance learner outcomes and patient safety. This chapter explores the benefits of INACSL endorsement, outlines the endorsement process, and provides actionable strategies for achieving this esteemed recognition.

11.1 Benefits of INACSL Endorsement

INACSL endorsement offers tangible and intangible benefits that extend beyond prestige. These advantages positively impact learners, faculty, and stakeholders while fostering continuous improvement.

1. **Recognition of Excellence** Programs with INACSL endorsement are recognized as leaders in simulation-based education. This distinction enhances credibility and attracts learners, faculty, and institutional partners.

Example: A nursing school with INACSL endorsement experienced a 30% increase in enrollment, as prospective students viewed the endorsement as a hallmark of quality.

2. **Enhanced Learner Outcomes** Endorsed programs align with the latest best practices, ensuring learners gain the skills and confidence necessary for real-world clinical challenges. **Statistic:** According to INACSL, programs that adopt its SOBP report a 25% improvement in learner competency scores (INACSL, 2021).
3. **Professional Development** Faculty and staff in endorsed programs benefit from opportunities to engage with INACSL's global community, accessing resources, conferences, and professional development activities.
4. **Global Networking and Collaboration** INACSL endorsement connects programs to a worldwide network of simulation professionals, fostering collaboration and the sharing of innovative practices.
5. **Continuous Improvement Framework** By adhering to the SOBP, programs establish robust quality improvement processes that support sustainable growth and excellence.

The Standards of Best Practice: Simulation℠ (SOBP) are the foundation of INACSL endorsement. These standards provide evidence-based guidelines for designing, implementing, and evaluating simulation activities.

11.2 Key Components of the SOBP

Simulation Design Simulation activities must have clearly defined objectives, realistic scenarios, and appropriate fidelity levels. The learner's needs and intended outcomes should guide the design process.

Outcomes and Objectives Each simulation should align with measurable learning outcomes, ensuring that activities address specific competencies or skills.

Facilitation Simulation facilitation must be learner-centered, with facilitators trained to guide participants through realistic scenarios and reflective debriefing.

Debriefing Debriefing is a critical component of simulation. It must follow structured frameworks like PEARLS or GAS to maximize learning and reflection.

Evaluation Programs must use reliable and valid assessment tools to evaluate learner performance and simulation effectiveness.

Professional Integrity Endorsed programs demonstrate ethical practices, transparency, and a commitment to advancing the field of simulation education.

Simulation Operations This standard emphasizes maintaining high-quality facilities, technology, and resources to support effective learning experiences.

11.3 The INACSL Endorsement Process

Achieving INACSL endorsement involves a multi-step process that requires careful planning, collaboration, and documentation. Programs must demonstrate alignment with the SOBP and provide evidence of their commitment to best practices.

Step 1: Self-Assessment
Before applying for endorsement, programs should conduct a thorough self-assessment to evaluate their alignment with the SOBP. This assessment identifies strengths and gaps, guiding improvement efforts.

Checklist for Self-Assessment:
- Are simulation scenarios designed with measurable objectives?
- Is debriefing conducted using evidence-based frameworks?
- Are learner outcomes consistently evaluated and documented?
- Are faculty trained in simulation pedagogy and facilitation?
- Do facilities meet safety, fidelity, and accessibility standards?

Step 2: Application Submission
Programs submit an application to INACSL, including:
- A detailed self-study report demonstrating compliance with the SOBP.
- Supporting evidence, such as policies, curricula, learner outcomes, and faculty training records.

Step 3: Peer Review
INACSL conducts a peer review of the submitted materials. Reviewers assess whether the program meets endorsement criteria and provide feedback on areas for improvement.

Step 4: Site Visit (Optional)
In some cases, INACSL may request a site visit to observe simulation activities, review facilities, and meet with faculty and staff.

Step 5: Decision and Feedback
Following the review process, INACSL makes a decision and provides constructive feedback. Endorsed programs receive certification and public recognition on INACSL's website.

11.4 Strategies for Achieving INACSL Endorsement

Achieving INACSL endorsement requires a multifaceted approach rooted in strategic planning, commitment to best practices, and continuous improvement. The following strategies provide actionable steps to help programs align with the Standards of Best Practice: Simulation℠ (SOBP) and demonstrate excellence in simulation-based education.

Align Policies and Practices with the SOBP
Ensuring that your program's policies and practices align with the SOBP is foundational for achieving INACSL endorsement. This process involves systematically reviewing and revising program documents to reflect best practices in simulation education.

> **Accreditation Tip:**
> When creating the standardized scenario template for your program, add the INACSL SOBP and any other AACN competencies or AAMC EPAs. That way, it is ready for review during the review, and the reviewers can quickly cross-reference.

Standardizing Scenario Design Templates: Develop templates for simulation scenarios that include:

- *Learning Objectives:* Clearly defined and measurable outcomes.
- *Participant Roles:* Detailed descriptions of roles to enhance realism.
- *Debriefing Guides:* Frameworks such as PEARLS or GAS for consistent, effective post-simulation discussions.

Embedding SOBP in Policies: Update program policies to explicitly incorporate elements of the SOBP, such as requiring faculty to use validated assessment tools or mandating annual reviews of simulation curricula. These updates demonstrate a commitment to ongoing alignment with INACSL standards.

Invest in Faculty Development
Faculty expertise is a cornerstone of high-quality simulation education. INACSL emphasizes well-trained and qualified educators who understand and apply simulation best practices.

Training on Best Practices: Provide faculty with training on simulation pedagogy, including:

- Scenario design and facilitation.
- Advanced debriefing techniques to foster reflective learning.
- Utilizing assessment tools like the Debriefing Assessment for Simulation in Healthcare (DASH).

Certification Support: Encourage faculty to pursue certifications such as the Certified Healthcare Simulation Educator (CHSE) or Certified Healthcare Simulation Operations Specialist (CHSOS). Offer financial support or study resources to incentivize participation.

Professional Development Opportunities: Fund attendance at INACSL conferences and webinars, enabling faculty to stay current with emerging trends and contribute to a culture of continuous learning.

Leverage Technology
Simulation technology is at the heart of effective experiential learning. INACSL endorsement often requires evidence of innovation and excellence in using simulation tools.

1. **Enhancing Realism with High-Fidelity Tools:** Invest in high-fidelity manikins, virtual reality platforms, and augmented reality tools replicating clinical environments. These tools engage learners, improve skill acquisition, and foster critical thinking.

2. **Maximizing Facility Utilization:** Use audiovisual technology to record and review simulation sessions, enabling detailed analysis and feedback. Highlight how technology supports learner-centered debriefing and performance evaluation.

3. **Technology Training for Staff:** Ensure that faculty and technical staff are proficient in operating and troubleshooting simulation equipment. Regular training minimizes downtime and maximizes the effectiveness of simulation activities.

Develop a Robust Quality Improvement Plan
Continuous Quality Improvement (CQI) ensures programs maintain excellence while adapting to changing needs and standards.

1. **Establishing CQI Processes:** Develop a formal CQI plan that includes:
   a. *Regular Data Collection:* Track learner outcomes, satisfaction scores, and scenario completion rates.
   b. Analysis and Reporting: Use dashboards to monitor performance and identify trends.

2. **Leveraging Feedback:** Collect feedback from learners, faculty, and external stakeholders to guide program enhancements. For example, post-simulation surveys can pinpoint areas for improvement in scenario design or facilitation.

3. **Documenting Improvements:** During the endorsement application, maintain detailed records of CQI initiatives to showcase your program's commitment to continuous improvement.

4. Engage Stakeholders
   Involving key stakeholders in the endorsement process fosters collaboration, builds support, and enhances the program's credibility.

5. **Faculty and Staff Engagement:** Involve faculty and staff in preparing for endorsement by assigning roles such as:
   a. Reviewing and updating documentation.
   b. Leading mock evaluations to simulate the endorsement review process.
   c. Developing professional development plans tied to SOBP criteria.

6. **Learner Involvement:** Encourage learners to provide feedback on their simulation experiences and participate in focus groups. Highlight how their insights have informed curriculum updates or new initiatives.

7. **External Partnerships:** Collaborate with local healthcare organizations, accrediting bodies, and other simulation programs to gain insights and resources. For example, a hospital partnership might provide funding for advanced simulation technology or access to clinical expertise for scenario development.

8. **Celebrating Achievements:** Recognize and celebrate milestones with stakeholders to maintain motivation and demonstrate progress. Publicly acknowledge faculty certifications, learner achievements, or infrastructure improvements.

Achieving INACSL endorsement is a testament to a simulation program's dedication to excellence, innovation, and continuous improvement. By aligning policies with the SOBP, investing in faculty, leveraging advanced technology, implementing CQI practices, and engaging stakeholders, programs can position themselves for success. These strategies facilitate endorsement and elevate the program's impact on learners, faculty, and the broader healthcare community.

Case Study: INACSL Endorsement at ABC University
ABC University's simulation program achieved INACSL endorsement after a two-year effort to align with the SOBP. The program:

- Conducted a comprehensive gap analysis to identify areas needing improvement.
- Implemented a faculty training initiative, resulting in 80% of educators earning CHSE certification.
- Upgraded its facilities with advanced audiovisual systems and high-fidelity manikins.
- Adopted the PEARLS framework for debriefing, enhancing learner reflection and competency scores.

Following endorsement, ABC University saw a 40% increase in learner satisfaction and secured a grant to expand its simulation lab. The program's success reinforced its reputation as a leader in nursing education.

11.5 Take Aways

- **Significance of INACSL Endorsement**
    - INACSL endorsement is a prestigious recognition affirming alignment with the Standards of Best Practice: Simulation^{SM} (SOBP).
    - It validates a program's commitment to excellence, innovation, and evidence-based simulation practices.
- **Benefits of INACSL Endorsement**
    - **Recognition of Excellence**: Enhances credibility, attracting learners, faculty, and institutional partners.

- **Improved Learner Outcomes**: Aligning with SOBP leads to measurable gains in competency and confidence among learners.
- **Professional Development**: Offers faculty and staff access to global resources, networking opportunities, and advanced training.
- **Global Networking**: Connects programs to a worldwide community of simulation professionals for collaboration and knowledge exchange.
- **Framework for Continuous Improvement**: Embedding SOBP into operations fosters sustainable growth and program excellence.

- **Core Components of the Standards of Best Practice (SOBP)**
  - **Simulation Design**: Scenarios must have clear objectives, realistic elements, and tailored fidelity levels.
  - **Facilitation and Debriefing**: Learner-centered facilitation and structured debriefing frameworks (e.g., PEARLS, GAS) are essential for reflection and learning.
  - **Evaluation**: Use valid tools to assess learner performance and simulation effectiveness.
  - **Professional Integrity**: Emphasize ethical practices, transparency, and continuous field advancement.
  - **Simulation Operations**: Maintain high-quality facilities, technology, and operational standards.
- **Steps in the INACSL Endorsement Process**
  - **Self-Assessment**: Evaluate alignment with the SOBP to identify strengths and gaps.
  - **Application Submission**: Provide a detailed self-study report and supporting documentation.
  - **Peer Review**: External reviewers assess compliance and provide feedback.
  - **Optional Site Visit**: Some programs may host reviewers for in-person evaluations.
  - **Decision and Feedback**: INACSL provides the endorsement decision and constructive suggestions.
- **Strategies for Achieving Endorsement**
  - **Align Policies with SOBP**: Update policies and procedures to integrate best practices, including scenario design templates and standardized assessment tools.

- **Invest in Faculty Development**: Provide training in simulation pedagogy, advanced debriefing techniques, and certification opportunities (e.g., CHSE, CHSOS).
- **Leverage Technology**: Incorporate high-fidelity simulation tools, virtual/augmented reality, and robust audiovisual systems for enhanced learner engagement and evaluation.
- **Implement Continuous Quality Improvement (CQI)**: Develop formal plans to track outcomes, analyze data, and document improvements.
- **Engage Stakeholders**: Foster collaboration with faculty, learners, and external partners to strengthen support and ensure alignment with endorsement goals.

- **Role of Continuous Improvement**
  - Regularly collect and analyze feedback to refine simulation activities and processes.
  - Use dashboards and data visualization to monitor performance and highlight areas for enhancement.
  - Maintain detailed CQI records to demonstrate a culture of ongoing development.
- **Importance of Stakeholder Collaboration**
  - Faculty, staff, and learners should actively participate in preparing for endorsement through documentation updates, mock reviews, and feedback sessions.
  - External partnerships with healthcare organizations and accrediting bodies can provide resources and insights to strengthen the program.
- **Celebrating Milestones**
  - Recognize achievements such as faculty certifications, learner successes, or technology upgrades to sustain motivation and highlight progress.
- **Long-Term Impact of Endorsement**
  - INACSL endorsement enhances a program's reputation, learner outcomes, and operational excellence.
  - Endorsed programs set benchmarks for innovation and quality in simulation-based education, influencing the broader healthcare community.

11.6 Summary

INACSL endorsement is a powerful affirmation of a program's dedication to simulation excellence. By aligning with the Standards of Best Practice: Simulation^{SM}, programs not only enhance their educational impact but also gain recognition as leaders in healthcare simulation. The journey to endorsement requires effort, collaboration, and strategic planning, but the rewards—improved outcomes, greater credibility, and expanded opportunities—are well worth the investment. As programs strive for endorsement, they advance their mission of shaping the future of healthcare education through innovation and quality.

Chapter 12

ASPE Accreditation

The Association of Standardized Patient Educators (ASPE) accreditation is a hallmark of quality for programs specializing in the education, training, and integration of standardized patients (SPs) into healthcare simulation. Earning ASPE accreditation demonstrates a program's adherence to best practices, commitment to continuous improvement, and dedication to advancing healthcare education through SP methodologies. This chapter provides a comprehensive guide to understanding ASPE accreditation, its benefits, and the strategies required to achieve and maintain it.

12.1 Understanding ASPE Accreditation

ASPE is a global leader in standardized patient education. It supports programs that use SPs to enhance healthcare education, assessment, and research. The organization has developed accreditation standards that emphasize excellence in SP training, program management, and ethical practices.

The Purpose of ASPE Accreditation

ASPE accreditation ensures that programs:
- Deliver consistent, high-quality SP education and experiences.
- Uphold ethical standards for SP engagement and learner interactions.
- Foster continuous professional development for educators and SPs.
- Advance the field of SP education through research and innovation.

12.2 Benefits of ASPE Accreditation

Achieving ASPE accreditation brings numerous advantages to programs, learners, faculty, and SPs. These benefits include:

1. **Enhanced Credibility and Recognition:** Accreditation signals to stakeholders—learners, faculty, and external partners—that the program meets rigorous industry standards. Accredited programs are viewed as leaders in SP education.
2. **Improved SP Program Quality:** The accreditation process provides a framework for assessing and enhancing every aspect of the program, from SP recruitment and training to curriculum integration and learner evaluation.
3. **Increased Stakeholder Confidence:** Accreditation builds trust among learners, faculty, and external partners, reassuring them of the program's quality and ethical practices.
4. **Opportunities for Collaboration and Funding:** Accredited programs are better positioned to establish partnerships, secure grants, and participate in research initiatives that advance SP education.
5. **Professional Development for Educators and SPs:** Accreditation encourages programs to invest in ongoing training, ensuring that faculty and SPs remain at the forefront of best practices.

12.3 ASPE Accreditation Standards

ASPE accreditation standards are designed to ensure the highest levels of excellence in SP education. These standards are categorized into the following key areas:

1. **Program Leadership and Governance**
   Accredited programs must have:
   - Clear organizational structures with defined leadership roles.
   - Policies and procedures to guide program operations and decision-making.
   - Ethical standards governing SP interactions with learners and faculty.

2. **SP Recruitment and Training**
   Programs must demonstrate:

- A robust recruitment process that selects SPs based on defined competencies and qualities.
- Comprehensive training protocols that prepare SPs for their roles in simulations, assessments, and debriefings.
- Ongoing professional development opportunities for SPs.

3. **Curriculum Design and Delivery**
   Accredited programs integrate SP methodologies into the broader curriculum, ensuring alignment with learning objectives and competency frameworks.

4. **Learner Assessment and Feedback**
   Programs must use SPs to assess learners effectively, incorporating:
   - Validated tools and rubrics for measuring clinical skills, communication, and professionalism.
   - Structured feedback processes to help learners improve performance.

5. **Continuous Quality Improvement (CQI)**
   Programs are required to engage in ongoing evaluation and improvement, including:
   - Collecting data on learner outcomes, SP performance, and program effectiveness.
   - Implementing changes based on feedback from learners, SPs, and faculty.

12.4 Strategies for Achieving ASPE Accreditation

Securing ASPE accreditation requires thoughtful planning, resource allocation, and an unwavering commitment to quality. By adopting a strategic approach, programs can ensure they meet accreditation standards while fostering an environment of excellence and innovation. Below is a detailed exploration of key strategies to achieve ASPE accreditation:

1. Establish Clear Policies and Procedures

Strong policies and procedures form the backbone of any successful SP program. These guidelines ensure consistency, transparency, and adherence to accreditation standards.

- **Develop Comprehensive Policies:** Craft policies covering SP recruitment, training, scheduling, and evaluation. Clear

documentation helps maintain uniform practices and sets expectations for all participants.
- **Integrate Ethical Guidelines:** Establish ethical standards to protect SPs and learners. Policies should address consent, confidentiality, and the boundaries of SP roles to ensure respectful and professional interactions.

2. Invest in SP Training and Development

The quality of SP performance directly impacts the effectiveness of simulations. Investing in comprehensive training ensures SPs can confidently and competently fulfill their roles.

- **Provide Initial and Ongoing Training.** Focus on areas such as role portrayal, feedback delivery, and cultural competency. Initial training establishes foundational skills for fulfilling roles and expanding SP capabilities.
- **Utilize ASPE Resources:** Use ASPE webinars, workshops, and resources to align training practices with industry standards.

> **From the Reviewer's Perspective:**
> The reviewers will want to examine the program's recruitment, orientation, training, and evaluation processes and ensure proper documentation is maintained.

3. Align Curriculum with SP Methodologies

Simulation programs must seamlessly integrate SP-based activities into their broader curriculum to maximize learning outcomes and meet accreditation standards.

- **Link SP Scenarios to Learning Objectives:** Ensure each simulation aligns with defined competencies, such as communication skills or clinical reasoning. Detailed scenario templates should include objectives, participant roles, and debriefing plans.
- **Use Role-Specific Guidance:** Provide SPs with scripts and case studies to clarify expectations and prepare them for specific scenarios.

4. Implement Robust Assessment Practices

Effective assessment practices are essential for evaluating learner performance and ensuring program effectiveness.

- **Use Validated Tools:** Adopt tools like the Objective Structured Clinical Examination (OSCE) to measure learner competencies objectively and consistently.

- **Train SPs for Feedback Delivery:** Equip SPs to provide constructive, learner-centered feedback. For example, SPs can use structured formats to discuss observed behaviors, focusing on improvement opportunities.

5. Engage Stakeholders

Collaboration among faculty, SPs, learners, and external partners strengthens the program and ensures alignment with accreditation standards.

- **Involve Stakeholders in Development:** Engage faculty, SPs, and learners in designing and refining program components, such as scenarios and evaluation tools.
- **Use Stakeholder Feedback:** Regularly solicit input through surveys, focus groups, and interviews to guide program improvements.

6. Leverage Technology

Technology can streamline operations, enhance learning experiences, and improve program management.

- **Adopt Scheduling Software:** Use software to efficiently manage SP assignments, availability, and performance tracking.
- **Incorporate Audiovisual Tools:** Record simulations for analysis, enabling detailed feedback for both learners and SPs.
- **Example:** A simulation center implemented a cloud-based system to schedule SPs and track their training progress, reducing administrative burdens and increasing operational efficiency.

7. Document Everything

Comprehensive documentation is critical for demonstrating compliance with accreditation standards and supporting continuous improvement.

- **Centralize Documentation:** Maintain a secure repository of SP training materials, program policies, learner assessment tools, and quality improvement reports.
- **Regularly Update Records:** Ensure documentation reflects current practices, such as recent training sessions or updated scenarios.
- **Example:** A program used a shared drive to store SP recruitment logs, training materials, and feedback reports, simplifying the accreditation review process.

8. Conduct Mock Reviews

Mock accreditation reviews provide a valuable opportunity to identify gaps, refine strategies, and build confidence among faculty and staff.

- **Simulate Accreditation Visits:** Use internal or external reviewers to assess compliance with ASPE standards. Mock reviews should mimic the structure and rigor of an actual site visit.
- **Address Identified Gaps:** Develop an action plan to resolve weaknesses highlighted during the mock review.
- **Example:** A program invited an external ASPE member to conduct a mock review, receiving constructive feedback that improved SP training protocols and documentation organization.

Achieving Excellence Through Strategic Planning

Implementing these strategies allows programs to approach ASPE accreditation as a structured and purposeful journey. Each step—refining policies, enhancing SP training, or leveraging technology—contributes to building a robust, high-quality SP program that aligns with ASPE's rigorous standards. Through careful planning and continuous improvement, simulation programs can achieve accreditation while advancing the field of standardized patient education.

12.5 Maintaining ASPE Accreditation

Earning ASPE accreditation is just the beginning. Programs must demonstrate ongoing compliance with standards and a commitment to continuous improvement. Key practices include:

- **Regularly Review Standards:** Stay informed about updates to ASPE accreditation criteria and adjust policies and practices accordingly.
- **Provide Ongoing Training:** Offer regular professional development opportunities for SPs and faculty to maintain their skills and knowledge.
- **Engage in CQI:** Use data from learner evaluations, SP feedback, and program assessments to drive improvements.
- **Prepare for Re-Accreditation:** Treat accreditation as an ongoing process, ensuring readiness for the next cycle through continuous monitoring and proactive management.

12.6 Case Example: Achieving ASPE Accreditation

Program: Bright Future Health Simulation Center

Challenge: Limited resources for SP training and curriculum integration.

Strategies:
- Developed a standardized SP recruitment and training process using ASPE resources.
- Integrated SP-based simulations into existing clinical courses, aligning them with learning objectives.
- Secured funding for SP workshops and professional development through local healthcare partnerships.

Outcome: The program achieved full ASPE accreditation, and it was commended for its innovative use of SPs to enhance learner outcomes. Accreditation also increased funding and institutional support for the program.

12.7 Summary

Achieving ASPE accreditation is a rigorous but rewarding process that positions simulation programs as leaders in standardized patient education. By adhering to ASPE standards, investing in faculty and SP development, and fostering a culture of continuous improvement, programs can deliver exceptional educational experiences that prepare learners for real-world clinical challenges. Accreditation is not just a validation of quality—it is a commitment to advancing healthcare education.

KEITH A. BEAULIEU

Chapter 13

ACS Accreditation

The American College of Surgeons (ACS) accreditation is a prestigious recognition of excellence in simulation-based surgical education and training. This chapter explores the significance of ACS accreditation, its standards, and the steps required for programs to achieve and maintain this distinguished status.

13.1 Introduction to ACS Accreditation

The ACS Accreditation Program for Simulation Centers is a benchmark for quality in surgical education. It ensures that centers meet rigorous standards in curriculum design, learner assessment, faculty qualifications, facilities, and quality improvement. Achieving ACS accreditation demonstrates a program's commitment to enhancing surgical training, improving patient safety, and advancing simulation-based education.

Why Pursue ACS Accreditation?

Achieving ACS accreditation is a milestone and a testament to a program's dedication to advancing surgical education and improving patient care. This prestigious recognition offers numerous benefits across educational, professional, and institutional dimensions.

1. Recognition as a Leader in Surgical Education

ACS accreditation positions a program as a trailblazer in surgical education. It signals to learners, faculty, healthcare institutions, and industry partners that the program adheres to the highest standards of quality and effectiveness.

- *Competitive Edge:* Accredited programs are often viewed as elite, attracting top-tier learners and faculty seeking opportunities to train or teach in high-caliber environments.
- *Institutional Prestige:* Accreditation elevates an institution's reputation, fostering stakeholder trust and reinforcing its status as a leader in healthcare education.

2. Validation of Program Quality and Effectiveness

ACS accreditation is an external endorsement of a program's quality and impact. By undergoing the rigorous accreditation process, programs demonstrate their ability to meet stringent benchmarks in curriculum design, faculty expertise, and learner assessment.

- *Credibility:* Accreditation reassures stakeholders, including healthcare employers, learners, and funders, that the program produces skilled, competent professionals who are well-prepared for the complexities of surgical practice.
- *Accountability:* The accreditation process encourages programs to establish robust policies and practices, ensuring consistency and reliability in delivering high-quality education.

3. Enhanced Learner Outcomes

Accreditation ensures simulation programs adopt evidence-based practices and innovative methodologies to enhance learning and skill acquisition.

- *Competency-Based Training:* Accredited programs align their curricula with ACS Core Competencies, emphasizing critical surgical skills, decision-making, teamwork, and communication.
- *Debriefing Excellence:* Accredited programs incorporate best practices in debriefing, such as structured feedback models, to help learners reflect on their performance, identify areas for growth, and achieve mastery.

4. Increased Opportunities for Partnerships, Funding, and Institutional Support

ACS accreditation opens expanded opportunities for growth and collaboration. Many organizations, including government agencies, healthcare institutions, and private funders, prioritize partnerships with accredited programs.

- *Funding Opportunities:* Accreditation strengthens grant applications and proposals by showcasing the program's commitment to excellence and its alignment with industry standards.

- *Collaborative Initiatives:* Accredited programs are more likely to secure partnerships with hospitals, research institutions, and technology developers to enhance their offerings.
- *Institutional Investment:* Achieving accreditation often leads to increased support from parent institutions, which recognize the value of having an accredited program within their portfolio.

The ACS Accreditation Advantage

Pursuing ACS accreditation is more than fulfilling a set of criteria—it is a strategic investment in the future of surgical education. Accredited programs enhance learner outcomes and advance surgical practices, improve patient safety, and foster innovation. By attaining this recognition, programs solidify their role as leaders in healthcare education, paving the way for transformative impact in the surgical field.

13.2 Standards and Guidelines for ACS Accreditation

The ACS accreditation process is guided by comprehensive standards that address all aspects of a simulation program. Key components include:

1. Organizational Governance

- A defined governance structure with roles and responsibilities for leadership and staff.
- Policies ensuring accountability, ethical practices, and effective decision-making.

2. Curriculum Design and Delivery

- Evidence-based curricula aligned with ACS Core Competencies and surgical standards.
- Integration of simulation into broader surgical education programs.
- Use of validated methodologies for scenario design, skills assessment, and debriefing.

3. Faculty and Staff Qualifications

- Faculty with advanced clinical and educational expertise in surgical simulation.
- Continuous professional development opportunities for faculty and staff.
- Adequate staffing to support simulation activities.

4. Facilities and Resources

- High-quality facilities designed for surgical simulation, including operating room replicas, procedural task trainers, and high-fidelity manikins.
- Advanced audiovisual systems for recording, reviewing, and debriefing.
- Adequate resources for equipment maintenance and upgrades.

5. Assessment and Evaluation
- Tools and metrics for assessing learner performance exist, such as Objective Structured Clinical Examinations (OSCEs) and competency-based evaluations.
- Mechanisms for collecting and analyzing data to evaluate program effectiveness.

6. Continuous Quality Improvement (CQI)
- A structured CQI process to monitor program performance, identify gaps, and implement improvements.
- Documentation of quality improvement initiatives and their impact on surgical education.

13.3 The Accreditation Process

Step 1: Readiness Assessment
Before applying for ACS accreditation, programs should conduct a comprehensive readiness assessment to evaluate their alignment with ACS standards. This involves reviewing policies, curricula, faculty qualifications, and facilities to identify areas for improvement.

Step 2: Application Submission
Programs must submit a detailed application demonstrating compliance with ACS standards. Required documentation typically includes:
- Organizational structure and governance policies.
- Curriculum maps, learner outcomes, and assessment tools.
- Faculty résumés, certifications, and professional development records.
- Facility descriptions, including equipment inventories and maintenance logs.
- Quality improvement plans and reports.

Step 3: Site Visit
The ACS conducts an on-site review to verify the program's compliance with accreditation standards. During the visit, reviewers:
- Tour the simulation facilities.
- Observe simulation sessions and debriefings.

- Review documentation and quality improvement records.
- Interview faculty, staff, and learners.

Step 4: Accreditation Decision
Following the site visit, the ACS provides a detailed feedback report outlining strengths, areas for improvement, and the accreditation decision. Programs may receive full accreditation, provisional accreditation, or a request for additional documentation or improvements.

13.4 Strategies for Achieving ACS Accreditation

Achieving ACS accreditation requires a structured and strategic approach to meet the rigorous standards of excellence in surgical education. Programs must address all aspects of their operations, from governance and curriculum to facilities and assessment practices. Below are detailed strategies to guide programs toward successful accreditation.

1. Align Policies and Practices with ACS Standards
ACS accreditation emphasizes alignment with its core standards, which cover program governance, curriculum design, and learner assessment. Programs must ensure their policies and practices reflect these priorities.

- *Document Governance Policies:* Develop comprehensive policies that define leadership roles, committee responsibilities, and decision-making processes. These policies should promote accountability and transparency.
- *Incorporate ACS Core Competencies:* Design simulation activities that align with competencies such as patient care, medical knowledge, professionalism, systems-based practice, and communication. For instance, a laparoscopic training session might include technical skills and teamwork components to prepare learners for real-world challenges.
- *Standardize Procedures:* Create templates for scenario development, debriefing guides, and learner evaluations to ensure consistency across all simulation activities.

2. Invest in Faculty Development
Faculty expertise is critical to meeting ACS accreditation standards. Programs must prioritize training and professional growth for their educators.

- *Support Certifications:* Encourage faculty to pursue certifications such as the Certified Healthcare Simulation Educator (CHSE) to validate their expertise in simulation-based education.

- *Ongoing Training:* Conduct regular workshops on debriefing techniques, assessment tools, and emerging surgical technologies. For example, faculty might attend training on virtual reality surgical platforms to incorporate them into their curriculum.
- *Foster Interdisciplinary Collaboration:* Engage faculty from different specialties to promote a holistic approach to surgical education, integrating perspectives from nursing, anesthesiology, and other fields.

3. Optimize Facilities and Resources

State-of-the-art facilities and equipment are vital for creating realistic surgical environments that prepare learners for clinical practice.

- *Realistic Simulation Environments:* Design simulation labs to mimic real operating rooms, complete with lighting, instrumentation, and ergonomic setups replicating clinical workflows.
- *Invest in High-Quality Equipment:* Provide advanced surgical simulators, such as laparoscopic trainers, robotic systems, and task trainers for suturing, knot-tying, and vascular anastomosis.
- *Maintenance and Upkeep:* Establish a schedule for regular maintenance and calibration of equipment to ensure reliability and functionality during simulations.

4. Implement Robust Assessment Practices

Assessment is a cornerstone of ACS accreditation, requiring programs to demonstrate that learners meet defined competencies.

- *Use Validated Tools:* Adopt assessment instruments such as OSATS, which provide objective measures of technical skill performance.
- *Train Faculty in Feedback Delivery:* Equip educators with the skills to provide constructive, learner-centered feedback during debriefings. This helps learners reflect on their performance and identify specific areas for improvement.
- *Track Learner Progress:* Use data dashboards to monitor learner performance over time, identifying trends and addressing gaps.

5. Establish a Continuous Quality Improvement (CQI) Plan

ACS accreditation requires programs to demonstrate a commitment to ongoing evaluation and improvement.

- *Data Collection and Analysis:* Regularly gather data on learner outcomes, faculty effectiveness, and program operations. For

instance, track metrics like pass rates, time to competency, and learner satisfaction scores.
- *Use Feedback to Drive Change:* Analyze data to identify areas for enhancement and implement targeted improvements. For example, the program might introduce additional practice sessions if learners report difficulty with advanced suturing techniques.
- *Document CQI Efforts:* Maintain detailed records of CQI initiatives to demonstrate the program's dedication to continuous improvement to ACS reviewers.

6. Conduct Mock Reviews
Mock reviews are a valuable tool for preparing for ACS accreditation, allowing programs to identify gaps and refine their strategies.
- *Perform Internal Audits:* Regularly evaluate compliance with ACS standards, reviewing documentation, facilities, and operational processes.
- *Invite External Reviewers:* Engage experts familiar with ACS accreditation to provide objective feedback and actionable recommendations.
- *Simulate the Accreditation Visit:* Rehearse the site visit process, including facility tours, document reviews, and faculty interviews, to build team confidence and address potential weaknesses.

Achieving ACS accreditation requires alignment with standards, faculty expertise, state-of-the-art facilities, rigorous assessment practices, and a commitment to continuous improvement. By implementing these strategies, programs can position themselves for accreditation success, ultimately enhancing their reputation, learner outcomes, and contributions to surgical education. ACS accreditation is not merely a badge of honor—it is a pathway to transforming surgical training and advancing healthcare quality.

13.5 Case Study: Achieving ACS Accreditation

The ABC Surgical Simulation Center: A Model of Excellence
The ABC Surgical Simulation Center faced significant challenges in preparing for ACS accreditation, including outdated equipment and a lack of formalized policies. Adopting a strategic approach, the center successfully transformed its operations and achieved full accreditation.

Challenges:
Limited budget for facility upgrades.
Gaps in documentation and quality improvement processes.

Solutions:
- Secured funding through institutional grants to purchase laparoscopic trainers and upgrade audiovisual systems.
- Established a documentation team to create and maintain comprehensive records of policies, curricula, and learner outcomes.
- Engaged faculty in professional development workshops, focusing on debriefing techniques and assessment tools.

Results: The ACS accreditation team commended ABC for its innovative curriculum, well-maintained facilities, and strong commitment to quality improvement. Accreditation enabled the center to attract new learners, form partnerships with local hospitals, and secure additional funding for expansion.

13.6 Benefits of ACS Accreditation

Achieving accreditation from the American College of Surgeons (ACS) offers transformative benefits for surgical education programs. Beyond the recognition of excellence, ACS accreditation validates the program's dedication to advancing surgical training and patient care. These benefits extend across multiple dimensions, enhancing credibility, outcomes, resources, and culture.

1. Enhanced Program Credibility

ACS accreditation serves as a mark of distinction, signaling to stakeholders that the program meets rigorous, internationally recognized standards of surgical education.
- *Validation of Quality:* Accreditation reassures learners, faculty, employers, and healthcare institutions that the program delivers training aligned with the highest benchmarks of excellence.
- *Competitive Advantage:* Programs with ACS accreditation stand out in a competitive educational landscape, attracting top-tier learners and faculty who prioritize quality.
- *Stakeholder Trust:* Accreditation strengthens relationships with external partners, fostering trust in the program's ability to produce skilled, competent surgeons.

2. Improved Learner Outcomes
The rigorous standards required for ACS accreditation ensure that learners receive high-quality, comprehensive training that prepares them for real-world surgical challenges.
- *Technical Skill Development:* Accredited programs emphasize validated assessment tools, such as OSATS, to ensure learners master critical surgical techniques.
- *Holistic Training:* Accreditation standards promote the integration of non-technical competencies, including teamwork, communication, and ethical decision-making, fostering well-rounded professionals.
- *Lifelong Impact:* Learners from accredited programs report increased confidence and preparedness, translating to improved patient outcomes and safer surgical practices.

3. Increased Funding and Partnership Opportunities
ACS accreditation opens doors to financial resources and collaborative opportunities that support the program's growth and innovation.
- *Grant Eligibility:* Accredited programs are often prioritized for grants and funding from government agencies, foundations, and industry partners.
- *Collaborative Initiatives:* Accreditation enhances the program's reputation and facilitates partnerships with leading healthcare institutions, research organizations, and technology providers.
- *Institutional Support:* Accreditation signals the program's value to parent organizations, often leading to increased budget allocations for facilities, technology, and faculty development.

4. Commitment to Excellence
Achieving and maintaining ACS accreditation fosters a culture of continuous improvement and innovation, ensuring that the program remains at the forefront of surgical education.
- *Quality Improvement:* Programs must regularly evaluate learner outcomes, curriculum effectiveness, and resource adequacy, leading to ongoing enhancements.
- *Adaptability:* Accreditation requires programs to stay current with emerging technologies, surgical techniques, and industry trends, fostering innovation and adaptability.
- *Professional Development:* Faculty and staff are encouraged to pursue advanced certifications and participate in professional development opportunities, elevating the program's overall expertise.

The benefits of ACS accreditation extend beyond formal recognition, offering tangible advantages that enhance every facet of a surgical education program. From bolstering credibility and improving learner outcomes to unlocking funding opportunities and fostering a culture of excellence, ACS accreditation is a powerful tool for driving growth and innovation. Programs that pursue and maintain this accreditation position themselves as leaders in surgical education, shaping the future of healthcare by preparing the next generation of highly skilled and competent surgeons.

13.7 Summary

ACS accreditation represents a hallmark of excellence in surgical simulation education. By aligning with ACS standards, investing in faculty and facilities, and embracing continuous quality improvement, programs can achieve accreditation and advance the field of surgical training. The journey to ACS accreditation is demanding but deeply rewarding, offering opportunities to enhance learner outcomes, build institutional credibility, and drive innovation in healthcare simulation. Through dedication and strategic planning, simulation programs can meet and exceed the rigorous expectations of ACS accreditation, setting a new standard for excellence in surgical education.

KEITH A. BEAULIEU

Chapter 14

SSH Accreditation

The Society for Simulation in Healthcare (SSH) is a leading authority in healthcare simulation, offering accreditation that signifies excellence in simulation-based education and training. Achieving SSH accreditation is a prestigious milestone that validates a program's commitment to high-quality education, innovation, and continuous improvement. This chapter explores SSH accreditation's significance, process, standards, and benefits, providing a roadmap for programs seeking to achieve this distinguished recognition.

14.1 The Importance of SSH Accreditation

SSH accreditation is highly regarded in the simulation field. It is a benchmark for excellence in education, operations, and program outcomes. SSH accreditation demonstrates that a simulation program meets rigorous international standards and is committed to advancing simulation-based training.

Why Pursue SSH Accreditation?

Pursuing accreditation through the Society for Simulation in Healthcare (SSH) is a transformative step for simulation programs aiming to elevate their quality, credibility, and impact. Accreditation is a hallmark of excellence, offering programs numerous benefits beyond the certification itself. Below are key reasons why pursuing SSH accreditation is essential for simulation programs.

1. Validation of Quality
SSH accreditation confirms that a simulation program adheres to internationally recognized standards and best practices. This validation

fosters trust among learners, faculty, and stakeholders by demonstrating a program's commitment to delivering consistent, high-quality education. Accreditation provides external assurance that the program's operations, curriculum, and outcomes align with the highest healthcare simulation benchmarks.

2. Enhanced Program Credibility
Accreditation distinguishes a simulation program as a leader in the field, setting it apart from non-accredited programs. This recognition strengthens the program's reputation and enhances its ability to attract top-tier learners, faculty, and institutional support. Stakeholders, including healthcare organizations and funding bodies, view accreditation as a mark of professionalism and accountability, further solidifying the program's standing in the simulation community.

3. Commitment to Continuous Improvement
The accreditation process fosters a quality enhancement culture, pushing programs to evaluate and refine their operations regularly. SSH standards emphasize curriculum design, faculty qualifications, resource management, and learner outcomes, requiring programs to engage in ongoing assessment and improvement. This commitment to continuous improvement ensures accredited programs remain dynamic, relevant, and responsive to changes in healthcare education.

4. Opportunities for Growth
SSH accreditation opens doors to new partnerships, funding opportunities, and collaborative initiatives within the simulation community. Accreditation enhances a program's visibility, making it more competitive for research grants, institutional investments, and strategic collaborations. Many organizations and funding bodies prioritize accredited programs, recognizing their demonstrated commitment to excellence and accountability.

SSH accreditation is more than a certification—it is a pathway to growth, credibility, and excellence. By pursuing and achieving this prestigious designation, simulation programs can validate their quality, build trust with stakeholders, and position themselves as leaders in the rapidly evolving field of healthcare education.

14.2 SSH Accreditation Standards

SSH accreditation is based on a comprehensive set of standards that evaluate various aspects of simulation programs. These standards ensure that accredited programs deliver high-quality education aligned with industry best practices.

Key Components of SSH Accreditation Standards

Achieving accreditation from the Society for Simulation in Healthcare (SSH) requires simulation programs to meet rigorous standards across several domains, reflecting their commitment to excellence and continuous improvement. The **SSH offers accreditation in various focus areas, including Assessment, Research, Fellowship Programs, Systems Integration, and Human Simulation**, catering to simulation-based education programs' diverse needs and objectives. Below is an expanded narrative of the core standards required for accreditation.

1. Mission and Governance

A clearly defined mission and governance structure are foundational to successful accreditation. Programs must articulate a mission and vision that align with their educational objectives and broader organizational goals. Leadership plays a pivotal role in demonstrating strategic direction, operational integrity, and a commitment to achieving the program's mission.

For example, a hospital-based simulation program might focus on improving patient safety through high-fidelity simulations. Its governance structure, including a dedicated advisory board, ensures alignment with institutional goals and provides strategic oversight for continuous improvement.

Why it Matters: Strong governance underpins the program's credibility, accountability, and ability to adapt to the evolving demands of healthcare education.

2. Programmatic Operations

Operational excellence is a cornerstone of accreditation. Programs must establish robust policies and procedures that define staff roles, resource allocation, and quality assurance processes. These policies should prioritize learner safety, professionalism, and ethical practices, ensuring a supportive and respectful learning environment.

Key Point: Effective operations management reflects a program's commitment to organizational efficiency and learner-centered practices, which is critical for accreditation in areas like Systems Integration or Human Simulation.

3. Curriculum and Instructional Design
Simulation activities must align with defined educational objectives, competency frameworks, and learners' diverse needs. Programs must employ evidence-based methodologies for scenario development, facilitation, and debriefing.

Why it Matters: Well-designed curricula ensure learners acquire transferable skills, fostering readiness for clinical practice while meeting accreditation expectations.

4. Assessment and Evaluation
Reliable and valid assessment tools are critical for evaluating learner performance and program effectiveness. Programs must demonstrate how assessment data inform decision-making and drive continuous improvement.

Impact: Robust assessment practices ensure that accreditation standards are met and that the program actively contributes to enhancing healthcare education.

5. Simulation Resources and Environment
Facilities and equipment must support realistic, effective simulation experiences. Programs are also required to maintain safety protocols and ensure proper functionality of simulation tools.

Why it Matters: A well-equipped and maintained environment enhances the program's credibility and aligns with SSH's emphasis on high-quality simulation delivery.

6. Continuous Quality Improvement (CQI)
Accreditation standards emphasize the importance of CQI, requiring programs to use data and feedback to continuously enhance education and operations. Programs must also demonstrate a systematic approach to identifying gaps, implementing changes, and evaluating the outcomes of their initiatives.

Significance: CQI fosters a culture of adaptability and growth, enabling programs to sustain accreditation and remain leaders in simulation-based education.

Tailored Accreditation Areas: Diverse Pathways to Excellence

SSH's accreditation options in Assessment, Research, Fellowship, Systems Integration, and Human Simulation allow programs to focus on their unique strengths and goals. For example:

- **Assessment** Accreditation emphasizes rigorous evaluation frameworks to measure learner competencies.
- **Research** Accreditation validates programs that contribute to the advancement of simulation science through innovative studies and publications.
- **Fellowship** Accreditation recognizes programs that prepare leaders in simulation education through structured training and mentorship.
- **Systems Integration** Accreditation supports programs that align simulation with broader organizational strategies, such as quality improvement and patient safety.
- **Human Simulation** Accreditation (forthcoming) focuses on programs utilizing SPs to enhance communication, empathy, and cultural competence in clinical training.

Each accreditation pathway requires programs to demonstrate excellence in their chosen focus area while meeting foundational SSH standards. SSH accreditation is a comprehensive process that elevates simulation programs to meet and exceed the highest standards in healthcare education. By addressing the core domains of governance, operations, curriculum design, assessment, resources, and CQI, programs can achieve accreditation in areas that align with their mission and goals. This multifaceted approach ensures that programs remain impactful, innovative, and aligned with the evolving demands of the healthcare industry. Pursuing SSH accreditation is more than a recognition—it's a commitment to excellence, collaboration, and continuous improvement.

14.3 The SSH Accreditation Process

The SSH accreditation process involves a series of steps designed to evaluate a program's alignment with accreditation standards and identify opportunities for improvement.

Steps in the Accreditation Process
1. **Application Submission:**
    - Programs submit an application outlining their mission, operations, and alignment with SSH standards.

2. **Self-Study Report:**
   - Programs prepare a detailed self-study report that includes evidence of compliance with accreditation standards, such as policies, curricula, and quality improvement initiatives.
3. **Site Visit:**
   - Accreditation reviewers conduct a site visit to evaluate the program's facilities, operations, and staff. The visit includes interviews with faculty, learners, and stakeholders.
4. **Accreditation Decision:**
   - Based on the self-study report and site visit findings, SSH provides an accreditation decision and feedback on strengths and areas for improvement.
5. **Maintenance of Accreditation:**
   - Accredited programs must submit periodic reports demonstrating ongoing compliance and quality improvement efforts.

14.4 Strategies for Achieving SSH Accreditation

Achieving accreditation from the Society for Simulation in Healthcare (SSH) signifies a commitment to excellence and adherence to the highest standards in simulation-based education. Here are detailed strategies to guide programs through the accreditation process:

1. Align Policies and Practices with SSH Standards

The foundation of accreditation lies in aligning program operations with SSH's rigorous standards.

- *Develop and Document Comprehensive Policies:* Create detailed guidelines that address key areas such as program governance, curriculum development, assessment protocols, and resource management. Clearly define processes to ensure consistency and accountability.
- *Mission-Driven Alignment:* Ensure all simulation activities directly support the program's mission and align with its educational goals. This alignment fosters coherence and reinforces the program's strategic objectives.

2. Invest in Faculty and Staff Development

The expertise of faculty and staff is critical to the success and credibility of a simulation program.

- *Training and Best Practices:* Provide faculty with professional development opportunities focusing on simulation pedagogy, debriefing techniques, and effective use of assessment tools.
- *Pursue SSH Certifications:* Encourage faculty and staff to attain SSH credentials, such as the Certified Healthcare Simulation Educator (CHSE) or Certified Healthcare Simulation Operations Specialist (CHSOS), to demonstrate expertise and elevate the program's reputation.

3. Optimize Simulation Facilities and Resources

State-of-the-art facilities and reliable equipment enhance the learner experience and reflect program quality.

- *Maintain High-Quality Equipment:* Invest in and regularly update simulation tools, such as high-fidelity manikins, task trainers, and audiovisual systems, to provide realistic and engaging scenarios.
- *Preventive Maintenance:* Establish and adhere to maintenance schedules to ensure equipment remains functional, safe, and ready for use. This proactive approach minimizes downtime and interruptions.

4. Implement Robust Quality Improvement Processes

Continuous quality improvement (CQI) is a hallmark of successful programs and a requirement for accreditation.

- *Data-Driven Insights:* Collect learner outcomes, program performance, and stakeholder satisfaction data. Employ robust analytics to identify trends and areas for enhancement.
- *Targeted Improvements:* Use feedback and assessment results to implement focused changes, demonstrating a commitment to excellence and adaptability.

5. Conduct Mock Accreditation Reviews

Preparation and self-assessment are key to a successful accreditation outcome.

- *Internal Audits:* Thoroughly review policies, procedures, and documentation to identify gaps or weaknesses.
- *Simulated Accreditation Visits:* Conduct mock site visits and interviews with faculty, staff, and learners to refine operations and build confidence in meeting SSH standards.

By adopting these strategies, simulation programs can achieve SSH accreditation and build a culture of continuous improvement and excellence, ultimately enhancing the learning experience and improving outcomes for all stakeholders.

14.5 Benefits of SSH Accreditation

1. Enhanced Program Credibility
Accreditation by SSH validates a program's commitment to quality and professionalism, fostering stakeholder trust and confidence.

2. Improved Learner Outcomes
Accredited programs deliver consistent, high-quality education, resulting in better preparation and performance of learners in clinical settings.

3. Increased Opportunities
SSH accreditation opens doors to funding, research partnerships, and professional collaborations, enabling programs to expand their impact and reach.

4. Commitment to Excellence
The accreditation process instills a culture of continuous improvement, ensuring that programs remain dynamic, innovative, and responsive to industry changes.

14.6 Research on ROI in Accreditation

In 2023-2024, the SSH Accreditation Council, composed of experienced healthcare simulation leaders, conducted an in-depth study to assess the perceived return on investment (ROI) of accreditation among programs that successfully underwent the accreditation process. This study aimed to comprehensively evaluate the tangible and intangible benefits of achieving accreditation, focusing on how it impacts program growth, operations, and outcomes.

Quantitative Findings

The study categorized quantitative data into three primary subgroups: **structure and governance**, **operations**, and **quality outcomes**. The analysis revealed that the perceived ROI was highest in areas related to structure and governance, highlighting the foundational importance of well-defined organizational frameworks. Below is a summary of the quantitative findings:

Subgroup	Perceived Positive Impact	Percentage Positive
Structure and Governance	Program Recognition and Awareness	89%
Structure and Governance	Strategic Vision	87%
Structure and Governance	Program Growth	81%
Structure and Governance	Governance and Structure	80%
Operations	Learner Satisfaction	69%
Quality Outcomes	Patient Safety	68%
Quality Outcomes	Clinical Quality Measures	62%

Programs reported the highest positive impact in **program recognition and awareness (89%)**, underscoring how accreditation enhances visibility and credibility within the healthcare community. Additionally, a significant percentage of programs acknowledged improvements in **strategic vision (87%)**, indicating that the accreditation process encourages long-term planning and alignment with institutional goals. Other notable impact areas included **program growth (81%)** and **governance and structure (80%)**, which are critical for sustainable development.

Qualitative Insights

In addition to the quantitative data, the study captured rich qualitative responses that highlighted the broader implications of accreditation on program sustainability and operational efficiency. These responses were categorized into three key themes:

Category	Predominant Themes
Sustainability	Increased credibility of the program
Sustainability	Increased resources
Operations	Improved processes in the program

Programs consistently reported that accreditation enhanced their credibility internally within their organizations and externally among stakeholders. The increased credibility often led to greater access to resources, including funding, equipment, and expanded facilities, enabling programs to grow and evolve. Additionally, many programs noted significant improvements in operational processes, with accreditation catalyzing the identification of inefficiencies and the implementation of best practices.

The findings demonstrate that accreditation is not merely a regulatory milestone but a transformative process that fosters growth, strategic alignment, and enhanced quality. Programs reported that the structured guidance provided during accreditation helped them conduct a comprehensive self-assessment, revealing improvement areas and innovation opportunities. The correlation between accreditation and resource allocation, including equipment acquisition and facility expansion, further underscores its role in building capacity and ensuring long-term sustainability.

Moreover, the study highlighted the direct and indirect benefits of accreditation on **learner satisfaction (69%)**, **patient safety (68%)**, and **clinical quality measures (62%)**. These outcomes emphasize how accreditation positively influences simulation programs' educational and clinical aspects, ultimately improving healthcare delivery and patient outcomes.

The results of this study affirm the substantial value that accreditation brings to simulation programs, with the highest perceived ROI observed in the areas of structure and governance. By providing a roadmap for excellence, accreditation equips programs with the tools to achieve strategic goals, enhance their reputation, and improve outcomes for learners and patients alike. This comprehensive evaluation underscores the importance of accreditation as a cornerstone of continuous quality improvement and a vital investment for healthcare simulation programs.

14.7 Case Example: Achieving SSH Accreditation

The ABC Healthcare Simulation Center is an example of a program that successfully achieved SSH accreditation. Facing challenges such as limited funding and outdated equipment, the center developed a strategic plan to align operations with SSH standards.

Strategies Employed:

- **Faculty Development:** Faculty attended SSH workshops on debriefing and simulation methodologies, earning CHSE certifications.
- **Facility Upgrades:** The center secured a grant to upgrade simulation tools and debriefing spaces.
- **CQI Initiatives:** Regular learner feedback informed curriculum updates, enhancing the quality and relevance of simulation activities.

Outcome:
The center achieved full SSH accreditation, earning commendation for its commitment to continuous improvement. Accreditation enhanced the center's reputation, increasing enrollment and new partnerships with local healthcare organizations.

14.8 Summary

SSH accreditation is a prestigious achievement that elevates a simulation program's quality, credibility, and impact. By adhering to SSH standards, investing in faculty development, and fostering a culture of continuous improvement, programs can achieve accreditation and position themselves as leaders in healthcare simulation. The journey to SSH accreditation is a validation of excellence and a catalyst for sustained growth and innovation.

Chapter 15

Case Studies and Success Stories

Real-world examples of successful accreditation efforts provide invaluable insights for healthcare simulation programs seeking to achieve or maintain accreditation. This chapter highlights case studies and success stories, showcasing how different programs overcame challenges, implemented best practices, and achieved accreditation. By learning from these experiences, your program can adopt proven strategies and avoid common pitfalls.

15.1 Case Study 1: Overcoming Resource Limitations

Program: ABC Nursing Simulation Lab

Challenge:
Operating on a limited budget with outdated equipment, ABC Nursing Simulation Lab faced significant obstacles in its pursuit of accreditation. With minimal staff and constrained resources, the lab must demonstrate its commitment to high-quality simulation-based education while navigating financial and operational limitations.

Background:
ABC Nursing Simulation Lab, a critical training hub for nursing students, had relied on aging high-fidelity manikins and makeshift debriefing spaces for years. Despite these challenges, the leadership team recognized the value of accreditation in solidifying the program's reputation and unlocking funding opportunities. Pursuing accreditation

was viewed as a validation of their efforts and a pathway to future growth and sustainability.

Strategies for Success
Faced with limited resources, the lab adopted innovative strategies to maximize its impact and effectively address accreditation requirements. These included conducting a resource audit, securing external funding, and optimizing staff roles to ensure compliance with accreditation standards.

1. Conducting a Resource Audit
The lab thoroughly audited its existing resources to make the most of their modest budget. This process involved:

- *Identifying Priorities*: The leadership team evaluated which elements, such as simulation manikins, debriefing spaces, and documentation systems, were critical for meeting accreditation standards.
- *Strategic Upgrades*: Instead of overhauling all aspects of the lab, the program focused its limited funds on replacing outdated high-fidelity manikins and enhancing the debriefing environment. By improving these high-impact areas, the lab ensured learners had access to realistic simulations and meaningful reflection sessions.

The audit revealed that some old equipment remained functional with minor repairs or adjustments. This approach allowed the lab to stretch its budget while meeting essential accreditation requirements.

2. Securing Grants and Partnerships
Recognizing that internal funding alone would not suffice, the lab pursued external support through strategic initiatives:

- *Grant Applications*: ABC Nursing Simulation Lab applied for simulation-specific grants, leveraging their plans for accreditation as evidence of their commitment to quality improvement.
- *Building Partnerships*: Collaborations with local healthcare organizations provided additional resources, including shared access to advanced simulation equipment and expertise. For example, a nearby hospital loaned the lab a state-of-the-art

birthing simulator, which was instrumental in achieving accreditation standards.

These efforts filled resource gaps and strengthened relationships with community partners, highlighting the lab's vital role in the local healthcare ecosystem.

3. Maximizing Staff Efficiency
With limited personnel, the lab adopted a cross-training approach to ensure all accreditation requirements were met:

- *Faculty Cross-Training*: Faculty were trained to perform multiple roles, such as facilitating simulations, maintaining equipment, and preparing documentation.
- *Streamlining Processes*: Administrative workflows were optimized to reduce redundancy and improve efficiency, allowing staff to focus on accreditation priorities.

The program maintained high education standards despite its staffing constraints by fostering a culture of adaptability and teamwork.

Outcome
The accrediting body awarded ABC Nursing Simulation Lab full accreditation, commending its innovative resource management and dedication to quality education. Reviewers noted the lab's ability to overcome significant challenges while maintaining a learner-centered approach and fostering strong community partnerships.

Post-Accreditation Success
Achieving accreditation had immediate and long-term benefits for the program:

- *Increased Funding*: The lab secured additional grants and institutional support, enabling further upgrades to facilities and equipment.
- *Enhanced Reputation*: Accreditation reinforced the program's credibility, attracting more learners and community partners.
- *Sustainability*: The experience of meeting accreditation standards created a framework for ongoing quality improvement, ensuring the lab's continued success.

Key Takeaways

The success of ABC Nursing Simulation Lab demonstrates that accreditation is achievable even with limited resources, provided programs take a strategic and resourceful approach:

- *Resource Audits Prioritize Impact:* Identifying critical needs and targeting upgrades ensures that limited funds deliver maximum value.
- *Leverage External Support:* Grants and partnerships can bridge funding gaps and enhance capabilities.
- *Efficiency Drives Success:* Cross-training and streamlined workflows enable programs to meet high standards despite staffing challenges.

By turning constraints into opportunities, ABC Nursing Simulation Lab transformed its limitations into strengths, achieving accreditation and laying the groundwork for sustained excellence. This case illustrates that any program can overcome obstacles to meet and exceed accreditation standards with creativity, determination, and strategic planning.

15.2 Case Study 2: Building a Culture of Quality Improvement

Program: ABC University Medical Simulation Center

Challenge: Lack of a structured quality improvement process.

Outcome: Achieved accreditation after developing a comprehensive CQI plan.

Background:
ABC University's simulation center excelled in delivering high-quality training but lacked formal processes for evaluating and improving program performance. This gap was identified during a mock review, prompting the program to focus on quality improvement before pursuing accreditation.

Strategies Used:

- *Implementing a CQI Plan:* The center established a CQI committee to oversee quality initiatives. Using Plan-Do-Study-Act (PDSA) cycles, the team addressed key areas such as learner feedback, faculty development, and equipment maintenance.

- *Engaging Stakeholders:* Faculty, staff, and learners were actively involved in identifying improvement opportunities and implementing solutions. Quarterly meetings provided a forum for discussing progress and challenges.
- *Leveraging Data Analytics:* The center introduced a dashboard to track key performance indicators, such as learner competency scores and scenario success rates, enabling data-driven decision-making.

Result:
Reviewers praised the center's robust CQI processes, noting their alignment with accreditation standards and positive impact on learner outcomes. Accreditation was granted with no deficiencies.

15.3 Case Study 3: Enhancing Faculty Development

Program: ABC Allied Health Simulation Program

Challenge: Limited faculty expertise in simulation-based education.

Outcome: Achieved accreditation by prioritizing faculty training and certification.

Background: ABC Allied Health Simulation Program recognized that its faculty lacked advanced training in simulation pedagogy, which posed a significant challenge for accreditation. Addressing this gap became a top priority.

Strategies Used:

1. *Developing a Faculty Development Plan:* The program created a structured plan that included funding for faculty to attend conferences, earn certifications (e.g., CHSE), and participate in workshops.
2. *Hosting Internal Training Sessions:* Senior faculty conducted regular training sessions on scenario design, debriefing techniques, and assessment tools, fostering peer learning and collaboration.
3. *Encouraging Certification:* The program incentivized faculty members to pursue professional certifications, covered associated costs, and provided time for study and preparation.

Result: The accrediting body highlighted the program's commitment to faculty development as a key strength. Faculty satisfaction and learner outcomes improved significantly, supporting the program's long-term success.

15.4 Case Study 4: Navigating Organizational Resistance

Program: ABC Hospital Simulation Program

Challenge: Resistance to accreditation from hospital leadership.

Outcome: Achieved accreditation after building stakeholder buy-in.

Background: The ABC Hospital Simulation Program's leadership resisted accreditation, viewing it as costly and unnecessary. To secure organizational support, program leaders needed to demonstrate its value.

Strategies Used:

- *Creating a Business Case:* Program leaders outlined the benefits of accreditation, including improved learner outcomes, increased institutional credibility, and access to funding opportunities.
- *Engaging Leadership:* The program invited hospital leaders to observe simulation sessions and meet with learners and faculty, providing firsthand insights into the program's impact.
- *Demonstrating ROI:* Leaders showcased data from other accredited programs, highlighting improved patient safety metrics and reduced clinical errors linked to high-quality simulation training.

Result: Hospital leadership ultimately supported the accreditation effort, allocating resources for documentation, facility upgrades, and faculty training. The program achieved accreditation and gained recognition as a leader in simulation education within the hospital network.

Lessons Learned from Success Stories
- *Start with a Readiness Assessment:* All successful programs conducted thorough readiness assessments to identify gaps and develop targeted improvement plans.

- *Engage Stakeholders Early:* Faculty, staff, learners, and leadership must be actively involved in the accreditation process to build support and ensure alignment with program goals.
- *Leverage Resources Wisely:* Whether through grants, partnerships, or internal reallocation, resourceful programs found creative ways to meet accreditation standards despite budgetary or logistical challenges.
- *Commit to Continuous Improvement:* Accreditation is not a one-time effort. Programs that embraced a culture of quality improvement demonstrated sustained success and positive outcomes.

15.5 Summary

This chapter's case studies, and success stories illustrate that achieving accreditation is possible, even facing challenges. By adopting a strategic approach, involving stakeholders, and committing to continuous improvement, your program can navigate the accreditation process successfully. As you reflect on these examples, consider how their strategies and lessons can be adapted to your program's unique context. In the final chapter, we will provide practical tools and resources to support you on your accreditation journey.

KEITH A. BEAULIEU

Chapter 16

Resources and Tools

Achieving and maintaining accreditation for a healthcare simulation program requires access to reliable resources, practical tools, and a supportive network. This chapter provides a curated collection of checklists, templates, and references to guide you through the accreditation process and ensure long-term success. By leveraging these resources, your program can streamline its efforts, enhance compliance with standards, and foster continuous improvement.

16.1 Accreditation Checklist

Creating and maintaining a detailed accreditation checklist is a cornerstone of successful preparation for initial accreditation and re-accreditation. A comprehensive checklist ensures that all accreditation components are accounted for, enabling simulation programs to track progress systematically, identify gaps, and meet requirements efficiently. Below is an expanded narrative for each key section of an accreditation checklist.

Organizational Structure

A clear and well-documented organizational structure is essential for demonstrating accountability and effective governance.
- ☐ **Organizational Chart:** Include an up-to-date chart showing reporting lines, leadership roles, and committee structures. This visual representation should reflect how responsibilities are distributed within the program.

> *Example:* A chart showing a Simulation Director overseeing faculty, technicians, and an administrative coordinator highlights how leadership ensures seamless operations.

- ☐ **Governance Policies and Procedures:** Outline policies guiding decision-making, conflict resolution, and operational oversight. These documents demonstrate transparency and adherence to best practices.

  > *Example:* A governance policy detailing the role of an advisory committee in curriculum updates shows a commitment to collaborative decision-making.

- ☐ **Leadership and Committee Roles:** Clearly define leadership roles and any standing committees, such as those responsible for quality assurance or curriculum design.

  > *Example:* Documentation of a Quality Improvement Committee's monthly meeting minutes highlights active engagement in program evaluation.

Program Mission and Objectives

A program's mission and objectives provide the foundation for its activities and alignment with accreditation standards.

- ☐ **Mission and Vision Statements:** Ensure these statements are clear, current, and reflect the program's goals and values.

  > *Example:* A mission focused on fostering interprofessional collaboration in healthcare aligns well with industry priorities.

- ☐ **Program Objectives:** Develop specific, measurable objectives that guide activities and demonstrate a commitment to educational excellence.

  > *Example:* Objectives such as "enhancing critical thinking through realistic simulations" link directly to learner outcomes.

- ☐ **Strategic Plan:** Align the program's strategic plan with accreditation standards and detail actionable steps to achieve long-term goals.

Example: A strategic plan outlining annual targets for faculty development and learner competency evaluations shows foresight and organization.

Curriculum Design and Delivery

The curriculum is the heart of any simulation program, and its design must reflect rigorous planning and alignment with professional standards.

- **Curriculum Maps:** Develop maps linking each simulation activity to specific learning objectives, ensuring clarity and consistency.

  Example: A curriculum map showing how simulations address competencies like communication, critical thinking, and technical skills demonstrates alignment with accreditation requirements.

- **Scenario Templates:** Use standardized templates that include learning outcomes, participant roles, and debriefing guides.

  Example: A scenario template for a pediatric emergency simulation might detail objectives like recognizing symptoms of sepsis and initiating appropriate interventions.

- **Professional Standards Alignment:** Provide evidence that the curriculum aligns with national and professional standards, such as AACN competencies or ACGME milestones.

  Example: Documentation showing how simulation activities incorporate the latest clinical guidelines ensures relevance and rigor.

Faculty and Staff

Accrediting bodies expect programs to employ qualified faculty and staff committed to ongoing professional growth.

- **Faculty CVs and Certifications:** Maintain up-to-date records of faculty credentials, including certifications like CHSE or CHSOS.

> *Example:* Highlighting a faculty member's CHSE certification emphasizes the program's dedication to employing skilled educators.

- ☐ **Training and Professional Development:** Document ongoing training efforts, such as workshops or conference participation.

  > *Example:* A record of faculty attendance at the International Meeting on Simulation in Healthcare (IMSH) demonstrates a commitment to staying current with best practices.

- ☐ **Staffing Levels:** Show evidence that staffing levels are sufficient to support program operations effectively.

  > *Example:* A staffing plan ensuring a technician is available for every simulation session highlights attention to operational needs.

Resources and Facilities

The facilities and resources available to a simulation program must meet safety, functionality, and educational standards.

- ☐ **Equipment Inventory:** Maintain a detailed inventory of simulation manikins, task trainers, and audiovisual equipment, along with purchase and maintenance dates.

  > *Example:* An inventory showing updated high-fidelity manikins demonstrates readiness for complex scenarios.

- ☐ **Maintenance Logs:** Keep thorough logs of equipment servicing and repairs to ensure functionality and compliance with safety protocols.

  > *Example:* A log documenting regular updates to a birthing simulator highlights a commitment to equipment reliability.

- ☐ **Facility Maps and Photos:** Prepare visual aids for site visits, including maps and photographs of simulation labs and debriefing spaces.

  > *Example:* A site map showing accessible pathways and emergency exits underscores attention to safety and inclusivity

Assessment and Quality Improvement

Assessing learner outcomes and demonstrating a commitment to continuous improvement are key components of accreditation.

- ☐ **Learner Assessment Tools:** Use validated tools like rubrics and checklists to evaluate learners consistently.

    Example: A checklist assessing teamwork during a surgical simulation shows an evidence-based approach to evaluation.

- ☐ **Program Effectiveness Data:** Collect and analyze data on learner outcomes, satisfaction rates, and competency achievements.

    Example: A dashboard tracking learner progress over time demonstrates the program's impact on education.

- ☐ **Quality Improvement Plans:** Document initiatives to enhance program quality, including goals, actions, and measurable outcomes.

    Example: A plan to address low learner satisfaction scores by revising debriefing techniques shows a commitment to improvement.

Conclusion

A comprehensive accreditation checklist is a roadmap for simulation programs, ensuring every detail is noted, and all standards are met. Programs can streamline preparation and confidently navigate the accreditation process by organizing efforts around key components like governance, curriculum, faculty, resources, and quality improvement. With this tool, programs transform accreditation from a daunting challenge into an achievable milestone, reflecting their commitment to excellence in healthcare simulation education.

> **Accreditation Tip:**
> Take this sample checklist and pair it with the standards for the accrediting body you are applying.

16.2 Templates for Documentation

Having standardized templates ensures consistency and professionalism in your accreditation submission. Below are examples of templates that can be customized for your program:

- **Self-Study Report Template**
  A structured format for documenting compliance with accreditation standards, including sections for each requirement, supporting evidence, and visual aids.

- **Scenario Template**
  Includes fields for learning objectives, setup instructions, case progression, and debriefing points.

- **Policy and Procedure Template**
  Provides a consistent structure for writing and updating policies, with sections for purpose, scope, responsibilities, and procedures.

- **Faculty Development Plan Template**
  Outlines training goals, timelines, and faculty and staff professional development resources.

- **Quality Improvement Dashboard Template**
  Tracks key performance indicators (KPIs) such as learner outcomes, satisfaction scores, and program improvements.

16.3 Recommended Tools for Accreditation

Leveraging technology and specialized tools can simplify the accreditation process and improve program operations. Below are some recommended tools and platforms:

- **Document Management Systems**
  - Google Drive, Dropbox, or OneDrive for centralized storage and easy sharing of accreditation documents.
  - Software like DocuWare or M-Files for advanced document tracking and version control.

- **Simulation Management Platforms**
  - SimCapture or LearningSpace for managing simulation scenarios, learner data, and audiovisual recordings.

- o Tools like CAE LearningSpace for integrating assessment and reporting functionalities.

- **Data Analytics Tools**
  - o Tableau or Microsoft Power BI for visualizing program data and tracking performance metrics.
  - o Excel templates for creating simple dashboards and reports.

- **Survey and Feedback Platforms**
  - o Qualtrics, QuestionPro, SurveyMonkey, or Google Forms are used to collect feedback from learners and stakeholders.

16.4 Professional Organizations and Networks

Joining professional organizations provides access to educational resources, networking opportunities, and industry updates. Below are some key organizations for healthcare simulation professionals:

- **The Society for Simulation in Healthcare (SSH)** Offers accreditation services, certification programs, and resources such as the SSH Academy and annual conferences.

- **International Nursing Association for Clinical Simulation and Learning (INACSL)** Provides evidence-based simulation standards, educational workshops, and networking events.
- **The Association for Simulated Practice in Healthcare (ASPiH)** promotes excellence in simulation-based education and offers resources tailored to the UK and European contexts.
- **The Global Network for Simulation in Healthcare (GNSH) facilitates international collaboration and resource sharing** among simulation educators and researchers.

16.5 Publications and Online Resources

Staying informed about best practices and emerging trends is critical for maintaining accreditation. Below are some recommended publications and online resources:

- **Simulation Journals**

- o *Clinical Simulation in Nursing*: Covers research and innovations in nursing simulation.
- o *Simulation in Healthcare*: Offers peer-reviewed articles on simulation education and technology.
- **Guidelines and Standards**
  - o SSH Accreditation Standards (available on the SSH website).
  - o INACSL Standards of Best Practice: Simulation™ (freely accessible online).
- **Books and Manuals**
  - o *Healthcare Simulation Education: Evidence, Theory, and Practice* by Debra Nestel et al.
  - o *Comprehensive Healthcare Simulation: An Interprofessional Approach* by Matthew Aldrich et al.
- **Online Courses and Webinars**
  - o SSH Learning Portal: Offers accreditation, simulation education, and leadership courses.
  - o INACSL Webinar Series: Features expert-led discussions on simulation standards and practices.

16.6 Funding and Grant Resources

Securing funding can support accreditation efforts, faculty development, and equipment upgrades. Below are potential funding sources:

- **Government Grants:**
  - o Health Resources and Services Administration (HRSA) grants for simulation-based training initiatives.
  - o National Science Foundation (NSF) funding for educational technology projects.
- **Private Foundations:**
  - o The Josiah Macy Jr. Foundation supports healthcare education innovations.
  - o The Robert Wood Johnson Foundation offers grants for healthcare improvement projects.
- **Institutional Support:**
  - o Seek funding from your organization's administration by presenting a business case for accreditation.

Case Example: Leveraging Resources for Accreditation

Achieving accreditation is a large feat, particularly for programs operating in resource-constrained environments. The ABC Allied Health Simulation Program exemplifies how strategic resource utilization can lead to accreditation success and recognition as a leader in allied health education. By combining technology, professional development, and external funding, the program transformed its operations, enhanced its educational offerings, and met rigorous accreditation standards.

Harnessing Technology for Organization and Accountability

One of the cornerstones of ABC's success was its adoption of cloud-based document management to streamline the organization and accessibility of accreditation evidence. This approach allowed the program to:

- *Centralize Documentation:* A cloud-based platform stored all necessary files—such as policies, learner assessments, and quality improvement reports—in a single location.

Example: Maintenance logs for simulation equipment and faculty résumés were updated in real-time, ensuring consistency and accuracy.

- *Facilitate Collaboration:* Faculty and staff could easily access and update documents, fostering teamwork and reducing duplication of efforts.

Outcome: This centralized system impressed accrediting reviewers, who praised the program for its meticulous record-keeping.

The program leveraged Tableau, a data visualization tool, to enhance its data analysis capabilities to track and display learner outcomes. Tableau enabled the program to:

- *Analyze Trends:* Data on learner competency, satisfaction scores, and scenario performance was visualized in dashboards, making it easy to identify strengths and areas for improvement.

Example: Analysis revealed that learners scored consistently higher in teamwork competencies after incorporating interprofessional simulation scenarios.

- *Demonstrate Impact:* During the accreditation review, the program used these dashboards to showcase measurable improvements in learner outcomes, reinforcing its commitment to evidence-based education.

Investing in Faculty Development

ABC recognized that the expertise and engagement of its faculty were pivotal to achieving accreditation. The program prioritized professional development by:

- *Attending INACSL Webinars:* Faculty participated in webinars on simulation best practices, such as scenario design and debriefing techniques, ensuring alignment with the latest industry standards.

Example: Training on the PEARLS debriefing framework led to more structured and effective post-simulation discussions, which learners reported as highly valuable.

- *Pursuing CHSE Certification:* Faculty members were encouraged and financially supported to earn Certified Healthcare Simulation Educator (CHSE) credentials, enhancing their credibility and expertise.

Outcome: The accrediting body commended the program for its highly qualified team and noted that certified faculty contributed significantly to learner success.

Securing Funding for Innovation
Understanding that outdated equipment could hinder both learner experiences and accreditation readiness, ABC aggressively pursued external funding. By applying for a Health Resources and Services Administration (HRSA) grant, the program secured critical funding to:

- Upgrade Simulation Equipment: The grant purchased advanced high-fidelity manikins, virtual reality (VR) tools, and updated audiovisual systems for debriefing sessions.

Example: Adding a VR module for allied health simulations allowed learners to practice rare scenarios, such as disaster response, in a controlled and realistic environment.

- *Enhance Facilities:* Funding supported renovations to create dedicated debriefing spaces facilitating reflection and collaboration.
- These upgrades improved the quality of education and demonstrated the program's commitment to maintaining state-of-the-art resources.

Aligning with Accreditation Standards

The program consistently used the Society for Simulation in Healthcare (SSH) accreditation standards to guide the preparation process. This alignment ensured that every initiative—whether related to governance, curriculum, or quality improvement—was purposeful and compliant. Specific actions included:

- *Curriculum Alignment:* The program revised its curriculum to ensure every simulation scenario mapped directly to learning objectives and professional competencies.

- *Continuous Quality Improvement:* The program leveraged learner feedback to implement targeted improvements, such as incorporating more diverse patient scenarios that reflected real-world challenges.

Achieving Accreditation and Beyond

The combined efforts of technology, faculty development, external funding, and strategic planning culminated in the full accreditation **of the** ABC Allied Health Simulation Program. Reviewers awarded accreditation without deficiencies and recognized the program as a leader in allied health education, citing its innovative practices and resourcefulness.

Key Outcomes:

- *Enhanced Reputation:* Accreditation elevated the program's standing, attracting new learners and fostering partnerships with local healthcare organizations.
- *Increased Funding Opportunities:* After accreditation, the program secured additional grants, enabling further advancements in simulation technology and curriculum design.
- *Sustainable Growth:* With a strong foundation, the program is well-positioned to maintain its accreditation status and drive innovation in allied health education.

Lessons Learned

The ABC Allied Health Simulation Program's success offers valuable insights for other programs pursuing accreditation:

- *Leverage Technology Strategically:* Tools like cloud-based document management and data visualization platforms simplify accreditation preparation and enhance program efficiency.
- *Prioritize Faculty Development:* Investing in faculty expertise boosts program quality and strengthens accreditation readiness.

- *Pursue External Funding:* Grants and partnerships provide the financial resources needed to overcome limitations and demonstrate a commitment to excellence.
- *Align Initiatives with Standards:* Accreditation standards serve as a framework to ensure that all efforts contribute directly to compliance and quality improvement.

By embracing resourcefulness and innovation, the ABC Allied Health Simulation Program turned challenges into opportunities, achieving accreditation and setting a benchmark for excellence in simulation-based education.

16.7 Summary

This chapter provides a comprehensive toolkit to support your program throughout the accreditation process and beyond. By effectively using these resources, your simulation program can achieve accreditation, maintain high standards, and deliver exceptional education and training. Accreditation is about meeting requirements and fostering a culture of excellence that benefits learners, faculty, and the broader healthcare community.

KEITH A. BEAULIEU

Conclusion

Achieving accreditation for a healthcare simulation program is far more than a procedural milestone—it is a testament to a program's commitment to excellence, innovation, and the advancement of healthcare education. Accreditation affirms that a program meets rigorous industry standards, delivering high-quality, impactful learning experiences while fostering continuous improvement and innovation. This concluding chapter reflects on the journey to accreditation, its profound benefits, and the enduring responsibility to maintain and elevate program quality.

The Journey to Accreditation
The path to accreditation is demanding yet transformative. It involves meticulous planning, thorough assessments, and a culture of collaboration. From conducting gap analyses to refining curriculum and resources, every step prepares the program for alignment with the standards of accrediting bodies such as the Society for Simulation in Healthcare (SSH) or the International Nursing Association for Clinical Simulation and Learning (INACSL). These standards are a blueprint for excellence, ensuring that programs deliver impactful, learner-centered experiences.

The accreditation process is not merely a series of tasks to complete but an opportunity to refine and innovate. Creating a self-study report allows programs to reflect on and evaluate their strengths and areas for growth. Mock reviews provide valuable rehearsal opportunities, enabling teams to address gaps and build confidence. Training faculty and staff fosters alignment and equips the team to articulate their roles during site visits.

Programs that embrace this journey with a mindset of growth and evolution often find rewards far exceeding the accreditation decision itself. As this guide shares, programs that leverage accreditation as a catalyst for improvement create lasting impacts on their learners, institutions, and healthcare systems.

The Benefits of Accreditation

Accreditation is more than a mark of compliance—it is a seal of distinction that communicates quality, professionalism, and a commitment to excellence. The benefits of achieving accreditation ripple across stakeholders and extend to the learners, educators, and healthcare systems that rely on simulation programs.

1. Enhanced Learner Outcomes

Accredited programs are designed to provide consistent, high-quality education tailored to real-world clinical challenges. Learners benefit from robust curricula, well-trained faculty, and cutting-edge technologies that prepare them to deliver safe, effective patient care.

2. Improved Program Credibility

Accreditation enhances a program's reputation, building trust among learners, faculty, and healthcare organizations. This credibility attracts top-tier faculty and learners and opens doors to partnerships and opportunities for growth.

3. Opportunities for Growth and Collaboration

Accreditation positions programs as leaders in simulation education, paving the way for global collaborations, participation in research, and access to grants. These opportunities help programs expand their reach and impact.

4. Commitment to Continuous Improvement

Accredited programs are committed to staying at the forefront of simulation education by integrating emerging technologies, evidence-based practices, and learner feedback into their operations.

Maintaining Excellence Post-Accreditation

Accreditation is not the finish line—it is the beginning of an ongoing journey toward sustained excellence. Accredited programs are responsible for maintaining standards, driving innovation, and preparing for re-accreditation. This commitment ensures that learners continue to benefit from high-quality education and that the program remains relevant and impactful.

Key Strategies for Sustaining Accreditation:

1. **Regular Reviews and Updates** Programs must continually evaluate and update their policies, curricula, and resources to ensure alignment with evolving accreditation standards and industry trends.
2. **Faculty and Staff Development** Ongoing training and certification opportunities for educators and staff are essential for maintaining expertise and delivering quality simulation experiences.
3. **Data-Driven Improvement:** Collecting and analyzing performance data helps programs identify strengths and address gaps, driving continuous quality improvement (CQI).
4. **Proactive Engagement with Standards** Staying informed about changes in accreditation requirements ensures that programs remain compliant and adaptable to new challenges and expectations.

Final Reflections

The accreditation process is undoubtedly challenging, but it is also deeply rewarding. It calls for strategic planning, resourcefulness, and a collaborative spirit. Programs that approach accreditation as an opportunity for growth and innovation often emerge stronger, more cohesive, and better equipped to serve their learners and the healthcare community.

The success stories shared in this guide—from overcoming resource limitations to fostering a culture of excellence—illustrate that programs of all sizes and circumstances can achieve accreditation. The common thread is a commitment to quality, creativity in problem-solving, and a willingness to grow.

A Call to Action

Accreditation is more than meeting a set of standards—it is a powerful tool for driving positive change in healthcare education. It inspires programs to elevate their practices, align with global benchmarks, and prepare learners to meet the complexities of modern healthcare.

To those embarking on the accreditation journey, approach it with purpose and determination. Use this guide's tools, strategies, and lessons to chart your path to success. Cultivate a vision beyond compliance that transforms your program into a beacon of innovation, quality, and excellence.

The journey to accreditation is a shared responsibility, but its rewards are transformative. With a clear vision, a committed team, and a relentless focus on improvement, your program can achieve accreditation and sustain its legacy as a leader in simulation-based education.

Glossary of Terms

This glossary defines key terms and concepts used throughout the guide. Familiarity with these terms will help readers navigate the accreditation process more confidently and clearly.

Accreditation
Accreditation is the formal recognition that a program meets established quality standards set by an accrediting body. It ensures consistency, effectiveness, and adherence to best practices.

Accrediting Body
An organization that establishes and enforces standards for education or training programs, such as the Society for Simulation in Healthcare (SSH) or the International Nursing Association for Clinical Simulation and Learning (INACSL).

Assessment
The process of evaluating learner performance, faculty effectiveness, or program quality using standardized tools, such as rubrics or checklists.

Certified Healthcare Simulation Educator (CHSE)
A professional certification that demonstrates expertise in healthcare simulation education, awarded by the Society for Simulation in Healthcare.

Certified Healthcare Simulation Operations Specialist (CHSOS)
A professional certification that recognizes expertise in healthcare simulation's technical and operational aspects.

Continuous Quality Improvement (CQI)
A systematic process for evaluating and improving program performance, often using data-driven methods such as Plan-Do-Study-Act (PDSA) cycles.

Curriculum Design
Planning and organizing educational content, activities, and assessments to achieve specific learning objectives.

Debriefing
After a simulation session, a reflective discussion is conducted to reinforce learning, address performance gaps, and promote critical thinking.

Evidence-Based Practice
The integration of the best available evidence, clinical expertise, and learner needs to guide decision-making in simulation design and delivery.

Facilitation

The process by which an instructor guides learners through a simulation activity, ensuring alignment with learning objectives and encouraging active participation.

Gap Analysis
A systematic comparison of a program's current practices and resources against accreditation standards to identify areas for improvement.

High-Fidelity Simulation
A type of simulation that uses advanced technology and realistic scenarios to mimic real-world clinical environments and patient interactions closely.

International Nursing Association for Clinical Simulation and Learning (INACSL)
A professional organization that provides best practices, resources, and standards for clinical simulation in nursing and healthcare education.

Key Performance Indicators (KPIs)
Quantifiable measures, such as learner outcomes, satisfaction scores, or scenario completion rates, are used to evaluate program performance.

Learning Objectives
Specific, measurable goals define what learners should know or be able to do after a simulation activity or educational program.

Maintenance Log
A record of equipment maintenance, repairs, and updates is often required as part of accreditation documentation.

Mock Accreditation Review
A practice run of the accreditation process is conducted internally or with external reviewers to assess readiness and identify areas for improvement.

Plan-Do-Study-Act (PDSA) Cycle
A CQI framework used to test and implement changes, involving planning, execution, evaluation, and adjustment based on results.

Policies and Procedures
Formalized documents that outline the rules, guidelines, and processes governing program operations, such as safety protocols or learner assessments.

Program Mission and Vision
Statements articulating a simulation program's purpose and long-term goals align with institutional values and accreditation standards.

Quality Improvement Dashboard
A visual tool used to track and display program performance metrics, such as learner competency scores or scenario completion rates.

Self-Study Report

A comprehensive document prepared by a program to demonstrate compliance with accreditation standards, including narrative explanations and supporting evidence.

Simulation

A method of training or assessment that replicates clinical scenarios to provide learners with experiential, hands-on learning opportunities in a controlled environment.

Society for Simulation in Healthcare (SSH)

A professional organization that offers accreditation, certification, and resources to advance the field of healthcare simulation.

Stakeholders

Individuals or groups interested in the simulation program, such as learners, faculty, administrators, healthcare institutions, and accrediting bodies.

Standards of Best Practice

Guidelines established by professional organizations, such as INACSL or SSH, to define best practices in simulation design, delivery, and evaluation.

Standardized Assessment Tools

Validated instruments, such as rubrics or checklists, used to objectively evaluate learner performance, scenario outcomes, or program quality.

Virtual Simulation

A type of simulation conducted in a digital environment, often using virtual reality (VR) or online platforms, to replicate clinical scenarios.

ACHIEVING PROGRAM ACCREDITATION FOR HEALTHCARE SIMULATION PROGRAMS: A Resource Guide

Contact Information

Accreditation is a pivotal step in affirming the quality and effectiveness of healthcare simulation programs. Engaging with established accrediting bodies provides access to standards, resources, and support essential for the accreditation journey. Below is the contact information for two prominent organizations in this field:

Society for Simulation in Healthcare (SSH)
- **Mailing Address:**
  - P.O. Box 856114
  - Minneapolis, MN 55485-6114
- **Phone:** 866.730.6127
- **Email:** membership@ssih.org
- **Website:** https://www.ssih.org/

SSH offers accreditation services, certification programs, and a wealth of resources to advance the healthcare simulation field. For specific inquiries related to accreditation materials, correspondence can be directed to:

- **Accreditation Materials Address:**
  - P.O. Box 0593
  - Dyersburg, TN 38025-0593

For more detailed contact information, please visit their contact page: https://www.ssih.org/Contact

International Nursing Association for Clinical Simulation and Learning (INACSL)
- **Address:**
  - 330 N. Wabash Ave, Suite 2000
  - Chicago, IL 60611
- **Phone:** 312.321.6813
- **Fax:** 312.673.6737
- **Email:** inacslinfo@inacsl.org
- **Website:** https://www.inacsl.org/

INACSL is dedicated to advancing the science of healthcare simulation and offers resources such as the Healthcare Simulation Standards of Best Practice™. For membership-related inquiries, please contact:

- **Membership Email:** inacslinfo@inacsl.org

For more detailed contact information, please visit their contact page: https://www.inacsl.org/contact-us

References

Introduction

Society for Simulation in Healthcare (SSH). (2022). *Benefits of Accreditation*. Retrieved from https://www.ssih.org

National League for Nursing (NLN). (2021). *Learner Confidence in Accredited Programs*. Retrieved from https://www.nln.org

International Nursing Association for Clinical Simulation and Learning (INACSL). (2020). *Barriers to Accreditation in Simulation*. Retrieved from https://www.inacsl.org

Chapter 1

International Nursing Association for Clinical Simulation and Learning. (2020). *INACSL standards of best practice: Simulation*. Retrieved from https://www.inacsl.org

Society for Simulation in Healthcare. (2022). *Society for Simulation in Healthcare accreditation manual*. Retrieved from https://www.ssih.org

Society for Simulation in Healthcare. (2021). *SSH impact report: Accreditation outcomes in healthcare simulation*. Retrieved from https://www.ssih.org

National League for Nursing. (2022). *NLN faculty development and accreditation guidelines*. Retrieved from https://www.nln.org

Simulation in Healthcare Journal. (2021). Clinical outcomes and accreditation standards in healthcare simulation. *Simulation in Healthcare*. Retrieved from academic databases such as PubMed or ScienceDirect.

International Nursing Association for Clinical Simulation and Learning. (2020). *Simulation in nursing education: Accreditation essentials* [White paper]. Retrieved from https://www.inacsl.org

American Medical Association. (2022). *Survey of simulation accreditation in U.S. healthcare education*. Retrieved from https://www.ama-assn.org

Journal of Nursing Education. (2021). Effects of accreditation on learner outcomes in simulation education. *Journal of Nursing Education*. Retrieved from academic databases such as PubMed or ScienceDirect.

ACHIEVING PROGRAM ACCREDITATION FOR HEALTHCARE
SIMULATION PROGRAMS: A Resource Guide

Chapter 2

International Nursing Association for Clinical Simulation and Learning. (2021). *Healthcare simulation standards of best practice: Simulation design*. Retrieved from https://www.inacsl.org

Society for Simulation in Healthcare. (2022). *SSH accreditation manual*. Retrieved from https://www.ssih.org

Society for Simulation in Healthcare. (2022). *Survey on accreditation readiness and outcomes in healthcare simulation*. Retrieved from https://www.ssih.org

Society for Simulation in Healthcare. (2021). *Stakeholder engagement in the accreditation process: Best practices and outcomes*. Retrieved from https://www.ssih.org

Journal of Clinical Simulation in Nursing. (2021). Simulation technician ratios and learner outcomes: A meta-analysis. *Clinical Simulation in Nursing*.

International Nursing Association for Clinical Simulation and Learning. (2020). *Building a quality improvement culture in healthcare simulation: Best practices*. Retrieved from https://www.inacsl.org

American Medical Association. (2022). *Accreditation benchmarks for healthcare simulation programs*. Retrieved from https://www.ama-assn.org

Chapter 3

International Nursing Association for Clinical Simulation and Learning. (2021). *Healthcare simulation standards of best practice: Simulation design*. Retrieved from https://www.inacsl.org

Society for Simulation in Healthcare. (2022). *Simulation program accreditation standards and guidelines*. Retrieved from https://www.ssih.org

International Nursing Association for Clinical Simulation and Learning. (2020). *Developing effective simulation curricula: Aligning with professional standards*. Retrieved from https://www.inacsl.org

Society for Simulation in Healthcare. (2021). *Certified healthcare simulation educator (CHSE): A guide for faculty qualifications*. Retrieved from https://www.ssih.org

American Medical Association. (2022). *Leveraging debriefing frameworks to enhance learner satisfaction and outcomes*. Retrieved from https://www.ama-assn.org

Lasater, K. (2007). *Clinical judgment development: Using simulation to assess student performance*. Nursing Education Perspectives, *28*(3), 126-133.

Society for Simulation in Healthcare. (2022). *Data dashboards in simulation programs: Improving KPI tracking*. Retrieved from https://www.ssih.org

International Nursing Association for Clinical Simulation and Learning. (2021). *The impact of standardized debriefing methods on learner outcomes*. Retrieved from https://www.inacsl.org

Chapter 4

International Nursing Association for Clinical Simulation and Learning. (2021). *Healthcare simulation standards of best practice: Simulation design*. Retrieved from https://www.inacsl.org

Society for Simulation in Healthcare. (2022). *Accreditation guide: Evidence checklist and submission process*. Retrieved from https://www.ssih.org

Society for Simulation in Healthcare. (2022). *Using dashboards to track learner competency milestones: A case study*. Retrieved from https://www.ssih.org

International Nursing Association for Clinical Simulation and Learning. (2021). *Plan-Do-Study-Act cycles in simulation-based education: Improving learner outcomes*. Retrieved from https://www.inacsl.org

Society for Simulation in Healthcare. (2021). *Accreditation standards and best practices: Faculty documentation and CQI initiatives*. Retrieved from https://www.ssih.org

International Organization for Standardization. (2020). *Guidelines for quality management in education and training programs*. Retrieved from https://www.iso.org

American Medical Association. (2022). *Documentation accuracy and version control in healthcare education programs*. Retrieved from https://www.ama-assn.org

Chapter 5

Nestel, D., et al. (2019). *Healthcare Simulation Education: Evidence, Theory, and Practice*. Wiley.

Society for Simulation in Healthcare (SSH). (2022). *Certified Healthcare Simulation Educator (CHSE)*. Retrieved from https://www.ssih.org

Chapter 6

Bryson, J. M. (2018). *Strategic planning for public and nonprofit organizations: A guide to strengthening and sustaining organizational achievement* (5th ed.). Wiley.

International Nursing Association for Clinical Simulation and Learning (INACSL). (2020). *Healthcare Simulation Standards of Best Practice: Operations*. Retrieved from https://www.inacsl.org

Society for Simulation in Healthcare (SSH). (2022). *Accreditation Standards and Self-Study Requirements*. Retrieved from https://www.ssih.org

Mintzberg, H. (1994). The rise and fall of strategic planning. *Harvard Business Review, 72*(1), 107–114.

Gaba, D. M. (2004). The future vision of simulation in health care. *Quality and Safety in Health Care, 13*(suppl 1), i2–i10.

Chapter 7
Society for Simulation in Healthcare (SSH). (2022). *Certified Healthcare Simulation Educator (CHSE)*. Retrieved from https://www.ssih.org

International Nursing Association for Clinical Simulation and Learning (INACSL). (2020). *Faculty Development in Simulation Programs*. Retrieved from https://www.inacsl.org

Nestel, D., et al. (2019). *Healthcare Simulation Education: Evidence, Theory, and Practice*. Wiley.

Chapter 8
Society for Simulation in Healthcare (SSH). (2022). *Accreditation Standards and Guidelines*. Retrieved from https://www.ssih.org

Rudolph, J. W., Simon, R., Dufresne, R. L., & Raemer, D. B. (2006). There's no such thing as "nonjudgmental" debriefing: A theory and method for debriefing with good judgment. *Simulation in Healthcare, 1*(1), 49-55.

Eppich, W., & Cheng, A. (2015). Promoting excellence and reflective learning in simulation (PEARLS): Development and rationale for a blended approach to healthcare simulation debriefing. *Simulation in Healthcare, 10*(2), 106-115.

International Nursing Association for Clinical Simulation and Learning (INACSL). (2020). *Healthcare Simulation Standards of Best Practice: Operations*. Retrieved from https://www.inacsl.org

Gaba, D. M. (2004). The future vision of simulation in health care. *Quality and Safety in Health Care, 13*(suppl 1), i2–i10.

Chapter 9: The Accreditation Site Visit
Society for Simulation in Healthcare (SSH). (2022). *Accreditation Site Visit Preparation*. Retrieved from https://www.ssih.org

International Nursing Association for Clinical Simulation and Learning (INACSL). (2020). *Engaging Stakeholders During Accreditation Visits*. Retrieved from https://www.inacsl.org

Chapter 10: Post-Accreditation: Maintaining Standards
Society for Simulation in Healthcare (SSH). (2022). *Maintaining Accreditation Standards*. Retrieved from https://www.ssih.org

International Nursing Association for Clinical Simulation and Learning (INACSL). (2020). *Continuous Quality Improvement in Simulation Programs*. Retrieved from https://www.inacsl.org

Chapter 11
International Nursing Association for Clinical Simulation and Learning (INACSL). (2021). *Standards of Best Practice: Simulation*^{SM}. Retrieved from https://www.inacsl.org

Society for Simulation in Healthcare (SSH). (2022). *Certified Healthcare Simulation Educator (CHSE) Guidelines*. Retrieved from https://www.ssih.org

Rudolph, J. W., Simon, R., Dufresne, R. L., & Raemer, D. B. (2006). There's no such thing as "nonjudgmental" debriefing: A theory and method for debriefing with good judgment. *Simulation in Healthcare, 1*(1), 49-55.

Eppich, W., & Cheng, A. (2015). Promoting excellence and reflective learning in simulation (PEARLS): Development and rationale for a blended approach to healthcare simulation debriefing. *Simulation in Healthcare, 10*(2), 106-115.

International Nursing Association for Clinical Simulation and Learning (INACSL). (2020). *Guidelines for Continuous Quality Improvement in Simulation Programs*. Retrieved from https://www.inacsl.org

Chapter 12
Association of Standardized Patient Educators (ASPE). (2021). *Standards of Best Practice for Standardized Patient Programs*. Retrieved from https://www.aspeducators.org

Harden, R. M., & Gleeson, F. A. (1979). Assessment of clinical competence using an Objective Structured Clinical Examination (OSCE). *Medical Education, 13*(1), 41–54.

Nestel, D., & Bearman, M. (2015). *Simulated Patient Methodology: Theory, Evidence, and Practice*. Wiley.

Association of Standardized Patient Educators (ASPE). (2020). *Best Practices for Standardized Patient Recruitment and Training*. Retrieved from https://www.aspeducators.org

Eppich, W., & Cheng, A. (2015). Promoting excellence and reflective learning in simulation (PEARLS): Development and rationale for a blended approach to healthcare simulation debriefing. *Simulation in Healthcare, 10*(2), 106-115.

Ziv, A., Wolpe, P. R., Small, S. D., & Glick, S. (2003). Simulation-based medical education: An ethical imperative. *Academic Medicine, 78*(8), 783–788.

Chapter 13

American College of Surgeons (ACS). (2021). *Standards for Accreditation of Simulation Centers*. Retrieved from https://www.facs.org

Martin, J. A., Regehr, G., Reznick, R., MacRae, H., Murnaghan, J., Hutchison, C., & Brown, M. (1997). Objective Structured Assessment of Technical Skill (OSATS) for surgical residents. *British Journal of Surgery, 84*(2), 273-278.

Gallagher, A. G., & Smith, C. D. (2003). Human-factors lessons learned from the minimally invasive surgery revolution. *Surgical Innovation, 10*(3), 127-139.

American College of Surgeons (ACS). (2022). *Continuous Quality Improvement in Simulation Programs*. Retrieved from https://www.facs.org

Ziv, A., Wolpe, P. R., Small, S. D., & Glick, S. (2003). Simulation-based medical education: An ethical imperative. *Academic Medicine, 78*(8), 783–788.

Rudolph, J. W., Simon, R., Dufresne, R. L., & Raemer, D. B. (2006). There's no such thing as "nonjudgmental" debriefing: A theory and method for debriefing with good judgment. *Simulation in Healthcare, 1*(1), 49-55.

Chapter 14

Society for Simulation in Healthcare (SSH). (2022). *Accreditation Standards*. Retrieved from https://www.ssih.org

Society for Simulation in Healthcare (SSH). (2022). *Certified Healthcare Simulation Educator (CHSE) and Certified Healthcare Simulation Operations Specialist (CHSOS) Guidelines*. Retrieved from https://www.ssih.org

Fanning, R. M., & Gaba, D. M. (2007). The role of debriefing in simulation-based learning. *Simulation in Healthcare, 2*(2), 115–125.

Rudolph, J. W., Simon, R., Dufresne, R. L., & Raemer, D. B. (2006). There's no such thing as "nonjudgmental" debriefing: A theory and method for debriefing with good judgment. *Simulation in Healthcare, 1*(1), 49-55.

International Nursing Association for Clinical Simulation and Learning (INACSL). (2020). *Healthcare Simulation Standards of Best Practice*. Retrieved from https://www.inacsl.org

Smith, M. K., Beaulieu, K., Kuszajewski, M., LeMaster, T., Nawathe, P., Schocken, D. M., Young, J., & Jaeger, J. (2024). Perceived return on investment of accreditation by accredited programs. Simulation in Healthcare: The Journal of the Society for Simulation in Healthcare. Advanced online publication. https://doi.org/10.1097/SIH.0000000000000801

Chapter 15: Case Studies and Success Stories

Journal of Clinical Simulation in Healthcare. (2021). *Case Studies in Simulation Program Accreditation*.

Society for Simulation in Healthcare (SSH). (2022). *Accreditation Success Stories*. Retrieved from https://www.ssih.org

International Nursing Association for Clinical Simulation and Learning (INACSL). (2020). *Innovations in Simulation Accreditation*. Retrieved from https://www.inacsl.org

Chapter 16: Resources and Tools

Society for Simulation in Healthcare (SSH). (2022). *Accreditation Resources*. Retrieved from https://www.ssih.org

International Nursing Association for Clinical Simulation and Learning (INACSL). (2020). *Healthcare Simulation Standards of Best Practice*™. Retrieved from https://www.inacsl.org

Power BI Documentation. (2022). *Data Visualization for Educational Programs*. Retrieved from https://powerbi.microsoft.com

Appendix A

Sample Policies and Procedures Outline

1. Introduction
- 1.1 Purpose of the Manual
- 1.2 Mission, Vision, and Goals of the Simulation Center
- 1.3 Scope and Applicability
- 1.4 Definitions and Key Terms

2. Governance and Oversight
- 2.1 Organizational Structure
- 2.2 Roles and Responsibilities
    - 2.2.1 Simulation Director
    - 2.2.2 Simulation Technicians
    - 2.2.3 Faculty and Instructors
- 2.3 Reporting and Decision-Making Processes
- 2.4 Committees and Stakeholders

3. Facility Operations
- 3.1 Facility Access and Security
    - 3.1.1 Visitor Policies
    - 3.1.2 Key and Badge Access
- 3.2 Scheduling and Utilization
    - 3.2.1 Reservation Process
    - 3.2.2 Priority Scheduling Guidelines
- 3.3 Equipment Maintenance and Management
    - 3.3.1 Preventative Maintenance
    - 3.3.2 Equipment Repair Protocols
- 3.4 Housekeeping and Cleanliness
- 3.5 Prioritization of Simulation Resources

4. Simulation Program Design
- 4.1 Simulation Curriculum Development
- 4.2 Learning Objectives and Outcomes
- 4.3 Scenario Creation and Approval
- 4.4 Debriefing and Evaluation Standards

5. Participant Policies
- 5.1 Code of Conduct
- 5.2 Confidentiality and Non-Disclosure

- 5.3 Dress Code and Safety Requirements
- 5.4 Attendance and Participation Expectations
- 5.5 Participant Photograph/Video Policy

6. Faculty and Staff Policies
- 6.1 Training and Certification Requirements
- 6.2 Professional Development Opportunities
- 6.3 Faculty of Record Responsibilities
- 6.4 Clinical Instructor Responsibilities
- 6.5 Conflict Resolution and Reporting

7. Health and Safety
- 7.1 Emergency Procedures
  - 7.1.1 Fire and Evacuation Plans
  - 7.1.2 Medical Emergencies
  - 7.1.3 Extreme Weather
- 7.2 Infection Control and Hygiene
- 7.3 Simulation Safety Protocols
  - 7.3.1 Use of Medical Gases
  - 7.3.2 Latex Allergies and Other Sensitivities
  - 7.3.3 Sharps
- 7.4 Separation of Equipment and Supplies (real vs. sim)
- 7.5 Psychological Safety

8. Technology and Media
- 8.1 Audio-Visual Recording Policies
- 8.2 Data Storage and Security
- 8.3 Data Retention
- 8.4 IT Support and Troubleshooting
- 8.5 Equipment Loan and External Use

9. Evaluation and Quality Assurance
- 9.1 Program Evaluation Metrics
- 9.2 Participant Feedback and Surveys
- 9.3 Continuous Improvement Processes
- 9.4 Accreditation and Compliance

10. Financial Management
- 10.1 Budget and Resource Allocation
- 10.2 Fees for Service and Billing Policies
- 10.3 Grant Management and Funding Opportunities

11. Special Circumstances
- 11.1 Research Use of the Simulation Center
- 11.2 Collaboration with External Partners
- 11.3 Simulation Center Closure and Downtime
- 11.4 Brand Use
- 11.5 Tours/outreach

12. Appendices

- A. Forms and Templates
- B. Emergency Contact List
- C. Glossary of Terms
- D. Relevant Laws and Regulations
- E. Simulation Center Map and Floor Plan

13. Revision History and Updates
- 13.1 Record of Changes
- 13.2 Update Process and Responsibilities

Appendix B

Sample Operational Trend Template

Operational Trend Projection Template for Simulation Programs (3–5 Years)
This template provides a structured framework for simulation programs to analyze current performance, project future trends, and identify resource needs and goals. Use this as a dynamic document to update regularly.

1. Executive Summary
- **Overview:** Briefly describe the program, including its mission, vision, and strategic goals.
- **Purpose:** State the objectives of the operational trend projection (e.g., resource planning, accreditation preparation, program expansion).
- **Timeframe:** Indicate the projection period (e.g., 2024–2029).

2. Key Performance Indicators (KPIs)
Define measurable KPIs to track operational and educational success. Example categories include:
- **Learner Metrics:**
    - Number of learners trained annually.
    - Learner satisfaction rates.
    - Learner competency scores (e.g., teamwork, communication).
- **Faculty Development:**
    - Number of faculty certifications (e.g., CHSE, CHSOS).
    - Percentage of faculty completing simulation-specific training.
- **Program Operations:**
    - Simulation sessions delivered per year.
    - Facility and equipment utilization rates.
- **Financial Performance:**
    - Annual budget and expenditure trends.
    - Revenue generated from external partnerships or grants.
- **Quality Improvement:**
    - CQI initiatives completed.

o Improvement rates in learner outcomes or process efficiency.

3. Current State Analysis
- **Strengths:** List current program strengths (e.g., state-of-the-art facilities, experienced faculty).
- **Weaknesses:** Identify operational gaps (e.g., outdated technology, insufficient staffing).
- **Opportunities:** Highlight growth opportunities (e.g., partnerships, new technologies).
- **Threats:** Note potential risks (e.g., funding challenges, competition).

4. Resource Planning

Category	Current Resources	Projected Needs (Year 1)	Projected Needs (Year 3)	Projected Needs (Year 5)
Faculty & Staff	# of faculty, technicians	Add X faculty; X technicians	Add Y faculty; Y technicians	Maintain or expand as needed
Technology	Current simulators, AV tools	Upgrade X technology	Introduce Y innovations	Replace aging equipment
Facilities	Simulation labs, debrief rooms	Add 1 lab	Expand debriefing space	Assess facility requirements
Budget	Current annual budget	Increase by X%	Increase by Y%	Adjust per operational needs

5. Projected Trends
Analyze and project trends across key areas:
- **Learner Volume:** Anticipated growth or decline in learner enrollment.
- **Simulation Activities:** Expected increase in demand for sessions, scenarios, or interprofessional education.
- **Technology Adoption:** Plan for introducing virtual reality, augmented reality, or AI-based tools.
- **Faculty and Staff Needs:** Growth in team size, development needs, or role diversification.
- **Facility Utilization:** Projections for lab and equipment usage.

6. Strategic Goals and Objectives
Outline SMART (Specific, Measurable, Achievable, Relevant, Time-bound) goals for the next 3–5 years:
1. **Goal:** Increase the number of learners trained by 25% over the next 5 years.
    - Objective: Develop 10 new scenarios tailored to interprofessional education.
2. **Goal:** Upgrade simulation technology within 3 years.
    - Objective: Invest in two high-fidelity manikins and virtual reality capabilities.
3. **Goal:** Enhance faculty expertise.

o   Objective: Certify 50% of faculty with CHSE by Year 3.

7. Financial Projection
- **Revenue Sources:**
    o   Tuition fees, grants, external partnerships.
- **Expense Categories:**
    o   Technology, staffing, training, facility upgrades.
- **Projected Budget:** Provide year-by-year estimates for revenue and expenses over 3–5 years.

Year	Projected Revenue	Projected Expenses	Surplus/Deficit
Year 1	$XXX	$XXX	$XXX
Year 2	$XXX	$XXX	$XXX
Year 3	$XXX	$XXX	$XXX
Year 5	$XXX	$XXX	$XXX

8. Risk Assessment and Mitigation

Risk	Likelihood	Impact	Mitigation Strategy
Funding shortfall	High	High	Pursue grants, diversify revenue sources
Staff turnover	Medium	High	Develop retention programs, training
Equipment failure	Medium	Medium	Implement preventive maintenance
Increased competition	Low	Medium	Focus on unique program strengths

9. Continuous Monitoring Plan
- Frequency of Updates: Quarterly or biannual reviews.
- Responsible Teams: Assign accountability for tracking and reporting on KPIs.
- Tools for Monitoring: Use dashboards, reports, and regular team meetings to assess progress.

10. Conclusion and Recommendations
Summarize the key findings, trends, and actions. Provide actionable recommendations to leadership or stakeholders to guide decision-making for the program's growth and sustainability.

Appendix C

Sample Simulation Scenario Template

Note: Standardized simulation templates may vary from center to center.

1. General Information
- **Scenario Title**:
- **Date Created/Updated**:
- **Authors**:
- **Target Learners**: (e.g., Medical Students, Nursing Students, Interprofessional Teams)
- **Simulation Modality**: (e.g., High-Fidelity Manikin, Task Trainer, Virtual Reality)
- **Duration**:
    - **Prebriefing Time**:
    - **Scenario Time**:
    - **Debriefing Time**:

2. Prebriefing
- Confidentiality
- Orientation to environment/equipment
- Flow/schedule of events
- Case stem

3. Learning Objectives
By the end of this simulation, participants will be able to:
1. *(Cognitive)*
2. *(Psychomotor)*
3. *(Affective)*

AACN Competencies

ACGME EPAs

4. Case Overview
- **Patient Name**:
- **Age**:

- **Gender**:
- **Weight/Height**:
- **Primary Diagnosis**:
- **Secondary Diagnoses**: (if applicable)
- **Clinical Setting**: (e.g., Emergency Department, Intensive Care Unit, Primary Care Clinic)
- **Scenario Complexity Level**: (e.g., Beginner, Intermediate, Advanced)

5. Case Description
   - **Presenting Complaint**: (e.g., "Chest pain for 2 hours.")
   - **History of Present Illness**:
   - **Past Medical History**:
   - **Medications**:
   - **Allergies**:
   - **Social History**:
   - **Family History**:

6. Pre-Simulation Requirements
   - **Knowledge or Skills Required**: (e.g., "Basic ECG interpretation, medication dosage calculation.")
   - **Preparation Materials**: (e.g., relevant guidelines, videos, or reading assignments.)
   - **Equipment Needed**:
     - Manikin/Simulator:
     - Medical Equipment:
     - Medications:
     - Technology: (e.g., monitors, defibrillators)

7. Scenario Flow
   - **Initial Patient Presentation**: (Include baseline vital signs, demeanor, and position.)
   - **Anticipated Actions by Participants**:
     - **Key Interventions**: (e.g., perform an ECG, administer medications.)
     - **Expected Decisions**: (e.g., escalate care, initiate a protocol.)
   - **Cueing Strategies**: (How facilitators can guide participants if needed.)
   - **Expected Outcomes**: (How the scenario should progress based on learner actions.)

8. Clinical Information
   - **Baseline Vitals**:
     - Heart Rate:
     - Blood Pressure:
     - Respiratory Rate:
     - Oxygen Saturation:
     - Temperature:

- **Dynamic Changes**: (Vital signs or conditions that change based on actions or time.)
    - **Cue 1**:
    - **Cue 2**:

9. Roles and Resources
- **Roles Required for Scenario**:
    - Participant Roles: (e.g., Primary Nurse, Physician, Respiratory Therapist)
    - Faculty/Staff Roles: (e.g., Scenario Lead, Voice of the Patient, Observer)
- **Additional Resources**: (e.g., lab results, imaging, family member calls.)

10. Debriefing Plan
- **Debriefing Framework**: (e.g., PEARLS, Gather-Analyze-Summarize)
- **Key Discussion Points**:
    - Clinical Reasoning:
    - Teamwork and Communication:
    - Technical Skills:
    - Emotional Reactions:
- **Learning Reinforcement Activities**: (e.g., review clinical guidelines, repeat key tasks.)

11. Scenario Evaluation
- **Assessment Tools**:
    - Checklist for Critical Actions:
    - Rubric for Performance Metrics:
- **Feedback Collection**:
    - Participant Feedback Form
    - Faculty Feedback Form

12. Notes and Additional Instructions
- **Special Considerations**: (e.g., cultural factors, patient family involvement.)
- **Adaptations for Different Learner Levels**:

13. References and Supporting Materials
- **Citations**: (e.g., clinical guidelines, journal articles.)
- **Attachments**: (e.g., lab reports, ECG strips, x-ray images.)
- **Documentation of Changes**

Appendix D

Sample Standardized Patient Script

Sample Standardized Patient Script
Aligned with Best Practices for Medical Education

Case Title
"Evaluation of Chest Pain in the Emergency Department"

1. Case Overview
Patient Name: Maria Hernandez
Age: 58
Gender: Female
Setting: Emergency Department
Chief Complaint: Chest pain

Objective: Assess the learner's ability to take a focused history, communicate effectively, and develop a preliminary differential diagnosis.

2. Patient Presentation
<u>Appearance</u>: Alert, slightly anxious. Sitting upright.
<u>Clothing</u>: Casual attire appropriate for a visit to the Emergency Department.
<u>Emotional Tone</u>: Cooperative but concerned. Voice may reflect mild anxiety.
<u>Non-Verbal Cues</u>: Frequently places hand on chest during the interview, shifts uncomfortably in the chair.

3. Script: Patient's Story
<u>Opening Statement</u>
When the learner asks, "What brings you in today?" respond:
"I've been having this pain in my chest, and I'm worried it could be something serious."
<u>History of Present Illness</u>
Provide details when prompted by the learner's questions:
<u>Location of Pain</u>
"It's right here in the middle of my chest." (Gesture to the sternum.)
<u>Character of Pain</u>
"It feels like a pressure, almost like something heavy is sitting on my chest."
<u>Onset and Timing</u>
"It started about an hour ago while I was watching TV. It's not constant, but it keeps coming back every few minutes."

Duration
"Each time it lasts maybe five minutes, then eases up a little."
Exacerbating/Relieving Factors
"It gets worse when I try to take a deep breath or when I move around."
"It doesn't seem to get better no matter what I do."
Associated Symptoms
"I feel a little short of breath, and I've been sweating more than usual. I also feel a little nauseous."
Severity
"I'd say it's about a 7 out of 10 when it's bad."

Past Medical History
If asked:
"I have high blood pressure, and I've been told I might have diabetes."
"I had my gallbladder removed a few years ago, but no other surgeries."

Family History
If asked:
"My father died of a heart attack when he was 60, and my mom had diabetes."

Social History
If asked:
Occupation: "I'm a retired teacher."
Living Situation: "I live with my husband."
Smoking: "I smoked for about 10 years in my 20s but quit a long time ago."
Alcohol: "I might have a glass of wine with dinner a couple of times a week."
Exercise: "I try to walk around my neighborhood a few times a week."
Diet: "I eat pretty healthy, but I do like sweets."

Medications
If asked:
"I take amlodipine for my blood pressure."
"I also take over-the-counter ibuprofen occasionally for headaches."

Allergies
If asked:
"I'm allergic to penicillin—it gives me a rash."

4. Non-Verbal Behaviors
Pain Gestures: Occasionally place your hand on your chest when describing symptoms.
Facial Expressions: Appear slightly anxious but not panicked.
Movement: Shift slightly in the chair, as though uncomfortable. Avoid sudden or exaggerated gestures.

5. Communication Style
Be forthcoming with information when asked directly.

Respond positively to empathetic statements, e.g., "Thank you for explaining that—I've been really worried."

Avoid volunteering unnecessary details unless prompted by the learner's questions.

6. Common Learner Pitfalls
If the learner:

<u>Fails to ask open-ended questions</u>, respond with brief answers to encourage them to dig deeper.

Example: If they ask, "Does it hurt when you breathe?" say, "Sometimes" instead of providing a full explanation.

<u>Misses key follow-up questions</u>, gently redirect:
"Should I be worried about this? My father had a heart attack."

7. Evaluation Checklist for Learners
<u>History-Taking Skills</u>
Asked about the location, quality, and severity of pain.
Inquired about associated symptoms (e.g., shortness of breath, nausea).
Explored relevant family, social, and medical history.
<u>Communication Skills</u>
Demonstrated empathy and active listening.
Used clear and patient-friendly language.
Maintained appropriate eye contact and non-verbal cues.
<u>Clinical Reasoning</u>
Identified key red flags (e.g., chest pain, shortness of breath, family history of cardiac disease).
Suggested appropriate next steps (e.g., ordering ECG, considering cardiac enzymes).

-

8. Debriefing Prompts for the Facilitator
What did you do well in gathering the patient's history?
What questions could you have asked to gain more information?
How did you demonstrate empathy and build rapport with the patient?
What would your next steps be based on this case?

-

9. Case Variations (Optional)
<u>For different levels of learners or scenarios:</u>
Beginner Level: Keep the symptoms straightforward with no unexpected findings.
Advanced Level: Introduce additional complexities (e.g., atypical presentation, language barriers, emotional distress).

Appendix E

List of Recommended Training and Certifications

Recommended Certifications
1. **Certified Healthcare Simulation Educator (CHSE)**
    o *Description*: Recognizes individuals with expertise in healthcare simulation education.
    o *Issuing Organization*: Society for Simulation in Healthcare (SSH).
    o *Who Should Pursue*: Educators and faculty involved in designing and implementing simulation-based learning experiences.
2. **Certified Healthcare Simulation Operations Specialist (CHSOS)**
    o *Description*: Validates proficiency in simulation operations, including technology management, scenario setup, and troubleshooting.
    o *Issuing Organization*: Society for Simulation in Healthcare (SSH).
    o *Who Should Pursue*: Simulation technicians, technologists, and operations managers.
3. **TeamSTEPPS Master Trainer Certification**
    o *Description*: Focuses on teaching teamwork and communication strategies in healthcare settings.
    o *Issuing Organization*: Agency for Healthcare Research and Quality (AHRQ).
    o *Who Should Pursue*: Educators, leaders, and facilitators incorporating teamwork training in simulations.
4. **Advanced Certified Healthcare Simulation Educator (CHSE-A)**
    o *Description*: An advanced-level certification for experienced simulation operators who demonstrate leadership and innovation in the field.
    o *Issuing Organization*: Society for Simulation in Healthcare (SSH).

- *Who Should Pursue*: Experienced simulation operators seeking to advance their credentials.
5. **Advanced Certified Healthcare Simulation Operations Specialist (CHSOS-A)**
   - *Description*: An advanced-level certification for experienced simulation educators who demonstrate leadership and innovation in the field.
   - *Issuing Organization*: Society for Simulation in Healthcare (SSH).
   - *Who Should Pursue*: Experienced simulation educators seeking to advance their credentials.
6. **Certified Simulation Healthcare Researcher (CSHR)**
   - *Description*: Recognizes expertise in simulation-based research methodologies.
   - *Issuing Organization*: Society for Simulation in Healthcare (SSH).
   - *Who Should Pursue*: Simulation professionals focused on research and evidence-based practice.
7. **Certified Clinical Simulation Educator (CCSE)**
   - *Description*: Validates the competency of educators specializing in clinical simulation.
   - *Issuing Organization*: National League for Nursing (NLN).
   - *Who Should Pursue*: Nurse educators and faculty specializing in clinical simulations.

Recommended Training Programs
1. **Simulation Instructor Training Course**
   - *Organization*: Center for Medical Simulation (CMS).
   - *Focus*: Simulation design, facilitation, debriefing techniques, and educator development.
2. **Harvard Macy Institute: Healthcare Simulation Essentials**
   - *Organization*: Harvard Macy Institute.
   - *Focus*: Advanced simulation-based education principles and best practices.
3. **INACSL Simulation Education Programs**
   - *Organization*: International Nursing Association for Clinical Simulation and Learning (INACSL).
   - *Focus*: Evidence-based simulation practices aligned with INACSL Standards of Best Practice.
4. **Laerdal SimCenter Courses**
   - *Organization*: Laerdal Medical.

- *Focus*: Hands-on training for Laerdal simulation technology, scenario design, and debriefing.

5. **Virtual and Augmented Reality in Healthcare Education Training**
    - *Organization*: Various vendors, including SimX and CAE Healthcare.
    - *Focus*: Integrating VR/AR technology into simulation programs.

Recommended Conferences

1. **International Meeting on Simulation in Healthcare (IMSH)**
    - *Organization*: Society for Simulation in Healthcare (SSH).
    - *Focus*: Advances in simulation technology, research, and best practices.
    - *Who Should Attend*: All simulation professionals.
2. **INACSL Conference**
    - *Organization*: International Nursing Association for Clinical Simulation and Learning (INACSL).
    - *Focus*: Nursing simulation, evidence-based practices, and research.
    - *Who Should Attend*: Nursing simulation educators and researchers.
3. **Simulation User Network (SUN) Conferences**
    - *Organization*: Laerdal Medical.
    - *Focus*: Hands-on training and user collaboration for Laerdal products.
    - *Who Should Attend*: Simulation operations specialists and Laerdal users.
4. **Health Professions Education Conference (HPEC)**
    - *Organization*: Harvard Macy Institute and Partner Organizations.
    - *Focus*: Innovative teaching methods and healthcare education trends.
    - *Who Should Attend*: Educators and faculty leaders.
5. **Interprofessional Education and Simulation Conference (IPE)**
    - *Organization*: Various academic and healthcare institutions.
    - *Focus*: Promoting interprofessional learning through simulation.

- *Who Should Attend*: Educators focusing on interprofessional collaboration.

6. **SimOPS Annual Conference**
    - *Organization*: Society for Simulation in Healthcare (SSH).
    - *Focus*: Simulation technology, operations, and troubleshooting.
    - *Who Should Attend*: Simulation technologists and operations specialists.

7. **SimGHOSTS Annual Conference**
    - *Organization*: Gathering of Healthcare Simulation Technology Specialists (SimGHOSTS).
    - *Focus*: Simulation technology, operations, and troubleshooting.
    - *Who Should Attend*: Simulation technologists and operations specialists.

8. **Association of Standardized Patient Educators (ASPE) Annual Conference**
    - *Organization*: ASPE.
    - *Focus*: Standardized patient programs and best practices.
    - *Who Should Attend*: Faculty and coordinators using standardized patients.

Appendix F

Tips for Writing the Self-Study

A self-study report is a critical component of the accreditation process. It demonstrates a program's alignment with accreditation standards, highlights strengths, and identifies areas for improvement. A well-organized and thorough report not only supports the accreditation process but also serves as a valuable roadmap for program development. Here are key tips and examples for writing an effective self-study report.

1. Understand Accreditation Standards
Tip:
Start by thoroughly reviewing the accreditation standards provided by the accrediting body, such as the Society for Simulation in Healthcare (SSH). Break these standards into manageable sections and ensure that each is addressed in the report.
Example:
If one standard focuses on governance, include a section that describes the program's leadership structure, decision-making processes, and advisory committees. Reference organizational charts and minutes from governance meetings as evidence.

2. Create a Structured Outline
Tip:
Follow a logical structure for the report that mirrors the accreditation standards. Use clear headings and subheadings to guide the reader. A typical outline might include:
- Executive Summary
- Program Overview
- Mission, Vision, and Strategic Plan
- Governance and Leadership
- Curriculum and Educational Outcomes
- Assessment and Evaluation
- Resources and Facilities
- Continuous Quality Improvement (CQI)
- Appendices

Example:
Under "Curriculum and Educational Outcomes," include subsections like simulation objectives, alignment with competencies, and learner feedback mechanisms.

3. Use Data to Support Your Narrative
Tip:
Provide quantitative and qualitative data to back up your claims. Data should be current, accurate, and relevant to the accreditation standards.
Example:
If the report addresses learner outcomes, include tables or charts that show pass rates, skill improvement metrics, or post-simulation evaluations over the past three years.

4. Provide Evidence for Every Claim
Tip:
Every statement in the self-study report should be supported with documentation. Include appendices or hyperlinks to policies, procedures, assessment tools, meeting minutes, or other evidence.
Example:
If you state that "The program has a robust CQI process," include examples of recent improvements made based on CQI findings, such as revising a scenario to better align with learning objectives.

5. Be Honest and Transparent
Tip:
Identify areas where the program is strong as well as areas needing improvement. Accreditation bodies appreciate transparency and a clear plan for addressing challenges.
Example:
"We identified a gap in faculty training related to advanced debriefing techniques. To address this, we implemented a faculty development program, with 80% of faculty completing training within the past year."

6. Highlight Strengths and Innovations
Tip:
Showcase unique aspects of your program that set it apart, such as innovative technologies, interprofessional collaboration, or research contributions.
Example:
"Our program is a leader in integrating virtual reality into nursing education, offering six VR-based simulation scenarios that have

improved learner confidence in clinical decision-making by 25%, as measured by post-simulation surveys."

7. Include Stakeholder Contributions
Tip:
Incorporate input from faculty, learners, and external stakeholders to show collaboration and engagement.
Example:
"In a recent stakeholder survey, 92% of clinical partners reported that our simulation-trained graduates demonstrated superior communication skills compared to peers trained in traditional settings."

8. Focus on Continuous Quality Improvement (CQI)
Tip:
Detail how the program uses CQI processes to evaluate and enhance performance. Include specific examples of changes implemented based on CQI findings.
Example:
"Through our CQI process, we identified that learners struggled with team communication during high-stress scenarios. As a result, we incorporated a TeamSTEPPS module, which improved communication scores by 18% over two semesters."

9. Use Clear and Concise Language
Tip:
Avoid jargon or overly complex language. Write in a way that is professional but accessible to reviewers unfamiliar with your program.
Example:
Instead of: *"Our pedagogical framework leverages a multimodal approach to foster cognitive synthesis in interprofessional competencies,"*
Write: *"Our program uses diverse teaching methods, such as hands-on simulations and interprofessional workshops, to improve teamwork and problem-solving skills."*

10. Proofread and Edit Thoroughly
Tip:
Errors in grammar, spelling, or formatting can detract from your program's professionalism. Have multiple people review the report for accuracy and clarity.
Example:
Enlist colleagues, administrators, or an external consultant to provide feedback on content and presentation before submission.

11. Incorporate Visuals and Summaries

Tip:
Use tables, charts, and infographics to present data succinctly. Include executive summaries at the beginning of sections to provide an overview.
Example:
A bar chart showing learner satisfaction scores over five years can quickly convey trends without requiring lengthy explanations.

12. End with a Forward-Looking Statement
Tip:
Conclude the report with a summary of your program's commitment to improvement and its goals for the future.
Example:
"Our program remains committed to excellence in healthcare simulation education. In the next five years, we plan to expand interprofessional simulation opportunities, incorporate cutting-edge technology such as AI-driven simulation, and enhance faculty development initiatives."

Appendix G

Sample CQI Plans

Sample CQI Plan 1: Enhancing Learner Performance
Objective:
Improve learner performance in critical simulation scenarios by 20% within 6 months.
Goals:
1. Identify gaps in learner skills and knowledge.
2. Provide targeted feedback to learners.
3. Monitor improvement trends over time.

Key Actions:
1. **Assessment Phase:**
    - Conduct pre-simulation knowledge and skill assessments.
    - Identify common challenges and errors in existing simulations.
2. **Intervention Phase:**
    - Develop targeted debriefing strategies emphasizing areas of improvement.
    - Provide learners with supplementary training materials, such as videos or handouts.
3. **Evaluation Phase:**
    - Implement post-simulation assessments to measure improvement.
    - Analyze performance data monthly.

Metrics:
- Pre- and post-simulation performance scores.
- Learner satisfaction with simulation-based training (measured via surveys).
- Number of critical errors reduced.

Responsible Parties:
- Simulation program manager.
- Instructors/facilitators.
- Data analyst.

Sample CQI Plan 2: Enhancing Simulation Scenario Realism
Objective:
Increase scenario realism by incorporating cutting-edge technology and updated protocols within the next year.

Goals:
1. Align scenarios with current industry standards and best practices.
2. Incorporate realistic equipment and environmental factors.

Key Actions:
1. **Review Phase:**
    - Conduct a literature review on best practices for high-fidelity simulations.
    - Gather feedback from stakeholders (learners, instructors, healthcare professionals).
2. **Development Phase:**
    - Upgrade simulation manikins and equipment.
    - Update simulation scripts to reflect the latest clinical guidelines.
3. **Implementation Phase:**
    - Pilot revised scenarios with a select group of learners.
    - Adjust scenarios based on pilot feedback.

Metrics:
- Feedback scores on scenario realism.
- Participant engagement levels during simulations.
- Alignment of scenarios with updated clinical protocols.

Responsible Parties:
- Simulation program coordinator.
- Technology specialist.
- Clinical advisors.

Sample CQI Plan 3: Improving Instructor Performance

Objective:
Enhance instructor facilitation skills through training and peer review by the end of the next quarter.

Goals:
1. Develop a standardized training program for simulation instructors.
2. Implement a peer-review system to provide constructive feedback.

Key Actions:
1. **Training Phase:**
    - Conduct workshops focused on debriefing techniques and learner engagement.
    - Provide access to online resources for skill development.
2. **Feedback Phase:**
    - Pair instructors for peer observation during simulations.
    - Use structured evaluation tools to assess performance.
3. **Recognition Phase:**
    - Recognize and reward instructors who demonstrate outstanding facilitation skills.

Metrics:
- Instructor evaluation scores (pre- and post-training).
- Peer review participation rates and feedback quality.

- Learner satisfaction with instructor performance.

Responsible Parties:
- Simulation training coordinator.
- Instructor peer review committee.
- Professional development team.

Appendix H

Sample Rubrics

Sample Rubric 1: Learner Performance in Simulation

Criteria	Excellent (4)	Good (3)	Satisfactory (2)	Needs Improvement (1)
Clinical Knowledge	Demonstrates comprehensive understanding and applies it accurately in all scenarios.	Shows good understanding but minor gaps in application.	Basic understanding; requires significant prompts or guidance.	Limited understanding; major errors or misconceptions.
Decision-Making	Consistently makes timely and effective decisions.	Decisions are generally appropriate but may lack efficiency.	Makes decisions with noticeable hesitation or errors.	Struggles to make decisions or makes inappropriate choices.
Communication Skills	Communicates clearly, effectively, and respectfully with the team and patient.	Communication is clear but occasionally lacks precision or confidence.	Basic communication; noticeable gaps in clarity or engagement.	Poor communication; unclear or inappropriate interactions.
Technical Skills	Executes all procedural and technical tasks flawlessly.	Performs most tasks well but has minor errors.	Struggles with some tasks; requires frequent assistance.	Unable to perform key tasks independently or safely.
Teamwork	Consistently collaborates and supports the team effectively.	Collaborates well but occasionally misses opportunities to engage.	Participates but shows limited teamwork or collaboration.	Does not engage effectively; disrupts team dynamics.

Sample Rubric 2: Scenario Design

Criteria	Excellent (4)	Good (3)	Satisfactory (2)	Needs Improvement (1)
Realism	Scenario reflects high fidelity and aligns with real-world practice.	Scenario is realistic but with minor gaps in detail.	Scenario is somewhat realistic but lacks depth or alignment with practice.	Scenario lacks realism; contains significant inaccuracies.
Learning Objectives	Objectives are clear, measurable, and fully aligned with the scenario.	Objectives are clear but not completely measurable or aligned.	Objectives are vague or inconsistently aligned with the scenario.	Objectives are unclear or unrelated to the scenario.

ACHIEVING PROGRAM ACCREDITATION FOR HEALTHCARE
SIMULATION PROGRAMS: A Resource Guide

Criteria	Excellent (4)	Good (3)	Satisfactory (2)	Needs Improvement (1)
Engagement	Scenario consistently engages participants and maintains interest.	Scenario is engaging but has occasional lulls in activity.	Scenario is somewhat engaging but participants lose focus at times.	Scenario fails to engage participants; lacks structure or flow.
Complexity	Scenario provides appropriate challenge for the target audience.	Scenario is slightly too easy or difficult for participants.	Scenario is overly simplistic or unnecessarily complex.	Scenario is poorly matched to participants' skill levels.
Debriefing Support	Scenario includes comprehensive debriefing tools and prompts.	Scenario has adequate debriefing tools but lacks depth.	Limited debriefing tools provided; lacks structure.	No debriefing tools or prompts included.

Sample Rubric 3: Instructor Evaluation

Criteria	Excellent (4)	Good (3)	Satisfactory (2)	Needs Improvement (1)
Facilitation Skills	Effectively engages learners, balances discussion, and maintains focus.	Engages learners well but occasionally struggles with time or focus.	Limited engagement or difficulty managing discussions.	Ineffective facilitation; learners are disengaged or confused.
Feedback Quality	Provides specific, constructive, and actionable feedback.	Feedback is constructive but lacks specificity or depth.	Feedback is vague or not actionable.	Feedback is unclear, overly critical, or unhelpful.
Scenario Management	Manages scenario flow seamlessly and adjusts dynamically as needed.	Manages scenario well but occasionally struggles with adjustments.	Has difficulty maintaining scenario flow or adjusting appropriately.	Scenario is poorly managed; significant issues disrupt learning.
Technical Proficiency	Operates simulation technology confidently and resolves issues quickly.	Operates technology well but with occasional delays or errors.	Basic proficiency; struggles with some aspects of technology.	Lacks proficiency; significant delays or errors in operation.
Professionalism	Consistently models professionalism and respect.	Generally professional but with occasional lapses.	Professionalism is inconsistent.	Lacks professionalism; inappropriate behavior or attitude.

Sample Rubric 4: Simulation Program Evaluation

Criteria	Excellent (4)	Good (3)	Satisfactory (2)	Needs Improvement (1)
Program Relevance	Program consistently meets current clinical and educational needs.	Program is relevant but could address emerging needs more effectively.	Program is somewhat relevant but lacks updates.	Program is outdated or fails to meet current needs.

Criteria	Excellent (4)	Good (3)	Satisfactory (2)	Needs Improvement (1)
Participant Outcomes	Participants consistently show significant knowledge and skill improvement.	Participants show noticeable improvement but with gaps.	Improvement is minimal or inconsistent.	No noticeable improvement; participants are dissatisfied.
Resource Allocation	Resources are used effectively and efficiently.	Resources are used well but with minor inefficiencies.	Resource use is inconsistent or occasionally wasteful.	Resources are poorly allocated; frequent shortages or waste.
Stakeholder Engagement	Stakeholders are actively involved and provide positive feedback.	Stakeholders are engaged but with occasional communication gaps.	Limited stakeholder involvement or mixed feedback.	Stakeholders are disengaged or provide negative feedback.
CQI Integration	Program has a strong CQI plan with measurable outcomes.	CQI plan is in place but lacks robust metrics.	CQI plan is limited or inconsistently implemented.	No CQI plan or evidence of quality improvement efforts.

Appendix I

Sample Student Feedback Form

This form is designed to gather feedback from students about their experience with the simulation activity. Your responses will help us improve the quality and effectiveness of our simulation program.

Student Information
Date of Simulation: _____
Course Title: _____
Simulation Title/Scenario Name: _____
Level of Learner (e.g., Undergraduate, Graduate): _____

Section 1: Simulation Experience
Please rate the following statements based on your experience with the simulation activity. Use the scale:
1 = **Strongly Disagree**
2 = **Disagree**
3 = **Neutral**
4 = **Agree**
5 = **Strongly Agree**

1. The simulation activity aligned with the stated learning objectives.
   1 | 2 | 3 | 4 | 5
2. The simulation scenario was realistic and engaging.
   1 | 2 | 3 | 4 | 5
3. I felt adequately prepared for the simulation.
   1 | 2 | 3 | 4 | 5
4. The simulation enhanced my understanding of the topic/skills.
   1 | 2 | 3 | 4 | 5
5. The simulation provided opportunities to apply critical thinking and decision-making skills.
   1 | 2 | 3 | 4 | 5
6. The simulation environment was supportive and promoted learning.
   1 | 2 | 3 | 4 | 5
7. I felt comfortable making mistakes and learning from them during the simulation.
   1 | 2 | 3 | 4 | 5

Section 2: Facilitation and Debriefing

1. The facilitator(s) provided clear instructions and guidance before the simulation.
   1 | 2 | 3 | 4 | 5
2. The facilitator(s) created a safe and supportive environment.
   1 | 2 | 3 | 4 | 5
3. The debriefing session helped me reflect on my performance and identify areas for improvement.
   1 | 2 | 3 | 4 | 5
4. The feedback provided during debriefing was constructive and actionable.
   1 | 2 | 3 | 4 | 5

Section 3: Skills and Confidence
1. The simulation activity improved my clinical skills (e.g., assessment, procedures, communication).
   1 | 2 | 3 | 4 | 5
2. The simulation increased my confidence in managing similar situations in real practice.
   1 | 2 | 3 | 4 | 5
3. I feel more prepared to work in a team-based healthcare setting.
   1 | 2 | 3 | 4 | 5

Section 4: Open-Ended Questions
1. **What did you find most valuable about this simulation activity?**

2. **What aspects of the simulation could be improved?**

3. **Were there any specific skills or knowledge areas you feel were not addressed but should be included?**

4. **Do you have any additional comments or suggestions?**

Section 5: Overall Rating
On a scale of 1 to 5, how would you rate your overall experience with this simulation activity?
1 (Poor) | 2 (Fair) | 3 (Good) | 4 (Very Good) | 5 (Excellent)

Thank You!
Your feedback is essential in helping us improve the quality of our simulation activities. Please submit this form to the designated collection point or electronically through the provided platform.

Appendix J

Sample SET-M Feedback Form

The Simulation Effectiveness Tool-Modified (SET-M) measures learners' perceptions of simulation effectiveness in achieving learning outcomes. Below is a sample SET-M template tailored for a healthcare simulation program.

Simulation Effectiveness Tool-Modified (SET-M)
Participant Information:
- Date of Simulation: _____
- Program/Discipline: _____
- Level of Learner: _____
- Simulation Title: _____

Instructions:
Please indicate the extent to which you agree with each statement below by circling the number that best represents your level of agreement. Use the following scale:
1 = **Strongly Disagree**
2 = **Disagree**
3 = **Neutral**
4 = **Agree**
5 = **Strongly Agree**

Section 1: Learning Outcomes
1. The simulation helped me understand the clinical concepts and skills being taught.
   1 | 2 | 3 | 4 | 5
2. The simulation provided opportunities to practice critical thinking and decision-making skills.
   1 | 2 | 3 | 4 | 5
3. The simulation experience enhanced my ability to apply theoretical knowledge to a clinical situation.
   1 | 2 | 3 | 4 | 5
4. The learning objectives of the simulation were clearly stated and met.
   1 | 2 | 3 | 4 | 5

Section 2: Realism and Engagement

5. The simulation environment (e.g., manikins, props, setting) was realistic and supported my learning.
   1 | 2 | 3 | 4 | 5
6. The roles and actions of facilitators or standardized patients enhanced the realism of the simulation.
   1 | 2 | 3 | 4 | 5
7. I felt engaged and actively involved throughout the simulation.
   1 | 2 | 3 | 4 | 5
8. The simulation created a safe environment where I felt comfortable to learn and make mistakes.
   1 | 2 | 3 | 4 | 5

Section 3: Communication and Teamwork

9. The simulation improved my ability to communicate effectively with the healthcare team.
   1 | 2 | 3 | 4 | 5
10. The simulation provided opportunities to practice interprofessional collaboration.
    1 | 2 | 3 | 4 | 5
11. The simulation helped me develop strategies to manage team dynamics and conflict resolution.
    1 | 2 | 3 | 4 | 5

Section 4: Debriefing and Feedback

12. The debriefing session provided valuable feedback to enhance my learning.
    1 | 2 | 3 | 4 | 5
13. The debriefing process allowed me to reflect on my actions and identify areas for improvement.
    1 | 2 | 3 | 4 | 5
14. The facilitators guided the debriefing effectively, creating a positive and supportive environment.
    1 | 2 | 3 | 4 | 5
15. I felt the feedback was specific, actionable, and aligned with the learning objectives.
    1 | 2 | 3 | 4 | 5

Section 5: Overall Experience

16. The simulation experience was effective in preparing me for clinical practice.
    1 | 2 | 3 | 4 | 5
17. I would recommend this simulation experience to other learners.
    1 | 2 | 3 | 4 | 5
18. The simulation increased my confidence in handling similar clinical scenarios in real practice.
    1 | 2 | 3 | 4 | 5

Open-Ended Questions:
1. **What aspects of the simulation were most beneficial to your learning?**

2. **What aspects of the simulation could be improved?**

3. **Do you have any additional comments or suggestions?**

Scoring and Analysis
1. **Quantitative Analysis:**
    - Calculate average scores for each section to identify strengths and areas for improvement.
2. **Qualitative Analysis:**
    - Review open-ended responses to gain insights into learner perceptions and potential program enhancements.

This SET-M template provides a structured approach to evaluating simulation effectiveness. It ensures that programs gather meaningful data to drive continuous improvement and meet accreditation standards.

KEITH A. BEAULIEU

Appendix K

Sample Mock Review Interview Template

This template provides a structured format for conducting a mock review interview for a simulation program. It is designed to simulate an accreditation site visit, enabling program leaders, faculty, and staff to practice answering questions and presenting evidence in accordance with accreditation standards.

Mock Review Interview Template
Program Name: *e.g., Clinical Simulation Program for Nursing Education*

Date of Mock Review: *MM/DD/YYYY*
Interview Panel:
- Lead Reviewer: *[Name and Role]*
- Panel Member 1: *[Name and Role]*
- Panel Member 2: *[Name and Role]*

Participants Being Interviewed:
- *e.g., Program Director, Simulation Specialist, Faculty Member, Learner Representative*

1. Interview Agenda

Time	Session	Participants	Location
9:00–9:30 AM	Welcome and Program Overview	Program Director	Conference Room
9:30–10:15 AM	Governance and Strategic Planning	Leadership Team	Conference Room
10:15–11:00 AM	Curriculum and Learning Objectives	Faculty	Simulation Lab
11:00–11:30 AM	Break		
11:30–12:15 PM	Resource Management and CQI	Operations Team	Simulation Lab
12:15–12:45 PM	Learner Feedback and Experience	Learner Representatives	Classroom

ACHIEVING PROGRAM ACCREDITATION FOR HEALTHCARE
SIMULATION PROGRAMS: A Resource Guide

Time	Session	Participants	Location
12:45–1:00 PM	Closing Remarks and Next Steps	Review Panel & All Staff	Conference Room

2. Interview Questions
A. Governance and Strategic Planning
1. Can you describe the governance structure of your simulation program?
2. How does the strategic plan guide the program's priorities and activities?
3. What is the process for reviewing and updating the mission and vision statements?
4. How do you involve stakeholders, such as faculty and learners, in decision-making?

B. Curriculum and Educational Objectives
1. How do you align simulation activities with the program's learning objectives?
2. Can you share an example of a scenario that supports interprofessional education?
3. How do you ensure that simulation scenarios are evidence-based and updated regularly?
4. How do you measure whether learners achieve the intended outcomes?

C. Assessment and Evaluation
1. What tools or methods do you use to assess learner performance?
2. How do you ensure fairness and consistency in evaluations?
3. How do you use learner performance data to improve the program?
4. Can you provide an example of how feedback has informed changes to assessments?

D. Faculty and Staff Development
1. What training opportunities are available for faculty and staff?
2. How do you ensure faculty are prepared for debriefing sessions?
3. What certifications (e.g., CHSE, CHSOS) have faculty members achieved?
4. How do you support professional development in simulation education?

E. Resource Management and Facilities
1. How do you ensure the simulation lab is adequately equipped to meet educational needs?
2. What is the process for maintaining and upgrading simulation equipment?

3. How do you allocate resources for different simulation activities?
   4. Can you describe any partnerships or funding sources that support the program?
F. **Continuous Quality Improvement (CQI)**
   1. What data do you collect to evaluate program effectiveness?
   2. Can you provide an example of an improvement made based on CQI findings?
   3. How do you document and share CQI outcomes with stakeholders?
   4. How does your CQI process align with accreditation standards?
G. **Learner Feedback and Experience**
   1. How do learners prepare for simulation activities?
   2. What feedback mechanisms are in place for learners to share their experiences?
   3. Can you provide examples of changes implemented based on learner feedback?
   4. How do you support learners who may feel stressed or overwhelmed during simulations?

3. Evidence Presentation
Instructions for Participants: Prepare to provide evidence that supports your responses. Examples of evidence include:
- Strategic plan documents.
- Organizational charts.
- Curriculum materials and simulation scenarios.
- Assessment rubrics and learner feedback forms.
- CQI reports and action plans.
- Equipment maintenance logs and resource inventories.

Reviewer Notes Section:

Question	Key Points	Supporting Evidence Provided	Follow-Up Needed
Question 1	Example notes.	Example evidence.	Example follow-up.

4. Feedback and Evaluation
After the mock interview, the review panel should provide constructive feedback based on the following criteria:
- **Clarity of Responses**: Were answers clear, concise, and well-organized?
- **Alignment with Standards**: Did responses demonstrate alignment with accreditation requirements?

- **Use of Evidence**: Was sufficient documentation provided to support claims?
- **Collaboration**: Did participants demonstrate teamwork and shared understanding of program goals?
- **Readiness**: Were participants confident and well-prepared?

Feedback Summary Table:

Category	Strengths	Areas for Improvement
Governance and Planning	Well-defined leadership roles.	Provide more detailed stakeholder input.
Curriculum and Objectives	Clear alignment with competencies.	Include more examples of interprofessional scenarios.
Resource Management	Excellent maintenance documentation.	Enhance funding diversification strategies.

5. Next Steps
Action Plan:
- Schedule follow-up mock interviews to address identified gaps.
- Develop a checklist for any missing or incomplete evidence.
- Refine interview responses and rehearse with participants.

Deadline for Updates: *e.g., Complete all follow-up actions by MM/DD/YYYY.*

Appendix L

Sample Mock Interview Questions

Mock interviews are critical to accreditation preparation, helping faculty, staff, and stakeholders articulate the program's strengths, processes, and alignment with accreditation standards. Below is a list of sample questions categorized by topic, designed to help simulation programs prepare for accreditation site visits.

General Questions

1. Program Governance and Leadership
- Can you describe the governance structure of your simulation program?
- How does your leadership ensure alignment between the program's goals and the institution's mission?
- What mechanisms are in place to involve stakeholders, such as faculty and learners, in program decision-making?
- How do you handle conflict resolution within the simulation team?

2. Mission, Vision, and Strategic Plan
- What is the mission of your simulation program, and how does it guide your activities?
- Can you share your program's vision for the next five years?
- How do your strategic goals align with your mission and vision?
- What are some specific examples of how your strategic plan has been implemented?

3. Curriculum Design and Educational Objectives
- How do you ensure that simulation activities align with the program's learning objectives?
- Can you provide examples of how your simulation curriculum supports interprofessional education?

- How do you incorporate learner feedback into curriculum improvements?
- What processes are in place to ensure scenarios are up-to-date and evidence-based?

4. Assessment and Evaluation
- How do you assess learner performance during simulation activities?
- Can you provide examples of assessment tools or rubrics you use?
- What steps do you take to ensure consistency and fairness in evaluations?
- How do you evaluate the effectiveness of your simulation program?

5. Faculty Development
- What training opportunities are available for faculty and staff in simulation-based education?
- How do you support faculty pursuing certifications such as CHSE or CHSOS?
- Can you describe the onboarding process for new simulation educators or technologists?
- How do you ensure faculty are prepared to conduct effective debriefing sessions?

6. Resource Management
- How do you manage and maintain simulation equipment?
- Can you describe your process for allocating resources to various simulation activities?
- What strategies are in place for securing funding or partnerships to support the program?
- How do you ensure the simulation lab environment meets safety and operational standards?

7. Continuous Quality Improvement (CQI)
- Can you describe your program's CQI process?
- How do you collect and analyze data to inform program improvements?
- Can you share an example of a program improvement that resulted from CQI findings?
- How do you track and document the outcomes of CQI initiatives?

8. Accreditation Preparation
- What steps have you taken to prepare for accreditation?
- How do you ensure that documentation aligns with accreditation standards?
- What challenges have you faced in the accreditation process, and how have you addressed them?
- How does your program demonstrate compliance with specific accreditation criteria?

9. Learner Experience
- How do you ensure learners are adequately prepared for simulation activities?
- Can you describe how debriefing sessions are structured to maximize learning?
- How do you support learners who may struggle during simulation exercises?
- What feedback have you received from learners about the program, and how have you responded?

10. Innovation and Future Directions
- What innovative technologies or methods have you integrated into your simulation program?
- How do you stay current with advancements in simulation-based education?
- What plans do you have to expand or enhance the program in the future?
- How does your program contribute to research in simulation-based healthcare education?

11. Stakeholder Engagement
- How do you involve the program's external stakeholders, such as clinical partners?
- What feedback have you received from external stakeholders, and how have you acted on it?
- How do you communicate the program's impact to institutional leadership?
- Can you provide an example of a collaborative project or partnership with external organizations?

12. Addressing Challenges

- What are the biggest challenges your simulation program currently faces?
- How have you addressed issues related to staffing, funding, or resources?
- Can you describe a situation where a simulation activity didn't go as planned and how you handled it?
- How do you manage resistance to change among faculty or staff when implementing new initiatives?

Executive Leadership Questions

Here are **sample questions reviewers might ask C-suite leadership** (e.g., CEO, COO, CFO, or other senior executives) during a simulation program accreditation site visit. These questions focus on strategic oversight, resource commitment, and alignment with institutional goals:

1. Strategic Oversight
- How does the simulation program align with the organization's overarching mission and strategic priorities?
- What role does the simulation program play in advancing the institution's commitment to patient safety, clinical excellence, or interprofessional education?
- How do you ensure that the simulation program remains a strategic priority within the organization?
- How is the impact of the simulation program evaluated at the executive level?

2. Financial Commitment
- What is the organization's financial strategy for sustaining and expanding the simulation program?
- How are budget decisions for the simulation program integrated into the broader financial planning process?
- Can you provide examples of recent or planned capital investments in the simulation program (e.g., technology, facilities, staffing)?
- How does leadership ensure that funding allocations for simulation align with institutional goals and accreditation standards?

3. Resource Allocation and Support

- How do you prioritize the simulation program's needs when allocating resources across the organization?
- What systems are in place to ensure the program has access to cutting-edge technology and adequate infrastructure?
- How does leadership ensure that faculty and staff working in simulation are adequately supported with training and professional development opportunities?
- Are there contingency plans for addressing resource shortfalls in the simulation program?

4. Impact on Institutional Outcomes
- How does the simulation program contribute to the organization's key performance indicators, such as patient outcomes, learner satisfaction, or clinical competencies?
- Can you share specific examples of how the simulation program has improved patient safety, staff training, or operational efficiency?
- How do you assess the simulation program's return on investment (ROI) in terms of outcomes and organizational goals?

5. Stakeholder Engagement
- How does the organization engage with internal and external stakeholders (e.g., learners, faculty, healthcare partners) to ensure the simulation program meets their needs?
- What is your strategy for leveraging the simulation program to build external partnerships or collaborations?
- How does leadership ensure that the program's outcomes are effectively communicated to key stakeholders, including board members, funders, and the community?

6. Commitment to Accreditation and Quality
- Why is achieving accreditation for the simulation program important to the institution's leadership?
- How does the C-suite support the program in meeting accreditation standards?
- What resources or initiatives has senior leadership provided to ensure accreditation success?
- How will leadership ensure ongoing compliance and continuous quality improvement post-accreditation?

7. Innovation and Future Vision

- What role does leadership see the simulation program playing in the organization's future, particularly in advancing innovation and adapting to emerging trends in healthcare education?
- How does the organization encourage the simulation program to explore innovative practices, such as integrating AI, virtual reality, or advanced analytics?
- What is your vision for the simulation program in the next five to ten years, and how do you plan to support its growth and evolution?

8. Institutional Integration
- How does the simulation program integrate with other organizational departments or initiatives, such as clinical training, quality improvement, or community outreach?
- What strategies are in place to ensure cross-departmental collaboration and maximize the simulation program's impact?
- How does leadership ensure that the simulation program supports the organization's accreditation and regulatory compliance goals?

Staff Questions

Here are **sample questions reviewers might ask staff and simulation technicians** during a simulation program accreditation site visit. These questions assess their roles, expertise, and alignment with accreditation standards:

1. Roles and Responsibilities
- Can you describe your specific role within the simulation program?
- How do you contribute to the day-to-day operations of the simulation program?
- What are your responsibilities in maintaining and setting up simulation equipment and environments?
- How do you collaborate with faculty and educators to support simulation activities?

2. Training and Professional Development
- What training or certifications have you completed to support your role (e.g., Certified Healthcare Simulation Operations Specialist (CHSOS), equipment-specific training)?

- How does the organization support your professional development, such as attending conferences, workshops, or pursuing certifications?
- Can you describe a recent professional development opportunity you participated in and how it enhanced your role?
- How do you stay updated on the latest technologies and best practices in simulation?

3. Simulation Operations and Maintenance
- How do you ensure that simulation equipment is functional and ready?
- Can you describe your process for performing routine maintenance and addressing equipment malfunctions?
- What procedures are in place to ensure simulation environments are safe, clean, and realistic for learners?
- How do you handle challenges or technical difficulties during simulation sessions?

4. Collaboration and Teamwork
- How do you work with faculty, educators, and learners to ensure the success of simulation activities?
- Can you provide an example of how you collaborated with a team member to resolve an issue or improve a simulation experience?
- How do you ensure that the simulation setup aligns with the learning objectives or scenario design provided by faculty?

5. Quality Assurance and Improvement
- What is your role in the program's continuous quality improvement (CQI) efforts?
- How do you collect and analyze feedback related to simulation operations and use it to make improvements?
- Can you share an example of a change or improvement you implemented based on feedback or operational needs?
- How do you ensure equipment and processes meet safety and accreditation standards?

6. Learner and Faculty Support
- How do you assist learners and faculty during simulation sessions?
- What role do you play in troubleshooting technical issues during live simulations?

- How do you ensure faculty and learners are comfortable using the simulation technology and equipment?
- How do you handle learner feedback related to simulation operations or environments?

7. Alignment with Accreditation Standards
- How familiar are you with the program's accreditation requirements, particularly those related to your role?
- What steps have you taken to ensure that simulation operations and equipment meet accreditation standards?
- Can you describe how you document simulation equipment maintenance, repairs, or updates?
- How do you contribute to preparing for accreditation site visits, such as organizing records or demonstrating equipment functionality?

8. Technology and Innovation
- What types of simulation technology and equipment are you responsible for, and how do you ensure they are used effectively?
- How do you integrate new technologies into the program, such as virtual or augmented reality?
- Can you provide an example of a recent technological upgrade or innovation and how you supported its implementation?

9. Challenges and Problem-Solving
- What is the most common challenge you face in your role, and how do you address it?
- Can you describe when you resolved a significant technical issue during a simulation session?
- How do you handle unexpected issues, such as equipment failure, while ensuring minimal disruption to learning?

10. Vision and Program Impact
- How do you see your role evolving as the simulation program grows?
- What do you think is the most important contribution simulation technicians make to the program's success?
- How do you ensure your work aligns with the program's mission and goals?

Faculty Questions

Here are **sample questions reviewers might ask faculty who teach in simulation** during a simulation program accreditation site visit. These questions are designed to evaluate their teaching practices, expertise, and alignment with the program's goals and accreditation standards.

1. Roles and Responsibilities
- What is your role in designing and facilitating simulation-based learning activities?
- How do you align simulation scenarios with course objectives and competency frameworks?
- Can you describe how you integrate simulation into the broader curriculum or clinical training program?
- What is your approach to engaging learners during simulation sessions?

2. Scenario Development and Implementation
- How do you develop simulation scenarios, and what factors do you consider in their design?
- Can you provide an example of a simulation scenario you created and how it addresses specific learner objectives?
- How do you determine the appropriate level of fidelity for each scenario?
- What steps do you take to ensure the scenarios are realistic and relevant to learners' future clinical roles?

3. Facilitation and Learner Engagement
- What facilitation techniques do you use to ensure learners are actively engaged in simulation activities?
- How do you tailor your facilitation style to accommodate diverse learner needs and experience levels?
- Can you describe a situation where you adapted your facilitation approach during a simulation session based on learner feedback or performance?
- How do you encourage critical thinking, teamwork, and decision-making in simulation-based learning?

4. Debriefing and Feedback
- What debriefing framework(s) do you use (e.g., PEARLS, GAS), and why?
- How do you ensure that debriefing sessions are learner-centered and promote reflective learning?

- Can you share an example of how you provided constructive feedback to learners during a debriefing session?
- How do you address challenges or conflicts that arise during debriefing?

5. Learner Assessment and Outcomes
- How do you assess learner performance during simulation activities?
- What tools or rubrics do you use to evaluate clinical skills, teamwork, or communication?
- Can you describe how you use assessment data to inform future simulations or learner feedback?
- How do you track and evaluate the impact of simulation activities on learner outcomes over time?

6. Faculty Development and Collaboration
- What training or certifications have you completed to enhance your teaching in simulation (e.g., CHSE, faculty development workshops)?
- How do you collaborate with other faculty or simulation staff to improve scenarios or teaching practices?
- What professional development opportunities have you pursued to stay current with simulation-based education best practices?
- How do you share your experiences and insights with colleagues to advance simulation pedagogy?

7. Alignment with Accreditation Standards
- How do you ensure your teaching practices align with the program's mission, goals, and accreditation standards?
- What role do you play in ensuring the program meets accreditation requirements related to curriculum design and learner outcomes?
- Can you provide examples of how your simulation activities contribute to the program's commitment to continuous quality improvement (CQI)?
- How do you document and report your contributions to simulation education for accreditation purposes?

8. Challenges and Problem-Solving
- What challenges have you faced while teaching in simulation, and how did you overcome them?

- Can you describe a time when you had to adapt a simulation activity on short notice to address unexpected issues?
- How do you manage resistance or anxiety among learners during simulation sessions?
- What strategies do you use to ensure learners feel supported while being challenged in simulation activities?

9. Impact on Learner Development
- How do you measure the effectiveness of simulation in improving learner knowledge, skills, and confidence?
- Can you share a success story where simulation significantly impacted a learner's clinical performance or professional growth?
- How do you ensure that simulation activities prepare learners for real-world clinical challenges?
- What feedback have you received from learners about your simulation teaching, and how have you used it to improve?

10. Vision and Future Goals
- How do you see your role evolving as the simulation program grows and develops?
- What innovative teaching practices or technologies do you hope to incorporate into your simulation sessions in the future?
- How do you plan to contribute to the simulation program's goals and long-term success?
- What do you believe is the most significant benefit of simulation-based education for learners?

Clinical Instructor Questions

Role and Responsibilities
1. What is your role in facilitating clinical activities within the simulation program?
2. How do you ensure that clinical scenarios align with the real-world experiences learners will encounter in practice?
3. What steps do you take to ensure that learners achieve the desired clinical competencies during simulation activities?
4. How do you balance the dual responsibilities of being a clinical instructor and a simulation educator?

Scenario Design and Implementation

5. How involved are you in designing clinical scenarios for the simulation program?
6. Can you provide an example of a clinical scenario you've developed or facilitated and its learning objectives?
7. How do you ensure that scenarios accurately reflect current clinical practices and evidence-based guidelines?
8. How do you determine the appropriate level of fidelity for clinical scenarios to match learner needs?

Learner Engagement
9. What strategies do you use to engage learners during clinical simulation activities?
10. How do you ensure that learners remain focused and take simulation scenarios seriously?
11. How do you encourage learners to reflect on their clinical decision-making during debriefing sessions?
12. How do you address learners' emotional reactions to challenging or high-stakes clinical scenarios?

Clinical Skills and Competency Assessment
13. How do you assess learners' clinical skills during simulation activities?
14. What tools or frameworks do you use to evaluate learners' performance in clinical scenarios (e.g., checklists, rubrics)?
15. How do you provide feedback to learners to help them improve their clinical skills?
16. Can you share an example of a time when a learner struggled during a clinical simulation and how you handled the situation?

Integration with Clinical Practice
17. How does the simulation program bridge the gap between simulated clinical activities and real-world practice?
18. Do you collaborate with clinical partners or institutions to ensure the scenarios align with current industry standards?
19. How do you incorporate interprofessional collaboration into clinical simulation activities?
20. What role do clinical simulation activities play in preparing learners for clinical rotations or actual patient care?

Debriefing and Reflection
21. What debriefing models do you use after clinical simulation activities (e.g., PEARLS, GAS)?

22. How do you guide learners in reflecting on their clinical decisions and actions during debriefing?
23. Can you describe how you handle situations where learners struggle to identify their own errors during debriefing?
24. How do you ensure that debriefing focuses on constructive feedback and fosters a growth mindset?

Collaboration and Communication
25. How do you collaborate with other faculty or simulation staff to plan and implement clinical activities?
26. Do you involve clinical partners or subject matter experts in the development or facilitation of clinical simulations?
27. How do you communicate learning objectives and expectations to learners before clinical simulation activities?
28. What role does learner feedback play in shaping or improving clinical simulation activities

Use of Technology and Resources
29. What simulation technologies or tools do you use to support clinical activities?
30. How do you incorporate simulation equipment, such as manikins or virtual reality, into clinical training?
31. What challenges have you faced with technology during clinical simulations, and how did you address them?
32. How do you ensure that learners are comfortable using technology in clinical simulations?

Continuous Improvement
33. How do you evaluate the effectiveness of clinical simulation activities?
34. What feedback mechanisms do you use to assess whether clinical activities meet learner needs and program goals?
35. Can you share an example of how you've improved a clinical simulation activity based on learner feedback or outcomes?
36. What ongoing training or professional development do you pursue to stay current in clinical education and simulation practices?

Program Alignment and Accreditation
37. How do the clinical activities you facilitate align with the program's mission and goals?
38. How do you ensure that clinical simulations meet accreditation standards for quality and effectiveness?

39. What role do clinical activities play in preparing learners for high-stakes assessments or certification exams?
40. What would you identify as the strengths and areas for improvement in the program's approach to clinical simulation?

Learner Questions

Here are **sample questions reviewers might ask learners and students** during a simulation program accreditation site visit. These questions assess the learners' perspectives on the program, its impact on their education, and alignment with accreditation standards.

1. General Experience with Simulation
- How have simulation activities been integrated into your curriculum or training program?
- Can you describe your experience participating in a simulation session?
- What do you find most valuable about learning through simulation?
- How do simulation activities help you feel better prepared for clinical practice?

2. Scenario Relevance and Realism
- How realistic are the scenarios you encounter in simulation sessions?
- Can you provide an example of a simulation activity that felt particularly relevant to your future clinical role?
- How well do the simulation scenarios reflect real-world healthcare situations?
- Are the simulation activities tailored to your current level of knowledge and skills?

3. Skills Development
- How has simulation helped you develop specific skills, such as clinical decision-making, teamwork, or communication?
- Can you share an example of a skill or competency you improved through simulation?
- How has simulation influenced your ability to work under pressure or manage critical situations?
- Do you feel more confident in your clinical skills after participating in simulation activities?

4. Feedback and Debriefing
- How does the debriefing process after a simulation session help you reflect on your performance?
- What kind of feedback do you receive from faculty or peers during debriefing?
- Do you feel that the feedback provided during debriefing is constructive and actionable?
- Can you share an example of how feedback from a simulation session helped you improve?

5. Assessment and Evaluation
- How are your skills and performance assessed during simulation sessions?
- Do you feel that the evaluation criteria used in simulation activities are clear and fair?
- Have you received feedback or scores on your performance that you found helpful for improvement?
- How does the program ensure that your learning needs are met through simulation?

6. Program Support and Resources
- Do you feel that the simulation facilities and equipment are adequate to support your learning?
- How accessible are simulation resources, such as practice labs or faculty guidance, outside of scheduled sessions?
- Have you experienced any issues with simulation technology, and if so, how were they resolved?
- What additional resources or support do you think could enhance your simulation experience?

7. Collaboration and Teamwork
- How do simulation activities encourage teamwork and interprofessional collaboration?
- Can you describe a simulation scenario where you worked as part of a team?
- How has simulation helped you understand the roles of other healthcare professionals?
- What have you learned about communication and collaboration through simulation?

8. Alignment with Learning Objectives

- How well do simulation activities align with the learning objectives for your program?
- Do you feel that simulation prepares you for assessments or clinical rotations?
- How do simulation activities address critical areas like patient safety or ethical decision-making?
- Are the scenarios designed to meet your educational and career goals?

9. Learner Satisfaction
- What do you enjoy most about participating in simulation sessions?
- Are there any aspects of the simulation program you find challenging or frustrating?
- How would you rate your overall satisfaction with the simulation program?
- What suggestions do you have for improving the simulation program?

10. Personal Growth and Future Impact
- How has simulation influenced your confidence in handling real-world clinical challenges?
- Can you share an example of how simulation helped you succeed in a clinical setting?
- What do you believe is the most significant benefit of simulation-based education for your future career?
- How do you plan to apply the skills and knowledge you've gained through simulation in your professional practice?

Standardized Patient Questions

Here are some sample questions that site reviewers might ask **Standardized Patients (SPs)** during a simulation program accreditation site visit. These questions assess the SPs' preparation, training, understanding of their roles, and how they contribute to the program's educational goals.

Training and Preparation
1. How were you trained for your role as a Standardized Patient (SP)?
    - Follow-up: Were you provided with scripts, scenarios, or performance guidelines?

2. What kind of feedback do you receive after your sessions?
   - Follow-up: How does this feedback help you improve your performance?
3. Can you describe the preparation process for a specific simulation scenario?
   - Follow-up: How much time do you typically spend preparing for a scenario?

Role Execution and Scenario Fidelity
4. How do you ensure your portrayal is consistent across multiple sessions?
5. What steps do you take if a scenario requires you to improvise within defined parameters?
6. How do you handle unexpected questions or behaviors from learners during simulations?
7. Can you share an example of how you maintained the realism of a scenario despite challenges?

Debriefing and Feedback
8. Are you involved in the debriefing process with learners?
   - Follow-up: If so, what is your role during debriefing?
9. How do you contribute feedback to learners about their performance?
   - Follow-up: Do you feel your feedback is valued by the program and learners?

Support and Professional Development
10. What support do you receive from the program to succeed in your role?
11. Are you given opportunities for professional development or additional training as an SP?
12. Do you feel adequately equipped to portray diverse patient scenarios, including cultural or linguistic variations?

Alignment with Program Goals
13. How do you see your role contributing to the learning objectives of the simulation program?
14. Are you familiar with the program's mission and vision? If so, how do you feel your work aligns with these goals?
15. Have you participated in scenarios designed to align with accreditation standards or specific program competencies?
    - Follow-up: Can you provide an example?

Ethical and Professional Considerations

16. How do you ensure patient confidentiality and professionalism during learner interactions?
17. What strategies do you use to maintain emotional boundaries while portraying emotionally intense scenarios?
18. Have you encountered any ethical challenges as an SP, and if so, how were they resolved?

Feedback and Continuous Improvement

19. Are you given opportunities to provide feedback on the scenarios or the program's operations?
20. Have you seen changes implemented based on feedback from SPs like yourself?

Faculty Questions (specific to assessment and evaluation)

General Philosophy and Approach

1. How does your program ensure that assessments align with learning objectives and desired competencies?
2. What frameworks or models (e.g., Kirkpatrick, Miller's Pyramid) do you use to structure your assessment and evaluation processes?
3. How do you balance formative and summative assessments in your simulation program?

Tools and Methods

4. What types of assessment tools (e.g., checklists, rubrics, OSCEs) are used to evaluate learner performance during simulations?
    - Follow-up: How were these tools developed or validated for use in your program?
5. Can you describe how you assess both technical and non-technical skills during a simulation?
6. How do you ensure objectivity and reliability in learner assessments, especially during high-stakes simulations?

Faculty Training and Calibration

7. What training do faculty members receive to ensure consistent and accurate assessment of learners?
    - Follow-up: Are calibration sessions conducted to align faculty scoring?
8. How do you handle discrepancies in evaluations among faculty assessors?

9. Are faculty required to maintain certifications, such as CHSE, to enhance assessment reliability and validity?

Learner Feedback
10. How do you provide learners feedback based on their simulation performance?
    o Follow-up: What strategies do you use to ensure feedback is constructive and actionable?
11. How do you engage learners in reflective practices after a simulation to complement the evaluation process?
12. Can you share an example of how feedback from a simulation session helped a learner improve?

Evaluation of Simulation Effectiveness
13. How do you assess the effectiveness of a simulation scenario in achieving its learning objectives?
14. What data do you collect to evaluate the overall impact of simulation activities on learner outcomes?
15. How do you use learner feedback to refine simulation scenarios and assessments?

Use of Data
16. How are assessment results documented and analyzed to track learner progress over time?
17. What role does data play in your program's quality improvement processes?
18. Can you provide an example of how assessment data has led to a significant program change or improvement?

Addressing Challenges
19. How do you handle situations where learners do not meet competency expectations in a simulation?
    o Follow-up: What remediation processes are in place?
20. How do you ensure inclusive and fair assessments for learners from diverse backgrounds?

Alignment with Accreditation Standards
21. How does your program ensure that assessment and evaluation practices align with accreditation standards?
22. What evidence do you provide to demonstrate that assessments are valid, reliable, and aligned with professional competencies?

Continuous Improvement

23. How do you review and update your assessment tools and strategies to keep pace with simulation and healthcare education advances?
24. Are faculty involved in research or initiatives to innovate assessment and evaluation methods in simulation?
25. How do you ensure that assessment practices support a culture of continuous improvement in both faculty and learners?

Faculty Questions (specific to systems integration activities)

General Understanding of Systems Integration
1. How does your program define and approach systems integration in the context of simulation?
2. What specific goals does your simulation program aim to achieve through systems integration activities?

Design and Implementation
3. Can you describe a recent systems based simulation activity designed to address organizational challenges (e.g., workflow optimization, patient safety)?
4. How do you ensure that systems integration simulations align with the healthcare institution's overall goals and priorities?
5. What interprofessional teams are typically involved in systems integration simulations, and how are their roles defined?
6. How do you incorporate realistic environmental and workflow conditions into systems-focused simulations?

Collaboration with Stakeholders
7. How do you engage stakeholders such as clinical leadership, IT teams, and quality improvement departments in systems integration activities?
8. What is the process for identifying systemic issues that can be addressed through simulation activities?
9. How do you involve participants from diverse professional backgrounds in the design and execution of systems-focused simulations?

Evaluation of Systems Integration Activities
10. What metrics or outcomes are used to evaluate the effectiveness of systems integration simulations?

11. Can you provide an example of how a systems-based simulation led to a measurable improvement in organizational processes?
12. How do you use systems-focused simulations to identify and mitigate latent safety threats?

Facilitation and Training
13. How are faculty trained to design and facilitate systems integration simulations?
14. What frameworks or methodologies (e.g., Lean, Six Sigma) are integrated into your systems-based simulations?
15. How do you ensure effective debriefing after systems integration simulations to capture actionable insights and foster interdisciplinary collaboration?

Feedback and Continuous Improvement
16. How do you collect and incorporate feedback from participants and stakeholders to refine systems-focused simulations?
17. Can you share an example of a systems-based simulation where feedback directly influenced subsequent program improvements?
18. How does your program ensure that identified system-level issues are communicated to and addressed by institutional leadership?

Integration with Quality and Safety Initiatives
19. How do systems integration activities support the institution's quality improvement or patient safety initiatives?
20. What role does your simulation program play in testing new processes, workflows, or technologies before their implementation in clinical practice?

Challenges and Solutions
21. What are the biggest challenges your faculty face when designing and conducting systems integration simulations, and how do you address them?
22. How do you balance the logistical and technical complexities of systems-based simulations with their educational objectives?

Alignment with Accreditation Standards
23. How do your systems integration activities align with accreditation standards and best practices?

24. What evidence do you provide to demonstrate the impact of systems-focused simulations on institutional outcomes and safety?

Examples and Case Studies
25. Can you describe a case where systems integration simulation uncovered a critical process gap and led to organizational change?
26. What is the most significant outcome or improvement your program has achieved through systems-based simulation activities?

Faculty Questions (specific to simulation-based research)

General Research Framework
1. What is the role of your simulation program in supporting research initiatives?
2. How do you align simulation-based research activities with the institution's overall priorities?
3. What are the main research themes or topics your simulation program focuses on (e.g., patient safety, interprofessional education, technology development)?

Research Design and Implementation
4. How are simulation-based research projects designed to address gaps in healthcare education, patient safety, or clinical outcomes?
5. Can you describe a recent research study in your simulation program, including its objectives, methodology, and findings?
6. What steps do you take to ensure the validity and reliability of data collected during simulation-based research?
7. How do you incorporate control measures in simulation research to eliminate biases?

Interdisciplinary Collaboration
8. How do you involve interdisciplinary teams in your simulation-based research initiatives?
9. What strategies do you use to foster collaboration between simulation faculty, clinical staff, and researchers from other disciplines?
10. Can you provide examples of partnerships with external organizations or institutions for simulation-based research?

Funding and Resource Allocation
11. How is simulation-based research funded within your program?
12. What resources (e.g., technology, staff, facilities) are allocated to support research activities, and how do you prioritize these resources?
13. Have you sought or received grants specifically for simulation-based research? If so, can you describe the grant objectives and outcomes?

Ethical Considerations and IRB Approvals
14. What processes are in place to ensure ethical standards are upheld in simulation-based research?
15. How do you manage Institutional Review Board (IRB) approvals for studies involving learners, faculty, or patients?
16. What steps do you take to protect participant confidentiality and ensure informed consent during simulation research?

Faculty and Staff Involvement
17. What role do faculty play in designing, implementing, and analyzing simulation-based research?
18. How are faculty trained to conduct high-quality simulation research?
19. What opportunities exist for faculty and staff to publish or present findings from simulation-based research?

Learner Involvement
20. How are learners involved in simulation-based research, and what safeguards are in place to prevent coercion?
21. Can you share an example of how learner feedback has informed the design or implementation of research studies?

Integration with Education and Practice
22. How does simulation-based research contribute to improving educational outcomes or clinical practices within your institution?
23. Can you provide an example of research findings that have directly influenced curriculum design or clinical protocols?
24. How are research findings disseminated to stakeholders, such as institutional leadership, clinical teams, or external partners?

Challenges and Solutions

25. What are the main challenges your faculty face in conducting simulation-based research, and how do you address them?
26. How do you balance research demands with teaching and operational responsibilities within the program?

Evaluation and Continuous Improvement
27. How do you measure the success or impact of your simulation-based research activities?
28. What systems are in place to evaluate the quality of research conducted in the simulation program?
29. Can you describe how research findings are used to inform future studies or improve simulation practices?

Innovation and Impact
30. What innovative research projects has your simulation program undertaken, and what were their outcomes?
31. Can you provide an example of a simulation-based research initiative that has had a measurable impact on healthcare education or patient safety?
32. How does your simulation program stay at the forefront of research trends and technologies in healthcare simulation?

Accreditation and Documentation
33. How do you document and showcase research activities for accreditation purposes?
34. What evidence do you provide to demonstrate the scholarly contributions of your faculty in simulation-based research?
35. How do you ensure your research aligns with accreditation standards and best practices in healthcare simulation?

Faculty Questions (specifically for fellowship and mentoring)

Program Structure and Objectives
1. What are the primary goals of your simulation fellowship program?
2. How does the fellowship align with the mission and vision of your simulation program?
3. What competencies or skills are fellows expected to develop during the fellowship?

4. How do you structure the fellowship program in terms of duration, curriculum, and learning activities?

Selection and Recruitment
5. What criteria do you use to select fellows for the simulation program?
6. How do you recruit candidates for the fellowship, and what strategies do you use to attract diverse applicants?
7. What is the typical profile of a fellow in your program (e.g., clinical background, prior experience, career goals)?

Fellowship Curriculum
8. What topics or skills are covered in the fellowship curriculum (e.g., scenario design, debriefing techniques, research)?
9. How do you incorporate hands-on simulation activities into the fellowship training?
10. What opportunities are provided for fellows to engage in teaching, research, or program development during the fellowship?

Mentoring Relationships
11. How are mentors assigned to fellows, and what qualifications do you look for in mentors?
12. What does a typical mentoring relationship look like in your fellowship program?
13. How do mentors provide feedback, guidance, and professional development support to fellows?

Assessment and Evaluation
14. How do you assess fellows' progress and competency throughout the program?
15. What tools or frameworks do you use to evaluate fellows' performance in key areas, such as scenario facilitation, debriefing, or research?
16. How do fellows receive feedback on their performance, and how is it used to support their growth?

Professional Development for Fellows
17. What opportunities do fellows have to present their work (e.g., conferences, workshops)?
18. How do you support fellows in achieving certifications, such as CHSE or CHSOS, during or after the fellowship?

19. What resources or funding are available to fellows for attending professional development events or pursuing advanced training?

Integration into the Simulation Program
20. How are fellows integrated into the broader activities of the simulation program?
21. What roles do fellows play in facilitating simulations, designing scenarios, or contributing to the program's strategic goals?
22. How do you ensure fellows are exposed to both clinical and educational aspects of simulation?

Fellowship Outcomes
23. What metrics do you use to evaluate the success of the fellowship program?
24. Can you share examples of where your fellows have gone after completing the program (e.g., leadership roles, academic appointments)?
25. How do you measure the long-term impact of the fellowship on fellows' careers and contributions to the field of simulation?

Mentoring Beyond the Fellowship
26. How do you maintain connections with fellows after they complete the program?
27. What ongoing mentoring or networking opportunities are available to alumni of the fellowship?
28. Do you track or document alumni achievements as part of your program's impact assessment?

Challenges and Continuous Improvement
29. What challenges have you encountered in running the fellowship program, and how have you addressed them?
30. How do you gather feedback from fellows about their experiences, and how is this feedback used to improve the program?
31. What initiatives have you implemented to enhance participants' fellowship or mentoring experience?

Accreditation and Documentation
32. How do you document fellowship and mentoring activities to meet accreditation standards?
33. What evidence do you provide to demonstrate the fellowship program's alignment with best practices in simulation education?

34. How do you ensure the fellowship program meets the expectations of accrediting bodies and advances the field of simulation education?

Faculty Engagement
35. What role do faculty play in shaping and delivering the fellowship program?
36. How do you train and support faculty who serve as mentors in the fellowship program?
37. How do faculty collaborate with fellows on projects, research, or other professional development activities?

Innovation and Impact
38. What innovations have you introduced to your fellowship or mentoring activities?
39. Can you share an example of a project or initiative developed by a fellow that has significantly impacted your simulation program?
40. How does your fellowship program contribute to advancing simulation-based education and research?

Fellow Questions

Fellowship Structure and Objectives
1. Can you describe the structure of your fellowship program and what you do on a typical day?
2. What were the primary goals of the fellowship, as explained to you during the onboarding process?
3. How well do you feel the fellowship aligns with its stated goals and objectives?
4. What competencies or skills have you developed during the fellowship?

Learning and Development
5. What specific areas of simulation have you been trained in (e.g., scenario design, debriefing, research, operations)?
6. What hands-on opportunities have you had to facilitate simulations or design scenarios?
7. How does the fellowship support your professional growth in simulation-based education or operations?
8. Have you received training in advanced debriefing techniques? If so, how has it impacted your practice?

Mentorship and Support

9. Who is your mentor in the fellowship program, and how often do you meet?
10. How has your mentor supported your learning and professional development?
11. Can you give an example of a time when your mentor provided guidance or feedback that significantly helped you?
12. Do you feel comfortable contacting faculty or staff for support when needed?

Assessment and Feedback

13. How is your performance as a fellow evaluated?
14. Do you receive regular feedback on your work? If so, how has this feedback helped you improve?
15. What tools or methods have assessed your progress during the fellowship (e.g., rubrics, performance reviews)?
16. How do you incorporate the feedback you receive into your practice or projects?

Opportunities for Growth

17. Have you had opportunities to attend conferences, workshops, or other professional development events?
18. Are you working toward any certifications, such as CHSE or CHSOS, as part of the fellowship?
19. What opportunities have you had to collaborate with other fellows, faculty, or external stakeholders?
20. Have you been encouraged to pursue research or scholarly projects during the fellowship? If yes, what support have you received?

Research and Scholarly Activities

21. Are you involved in any simulation-based research projects as part of your fellowship?
22. What resources or mentorship have been provided to support your research endeavors?
23. Have you had opportunities to present your work at conferences or publish in peer-reviewed journals?
24. Can you describe a research project or scholarly activity you're currently working on and how it aligns with the fellowship's goals?

Fellowship Experience

25. What has been the most rewarding aspect of your fellowship experience so far?
26. What challenges have you faced during the fellowship, and how were they addressed?
27. How has the fellowship prepared you for your future career in simulation or healthcare education?
28. Can you share an example of a project or simulation activity you've led or contributed to during the fellowship?

Integration and Collaboration
29. How are fellows integrated into the simulation program's operations and decision-making processes?
30. Do you feel like a valued member of the simulation team? Why or why not?
31. What opportunities have you had to work with interdisciplinary teams during the fellowship?

Continuous Improvement
32. How does the fellowship program incorporate your feedback as a fellow?
33. Have you had opportunities to suggest improvements to the program? If so, were those suggestions acted upon?
34. What changes or enhancements would you recommend for future fellows in this program?

Impact and Outcomes
35. How has the fellowship shaped your understanding of simulation-based education or healthcare simulation operations?
36. Do you feel more prepared to take on leadership roles in simulation after completing this fellowship? Why or why not?
37. What specific skills or experiences gained during the fellowship do you think will have the greatest impact on your career?
38. Would you recommend this fellowship to others interested in simulation? Why or why not?

Program Alignment with Goals
39. Do you feel the fellowship is meeting its stated goals? If not, where do you think it falls short?
40. How does the fellowship align with your personal and professional goals in simulation?

List of Figures

Figure 1 Steps to Perform a Gap Analysis 18
Figure 2 Steps to Engage Stakeholders 19
Figure 3 Steps to Evaluate Resources and Infrastructure 20
Figure 4 Steps for building a timeline 21
Figure 5 Steps to Assess Organizational Readiness 21
Figure 6 Developing a Strategic Plan 66
Figure 7 Steps for Conducting a Mock Review 104
Figure 8 Benefits of Maintaining Accreditation 126
Figure 9 Strategies for Maintaining Accreditation 129
Figure 10 The Mindset of Ongoing Preparation 132
Figure 11 Steps for Maintaining CQI 139

KEITH A. BEAULIEU

About the Author

Keith A. Beaulieu, MBA, CHSOS-A

Keith A. Beaulieu is an accomplished professional with extensive experience in healthcare simulation, accreditation management, and operational leadership. Currently serving as the Accreditation and Operations Manager at the Sue & Bill Gross School of Nursing, University of California, Irvine, Keith oversees accreditation processes and ensures operational excellence within the simulation programs.

With a career spanning over a decade in healthcare simulation, Keith has held pivotal roles, including Director of Operations for the Medical Education Simulation Center and Simulation Curriculum Coordinator at prominent institutions. His contributions have directly supported program growth, quality improvement, and alignment with accreditation standards. At the Sue & Bill Gross School of Nursing, Keith has ensured continued program accreditation and approval from the Commission on Collegiate Nursing Education (CCNE) and the California Board of Registered Nursing.

Keith is a Certified Healthcare Simulation Operations Specialist – Advanced (CHSOS-A) and a respected Society for Simulation in Healthcare (SSH) Accreditation Council member. He has performed over 30 accreditation site reviews globally for SSH, applying his expertise to enhance simulation programs across diverse healthcare settings. In addition to his site review experience, he has been instrumental in supporting accreditation research and standards development, contributing to the field's growth and innovation.

Keith is also a published author, contributing to **Achieving and Maintaining Accreditation for Nursing School Programs: A Comprehensive Guide** and writing a chapter in the most recent edition of **Defining Excellence in Simulation Programs**. These works reflect his deep knowledge and thought leadership in accreditation and healthcare simulation.

Keith's educational background includes an MBA and multiple leadership, quality improvement, and simulation education certifications. Through his strategic vision, extensive accreditation experience, and scholarly contributions, Keith has become a leading figure in advancing the quality and impact of healthcare simulation worldwide.

KEITH A. BEAULIEU

Other Titles Available by this Author

BARNES&NOBLE
BOOKSELLERS

IngramSpark

Other Titles Coming Soon

Simulation Operation in Healthcare Education: A primer into the role of Operations in Medical and Nursing Training

Mapping Success: Aligning Nursing Curricula with the AACN Essentials

Mastering Healthcare Management and Operations: Insights, Case Studies, and Practical Strategies

Nursing Administration for the Non-Nurse in the Academic Environment: A Primer

www.ingramcontent.com/pod-product-compliance
Lightning Source LLC
Chambersburg PA
CBHW072149070526
44585CB00015B/1063